W9-ATH-692

THOMAS HARDY
THE WILL AND THE WAY

THOMAS HARDY

THE WILL AND THE WAY

ROY MORRELL

823.
09
HARDY

FINKELSTEIN
MEMORIAL LIBRARY
SPRING VALLEY, N. Y.

KUALA LUMPUR
UNIVERSITY OF MALAYA PRESS
SINGAPORE

69-12762

Sole Distributors
Oxford University Press, Ely House, London W.1

GLASGOW NEW YORK TORONTO MELBOURNE WELLINGTON
CAPE TOWN SALISBURY IBADAN NAIROBI LUSAKA ADDIS ABABA
BOMBAY CALCUTTA MADRAS KARACHI LAHORE DACCA
KUALA LUMPUR HONG KONG TOKYO

Bangunan Loke Yew, Kuala Lumpur

● University of Malaya Press 1965
First published 1965
Reprinted with a new Foreword 1968

*The University of Malaya Press is a joint
enterprise of the University of Malaya and
the University of Singapore*

First printed in Great Britain
Reprinted by
Art Printing Works,
Kuala Lumpur

Contents

Foreword

SOME SECTIONS of this book were first published as separate essays; a few changes have been made to avoid too much repetition within the covers of a book, and some chapters have been added. The result is a series of notes and essays which may be regarded as preliminary studies to a more exhaustive book which I hope to publish later.

In my original foreword I referred to Samuel Butler's remark that he would never have written on any subject if he had not found himself in disagreement with the accepted authorities, and I suggested that this was my own reason for writing. This meant just what it said. Not that I disagreed with all Hardy's critics; but that the few with whom I agreed seemed to me comparatively uninfluential. I conceded, however, that even in two or three of those critics with whom I was in fundamental disagreement, there were points to admire.

Harold Child's book seems to me a good short introduction to Hardy's novels; but it is seldom quoted and has long been out of print. I admire H. C. Webster's *On a Darkling Plain*; but when I was writing this book, his was remaindered in the Charing Cross Road. It has since been reprinted; and if this means he is now an 'accepted authority', I can only say that I am delighted, but that I feel that on this matter of Hardy's 'meliorism' much remains to be said: opinion is still weighted on the other side. Mr. M. A. Goldberg is another writer with whom I agree; but I know only his short article on *The Return of the Native*, 'Hardy's double-visioned Universe'. I like Blunden's sympathetic book in the English Men of Letters series, wishing, however, that he had written a little more fully. In the main, too, I agree with J. I. M. Stewart's rather inaccessible essay, 'The Integrity of Hardy': it is a splendid refutation of Eliot's strictures in *After Strange Gods*,[1] and also a defence

---

[1] Eliot regretted *After Strange Gods*, and did not wish the book to be reprinted. He wrote to me in 1964: '... I regret in particular what I said about Hardy ... nor do I feel that dislike of Hardy's novels which I then felt.' But he did not, I believe, overcome his dislike of *Barbara of the House of Grebe*; nor does Mr. Stewart defend this piece of 'pasteboard Gothic', as he calls it. It is rather more than this, however: see my analysis on pp. 114–18, below.

against those who suggest there is an inconsistency in Hardy, a disjunction between conscious artist and unconscious 'personality'.

I mentioned three others, Guerard, Hawkins and Wing, who have written freshly about Hardy, and to some extent with an open mind. And to these I ought to add Lord David Cecil, the merits of whose book I had forgotten. By the qualification 'to some extent', I mean that even these writers take over certain basic assumptions about Hardy from earlier critics: almost universal assumptions and preconceptions which they fail to question, and which at best lead to omissions and false perspectives, and, at worst, in many of Hardy's other critics, to distortions and complete misunderstanding. Few writers can have suffered so much, it seems to me, from misrepresentation.

In trying to show that the main lines of Hardy criticism were misleading, I received very much more sympathy than I had a right to expect. The tide of opinion may well be slowing up; although it has certainly not turned. One anonymous reviewer, indeed, affected to think that this tide did not exist; that I had invented it. At the end, however, he privily swallowed his words and invoked against me that very tide of opinion the existence of which he had denied.

Certainly it exists. But in opposing it I claim no originality. A handful of critics, as I have said, have interpreted Hardy sensibly enough; and first on the scene, with certain explicit but quiet comments, was Hardy himself. I am not referring now to his occasional 'philosophical' intrusions, reflections on the 'ill-judged execution of a well-judged plan of things' or on happiness being 'an occasional episode in a general drama of pain'. Such reflections are rarer and less intrusive than one should judge from the insistence with which they are quoted by critics and seized on by students as short cuts to 'understanding' Hardy; and, as I shall show, they usually bear a meaning quite different from that which they assumed to bear or that which continual re-iteration out of their context seems to have forced upon them.[2] I am referring rather to Hardy's protests that he was a pessimist, not in the sense of 'fatalist' or 'defeatist', but in believing that a man can be successful in the long run only if he is prepared for the worst contingencies, and happy

---

[2] The second was never asserted by Hardy: see p. xv below. The first is often quoted as if it indicates Hardy's fatalism. But might it not mean just what it says? That the world has many potentialities for good, but that these are either neglected, or frustrated by secondary causes—by the inefficiencies and limitations of social systems, by conventions, in fact by mankind generally?

only if his demands on life are modest: I cannot recall that Hardy ever precisely quoted Pope's 'ninth Beatitude': Blessed is the man who expects nothing . . . but he never tired of this theme, and did actually say that 'Pessimism' was 'playing the sure game' . . . the only view of life 'in which you can never be disappointed'.

That the explicit 'philosophy' of an author has no relevance to the interpretation of his novels or poetry is a principle of more than usual importance, it is sometimes argued, in reading Hardy. Thus Miss Evelyn Hardy (no relation of Hardy's) discounts what he says when he disclaims any gloomy fatalism, by insisting that 'something remains unexplained'. And this argument, that Hardy must mean something different from what he says, and that we must be sensitive to his 'overtones', has often been used in one form or another. It has been used against one of the essays in this book: 'Yes: Hardy says this. But what of the *way* he says it?' This seems to me naive, even as a debating point. 'Overtones', what the reader feels over and beyond the bare words he reads, may derive as readily from a bias in himself as from a pressure of feeling in the author. There are certainly 'overtones' in Hardy; but are these overtones likely to be conveyed to the reader in anything remotely resembling their original form, if they have to penetrate a filter of preconceived notions? I have discussed this further in the opening chapter; for the moment I need only return to my point that preconceptions about Hardy are widespread. Even people who have read none of his books 'know' that he is a pessimist. 'I have not read this novel, nor any of Hardy's books; but of course I know all about him' are the exact words of one undergraduate to me, and virtually what I have been told by other people. Apart from the usual prefaces, critical studies and literary histories, comments on Hardy's 'philosophy' appear in Dorset guide books, in the pages of other novelists, and in Mr. Betjeman's verse. And the casualness of most of the references is significant: his pessimism, or fatalism, is accepted; it is no longer something one questions.

Critics are not so unanimous in condemning the 'intentionalist fallacy' as they were ten or twenty years ago. But even if we concede the general principle that the novel or poem matters, not the author's 'ideas', the conditions for applying this principle do not exist in Hardy's case. For the last seventy or eighty years, critics have been discussing what they took to be Hardy's ideas: it is too late to rule me out of court; to get an unbiased decision, the rest would have

to be ruled out too. It cannot be done. All we can do is to re-open
the case, and try to get the ideas right. Ironically it was Hardy
himself who tried first to discredit this talk of his 'creed' or his
'philosophy', claiming that his novels and poems were only 'impressions'. We must remember, though, that these protests were
defensive: the 'philosophy' he disclaimed was that which the critics
were foisting upon him. He never thought the protests might be used
to discredit his own very tentative and questioning formulations.

My approach to Hardy was unusual; or would be today. I read
Hardy's novels, and many of his poems, before encountering any
Hardy criticism. I had read some Schopenhauer; and it seemed to
me that when Hardy wrote on some of Schopenhauer's themes,
he was not echoing the German writer so much as ironically commenting or questioning. So the typical criticism, when I came to
it, puzzled me. It seemed to me right off the target. I had not read
The Dynasts; but I could not believe that the author I thought I
knew so well had committed himself to the narrow views so often
quoted from that book. I read it at last: to find there was at least a
different way of taking it.[3] Re-readings of the novels, the poems, and
Mrs. F. E. Hardy's biography (written mainly by Hardy himself)
have confirmed my original impression, and led me to sympathize
deeply with Hardy in his protests (in letters, in notes, and occasionally more publicly in prefaces such as the 'Apology' prefixed to
Late Lyrics and Earlier) that he was persistently misrepresented.

In an interesting passage quoted in *The Later Years of Thomas
Hardy*,[4] Charles Morgan discusses Hardy's vitality ('sprightly,
alert, birdlike'), but then mentions what he regards as Hardy's
painful oversensitiveness to criticism, and his dislike of literary
criticism in general:

The origin of this bitterness was in the past ... but it was directed now
against contemporary critics of his own work, and I could not understand

[3] Brennecke, in *Thomas Hardy's Universe* drew close parallels between Hardy's
thought and Schopenhauer's, referring especially to *The Dynasts*. In the Max Gate
copy, now in the Dorchester Museum, the marginal comment 'Too much Schopenhauer
for truth' and other disclaimers, are pencilled in Hardy's hand. But it is an odd book:
at the end the reader finds Brennecke writing of 'Hardy's basic optimism', and he may
well wonder what kind of book it might have been had Brennecke rewritten it, from
the beginning.

[4] The two volumes of biography will henceforward be referred to as *Early Life* and
Later Years. But as they have recently been republished in a single volume, with the
chapters numbered separately and with different pagination, I will give page references
to both editions, calling the one volume *Life of Thomas Hardy* simply *Life*. Thus the
present reference is *Later Years*, p. 208; *Life*, p. 402.

what general reason he had to complain of them. He used no names; he spoke with studied reserve, sadly rather than querulously; but he was persuaded—and there is evidence of this persuasion in the preface to the posthumous volume of his verse—that critics approached his work with an ignorant prejudice against his 'pessimism' which they allowed to stand in the way of fair reading and fair judgment.

This was a distortion of the facts as I knew them. It was hard to believe that Hardy honestly thought that his genius was not recognised. . . .

The *non sequitur* of the last sentence shows that the possibility never occurred to Morgan that Hardy was distressed not by lack of 'recognition' but by lack of understanding. Once this is grasped, and it is fairly obvious even from Morgan's account, Hardy's attitude presents no puzzle.

Blunden gives a vivid account of Hardy in old age, recording his own impression, and reporting those of others. Here is that of Edmund Gosse:

He is a wonder if you like. At $87\frac{1}{2}$ without a deficiency of sight, hearing, mind or conversation. Very tiny and fragile, but full of spirit and gaiety not quite consistent in the most pessimistic of poets.

The reader will, I hope, find this 'gaiety' not quite irreconcilable with the Hardy I present in this book. I am not saying that Hardy's writings are gay; they are not. But nor are they steeped in the fatalistic gloom or settled sadness which is sometimes associated with his name and which would, surely, have precluded this love of company and conversation and human contacts. The love was, by all accounts, a genuine one; and it showed great resilience. For we also know of those moments of sadness and reserve, such as Charles Morgan mentions, when he was reminded that his books, and the aims of his life, had been largely misunderstood. His frustration at these times may easily be imagined. But it is not a matter simply of being fair to Hardy, better posthumously than never; it is a matter of making the most sense. For when all those who interpret Hardy as a gloomy fatalist have sensitively responded to the overtones of fatalism, the difficulties do not disappear; they are much greater; much more 'remains unexplained'. Insisting that Hardy believes in a malign and powerful fate brings in its train a whole series of contradictions and inconsistencies, which indeed the critics do not fail to notice, but for which they lay the blame on Hardy himself!

The contradictions disappear only when we accept Hardy's own ideas; properly understood they radiate significance upon every page. And it is this, not the fact that they are Hardy's, that makes them valuable. But there is another point here: the narrowly deterministic creed which he is said to have held would indeed be restrictive to any author, as restrictive to his creative imagination as the mystique of sadness and suffering has been to the criticism. Hardy would have been able to write well only by jumping its bounds, by denying such a creed. But this is not true of the far less rigid ideas, indeed rather wary and non-committal ideas, that Hardy held in fact. He did not believe, for instance, that the worst *must* happen, but that it *could* happen; and so could the best. Anything could happen; and even what did happen could change. A realm of the 'unknowable' was a fundamental conception of Hardy's, so that every discovery and every 'impression' was for him provisional. His impressions—about nature and Providence, about the will of the individual and its function in the rest of the world, about time, and chance, and love, have a certain coherence, but they are complex too. Such words as 'creed' and 'philosophy' are misleadingly rigid. His art was not a blinkered following of a trail, but a true exploration, a series of 'questionings' to use a word of Wordsworth's that Hardy himself borrowed to describe his own writing.[5]

If modern critics misrepresent Hardy, I believe it is because in all good faith they are unable to set aside the bulk of established criticism. In the 1880's and 1890's, when Hardy was publishing his later novels, the matter was different. Then, some reviewers may have misrepresented him deliberately or at least impatiently, since this was an effective way of discrediting his 'atheism'. And in all fairness to these reviewers, it must be admitted that for many Christians there is a fundamental ambiguity in Hardy's attitude: to believe that anything can happen is to deny the existence of Providence, and this, to many of Hardy's contemporaries, was to deny all hope to mankind. The exclusion of Providence also offended the Victorian novel reader who demanded a happy ending; again and again one reads, in the older reviewers and critics, the objection that Hardy creates persons with whom he sympathizes and asks the reader to sympathize, and then shows them failing

[5] In the 'apology' prefixed to *Late Lyrics and Earlier*, and reprinted in all editions of the *Collected Poems*.

to achieve the happiness they 'deserve'. We may feel impatient with this kind of objection today, but I suspect it counted for a good deal with many readers, and that in it lies the germ of much critical misconception. Yet another ground of genuine misunderstanding, perhaps, is the fact that any writer who sets out to map the territory of human freedom inevitably finds himself marking the boundaries: the timid and conservative critic may well persuade himself that human bondage, and not human freedom, is the theme. But this subject I approach from several different angles in the pages that follow, and I need not discuss it here.

A similar argument might be used for that other stand-by of Hardy criticism today: that Hardy's aim was to record the old agricultural way of life, and that his pessimism was despair as he saw the old order defeated by the machine. Again there is just enough ambiguity in Hardy's attitude to lend momentary plausibility to the interpretation. Like most normal people, Hardy had an affection for old and familiar things; he felt sorrow when they were discarded; and he felt nostalgia for old times and old customs. There is evidence of this. But this is different from saying that the Wessex Novels are centred upon, and largely motivated by, a deep loyalty to the agricultural community, a hatred of innovators and intruders, and a dismay and horror at the changes taking place in rural England in the last half of the nineteenth century. This view has been put forward, not just on insufficient evidence, but in the face of much evidence to the contrary. I shall deal with some of the points later. Meanwhile it may be said that the view is in conflict with Hardy's own account of himself as an 'evolutionary meliorist' and impossible, surely, to reconcile with the most moving experience of reading any of Hardy's masterpieces: the sense he conveys to us of the preciousness of the individual and the sometimes desperate need of that individual for love and understanding. That the novels and stories are much more intimately concerned with personal and human dilemmas than with the documenting of social conditions seems to me incontrovertible. And the danger of seeing Tess not as a woman but as a representative of the peasantry in decline, and Henchard as an incarnation of 'agricultural man' instead of as a lonely individual, is that we shall thereby miss Hardy's deeper insights into those human dilemmas.

This book, then, is a plea for a reconsideration of Hardy. The introductory chapter deals with some general points first, and then endeavours to show that there is at least a *prima facie* case for thinking that Hardy has been seriously misunderstood. Here, and in the two 'Notes' that follow, I am largely clearing the ground. In the fourth section, I suggest how Hardy came to adopt his somewhat indirect method, changing his tactics after the criticisms that were levelled at *The Poor Man and the Lady* but trying none the less to preserve his aims; trying to 'speed' the Truth 'but in phrase askance', to borrow his own words from the *Lausanne* poem. Of the arrangement of the rest of the book, I need only say that comment on *The Dynasts* comes fairly early because the poem often proves a stumbling block, and that, towards the end of the book, I have elaborated a comparison between Hardy and some living writers to suggest the great interest Hardy can have for us today, and as a way of combating the common assumption that a large part of Hardy's appeal is to the curiosity of the literary or social antiquarian. His place in English literature means more than that. It means that as a true author of his time he enlarged human experience and human sensibility, and increased the scope of poetry and of fiction. To appreciate Hardy properly is also to appreciate better the writers of generations before and after him. To understand him, as to understand any of the writers in the main tradition, is to understand ourselves better.

Hardy has made his own rich contribution to the variety of our literature. We cannot afford to lose this by misunderstanding and misrepresenting him. I regret the attacks upon critics in the following pages; I find no other way to appeal for another hearing. To vindicate Hardy, to rescue even a part of his meaning, is more important, surely, than to spare the feeling of critics; for although authors have been known to succumb to critical attacks, critics are made of tougher stuff; and the charge of being 'destructive' can hardly be brought against me, with any justice, for what is after all an attempt at salvage.

What are the essentials that one hopes to salvage? What should one find in Hardy, and most value? To set in perspective what I have to say in the following pages, I should like to expand my remark about Hardy's sense of the value of the individual and his deep sympathy with his characters; a sympathy we can measure by his unmatched power to involve us too.

It is a truism that many novelists find it easier to portray wickedness, or at least sin and human weakness, than virtue. Their rogues

are more 'round' and alive than their good people. The opposite
is true of Hardy. He excels in depicting characters who, whatever
their faults, are on the whole good and kind. Even someone with
great faults, like Michael Henchard, deeply engages our sympathy.
We do not forget that he is rash-tempered and egocentric while we
desperately wish for him the happiness he himself desires but seems
bent on destroying. So too with Eustacia: knowing all her faults,
we still wish her happiness; not the success of her romantic dreams,
but that measure of real happiness that would follow from an acceptance of reality. And we wish her this not for Clym's sake, but for
her own.

But if Hardy manages to convey to the reader his conviction that
'no human being deserves less' in the way of happiness 'than is
given' in the cases of these rather flawed characters, he pleads even
more successfully on behalf of his greater heroes and heroines.
With Tess and Jude and Sue, with Oak, Bathsheba and Giles, and
with many of the more sympathetic characters in his minor novels
such as Viviette and Elfride, our urgent concern for their happiness
becomes almost painful. A simple fatalistic pattern—an irrevocable
mistake followed by disaster—would be bearable. We could accept
with resignation, even with relief, this harsh and simple statement
of life's meaning. But the pattern we find is quite different. There
are disasters it is true. But just as 'an anticipated heap of happiness'
dwindles as it comes within reach, so a disaster too, however dark
and terrifying in prospect, is not quite so bad once a man faces it
squarely and starts to live through it. Hope is renewed; opportunities recur . . . and then, again, setback and disappointment: not
through any folly or real fault so much as through a simple unawareness of the conditions of life, something which might have been
prevented. Again the mistake is not irrevocable. . . .

The way life treats Hardy's characters is not quite the same as the
way the 'Doomsters' treat the poet in that much misunderstood
poem *Hap*. But it is comparable. And the effect upon the reader is
much more harrowing than the story of a plain disaster. It keeps
alive our sympathy and hope, and at the same time distresses us
that the game of life should be played without that modicum of
vigilance that might turn the balance.

Hardy's aim is to move the reader to pity and to protest. But the
more successful he is in arousing our sympathy for his heroes and
heroines, and in keeping our hopes alive, the more pain we feel in

their eventual disaster. The point, one would have thought, was obvious; yet surely it is from misunderstanding it that the grotesque notion has arisen that there is a sadistic streak in Hardy. From the days when Tinsley tried to make Hardy change the end of *A Pair of Blue Eyes*, and six Americans visited Hardy to protest against his cruelty to the dog that helped Fanny Robin, and to ask him to omit those few sentences, to Mr. Stewart's uneasiness over Hardy's 'extra turns of the screw' and Larkin's fatuous accusation of 'sensual cruelty', such comments have been made—comments that hint at a man totally different from the one we know from other evidence. The concern of Tess, Jude and Gabriel over the sufferings of animals will be recalled; and Giles's 'gentle conjurer's touch' with the roots of the young trees. That the creator of such characters depicted suffering not for the relish of it but in order to move the reader to compassion, and to such action as might alleviate or prevent unnecessary pain, seems obvious enough, even if we did not have his protest to William Archer: 'What are my books but one plea against "men's inhumanity to man"—to woman—and to the lower animals?'[6]

If Hardy's 'meaning' be seriously disputed, it is relevant to consider his effect. Any attempt to do so must be inconclusive, but Professor Weber, in *Hardy of Wessex* and again in his introduction to the Modern Library edition of *Tess*, brings forward much evidence to suggest that Hardy's books, especially *Tess* and *Jude*, have exerted a wide influence and done much to modify our attitudes towards women and sex. On the matter of Hardy's compassion, he quotes a number of tributes, including Virginia Woolf's:

It is no mere transcript of life at a certain time and place that Hardy has given us. It is a vision of the world and of man's lot, as they revealed themselves to a powerful imagination, a profound and poetic genius, *a gentle and humane soul*.[7]

And Weber himself testifies to the encouraging and 'moral quality' of Hardy's writing: 'Against the challenge of despair ... Hardy had steadfastly vindicated the soul of man.'

[6] W. Archer, *Real Conversations*. One supposes that Hardy usually regarded such pleas commonsensically enough. Occasionally, however, as at the end of *The Dynasts*, and as in the following note, he thought in terms of a group conscience:
Altruism, or The Golden Rule, or whatever 'Love your Neighbour as Yourself' may be called, will ultimately be brought about I think by the pain we see in others reacting on ourselves, as if we and they were a part of one body. (*Early Life*, p. 294; *Life*, p. 224.)
[7] My italics.

With this point, which seems to me incontrovertible, J. I. M. Stewart agrees, saying that Hardy's novels 'do not leave us despairing nor debilitated as after sojourn in some unwholesome place'. Even those who, in my view, mistake the whole tone of Hardy's writing, and see in what they call his 'pessimism' an invitation to despair, do not accept that invitation: they protest, react against it. And Hardy himself never despaired. He continued to believe in 'some blessed Hope'. When asked, in September 1918, what he thought about prophecies of even more frightful future wars, he wrote: 'As a meliorist (not a pessimist as they say) I think better of the world'. His writings continually assert the virtue of re-engagement in life, rather than a withdrawal from it; his eye was ever upon the 'chink of possibility' of mankind's betterment and happiness. 'Hardy never came not to care,' Stewart says rightly. 'To the end he did, as a man, care intensely—"Hoping it might be so".'

Acknowledgements

MOST of the first chapter is reprinted from 'An Essay on Criticism' published by the Humanities Division of the International Christian University of Japan; the chapter on *Far from the Madding Crowd* appeared first in *Studies in English Literature* (Tokyo University); 'Nature, the Garden and "God's Gardener" ' has been adapted from an essay 'Hardy in the Tropics' printed in *The Review of English Literature*; 'Remorse and Memorials: Romance or Reality' appeared in *The Makerere Journal*; and '*The Dynasts* reconsidered', in *The Modern Language Review*. I should like to thank the editors of these journals for permission to reprint.

Messrs. Macmillan and Company and the Trustees of the Hardy Estate have permitted me to quote freely from Hardy's books and from Mrs. F. E. Hardy's biography of Hardy. I am very grateful to them, and also to the following: Messrs. Hamish Hamilton and Company and M. J-P. Sartre for permission to quote from *The Flies*; Messrs. Jonathan Cape for allowing me to quote lines from A. E. Housman's poetry; and Miss Iris Murdoch and Messrs. Chatto and Windus for permission to quote from *The Bell*.

Finally I should like to thank all those who have, at one time or another, helped me with encouragement and guidance; especially Mr. Beda Lim, Librarian of the University of Malaya, and also the Council of the University who, longer ago now than I like to think, granted me study leave to pursue my research.

I

Hardy and the Critical Confusion

> How strangely all of them read! I suppose that instead of
> following the road laid out for them, most go wandering blind-
> ly through the pages; from time to time a word strikes a chord
> in them, awakening God only knows what memories or what
> longings. Or else they think they see a reflection of themselves
> in some image or other. . . .
>
> Henri in *Les Mandarins*

THE MAIN lines of my approach to Hardy's writings will, I hope, be
clear even in this opening chapter; but my first task is to try to clear
the ground: to explain why much of the current criticism of Hardy
must be rejected.

It is not enough, however, to show that misconceptions have arisen.
To keep such mistakes within bounds, we must see how they arise.
How does it happen that intelligent scholars can approach a fairly
straightforward writer, in good faith, and distort the meaning?
That Hardy is misunderstood, this chapter will supply ample evidence; that he is a 'fairly straightforward writer' is usually taken for
granted: indeed there are still critics who regard him as little more
than a simple-minded countryman. And absurd as this last view may
be, Hardy is certainly not obscure; one would have thought it was
no great feat to understand him.

The reader will have noticed that I am already begging certain
questions about 'meaning', and communication, and the function of
criticism. Before going much further I must offer some general
remarks by way of clarification; but I will make these as brief as
possible.

As far as Hardy is concerned, I shall deal mainly with the criticism
of Dr. John Holloway,[1] since this is admirably representative of the
two most typical lines of interpretation today: those which assume
in Hardy, first, a narrow belief in pessimistic determinism, a denial
of man's freedom, and, second, an abiding faith in the goodness of

[1] In *The Victorian Sage* (1953) and *The Charted Mirror* (1960).

nature and of the old agricultural order. Other critics, among them, D. H. Lawrence[2] and James Stephens,[3] Douglas Brown[4] and Arnold Kettle[5]—have put forward these views, but none of these is so suitable for my purposes as Dr. Holloway.

Dr. Kettle insists that *Tess* is not the story of a girl but a thesis on the decline of the peasantry. Only if we take it in this way, he argues, can we overlook the gross flaws: the accidents and improbabilities. I do not follow this; it seems to me that if we follow Dr. Kettle's approach, and only then, do these 'flaws' become real stumbling blocks, and that he admits as much when he says that a *typical* peasant girl would not have reacted to the 'accidents' as Tess did. In any case we do not solve the problem of the 'accidents' by wishing them out of the way, but by noticing how Tess reacted, and what Hardy intended by them. Dr. Kettle makes some good points, but not, I think, in support of his main thesis. I return to the peasantry later; but meanwhile I pass on from Dr. Kettle since he confines his attention to *Tess of the d'Urbervilles*.

Professor Brown's is a general case; but in one respect it is not typical, for he sees an affirmation in Hardy, a strength, despite the 'apparent pessimism'. This is splendid; but he then attempts the impossible—to reconcile this valid personal impression with the views of other critics. He thus finds himself in the paradoxical position of seeing this 'strength' of Hardy's in the very surrender of his characters to Fate. He sees it in the remark of Joan Durbeyfield, Tess's mother, when Tess returns home pregnant: "'Tis nater, after all, and what do please God.'[6] Brown sees no irony here; although the reader of those early chapters[7] will remember that the person whose vanity and silliness had caused all the trouble was Mrs. Durbeyfield herself. It had been her idea to send Tess to 'claim kin', to deck her out as a bait for Alec; she had given Tess no word of warning, and had indeed suppressed her own misgivings in her dreams of what might happen. Hers was the main moral failure, and that she could so easily shift the blame to 'nater' and 'God' is the point of Hardy's bitter joke. But from this, and other references detached from their contexts, Brown sees Hardy as finding a refuge

---

[2] In *Phoenix*.
[3] *Spectator*, March 1942. Ostensibly a review of Blunden's book in the *English Men of Letters* Series.   [4] *Thomas Hardy*, 1954.
[5] *Introduction to the Novel*, II (1954).
[6] *Tess*, XII (I give chapter, not page, references to Hardy's novels since the pagination differs widely in the various editions available).   [7] See especially chapters III–VII.

in nature and Providence that is essentially Wordsworthian. Indeed he affirms this explicitly at one point, although later, wishing to have it both ways, he talks of Hardy's sense of 'nature's indifference'. Such major contradictions and some falsifications (as when he quotes Hardy's description of Marty South but omits sentences that weaken his case) are easier to define than the book's real weakness. Something in the tone, that earnestly urges upon us Hardy's devotion to agricultural and rural sanctities, but says more than it proves, and suggests more than it says, makes it a difficult book to discuss. Perhaps one's embarrassment indicates that Professor Brown has not convinced himself; perhaps the book is a parody: certainly it discredits a certain critical attitude as effectively as *Cold Comfort Farm* discredited a certain kind of fiction.

James Stephens's review is now doubtless forgotten: it was perhaps the bitterest attack on Hardy, the man and the writer, since reviewers sank their teeth into *Jude the Obscure* in the nineties. The animosity makes the review unsuitable for detailed reference here; none the less it has an interest: it presented what is basically the modern view, except that it blamed Hardy for a devotion to the old and rural, where Holloway and Brown praise.

There would be a real point in taking Lawrence, since much modern criticism of Hardy seems to stem from him. I am not doing so because Lawrence was not primarily a critic: he had the creative artist's right to express his views without having their soundness, as literary criticism, called in question. Many of his remarks on Hardy are brilliant, and even the absurdities (his liking for Arabella, for instance) are justified because what they obscure about Hardy is counterbalanced by what they reveal about himself. 'What Hardy wrote,' Lawrence seems to say in effect, 'is no concern of mine. I am concerned with what he *ought* to have written'.[8] In a critic this would be unforgivable; but in Lawrence it is clearly no basis for a quarrel.

So we are left with Dr. Holloway, whose arguments seem to me the best. They are supported by a formidable range of references to most of Hardy's books; he is consistent; and, the most important point, he takes Hardy much more seriously than the others do, and more seriously, it need hardly be said, than the majority of critics today.

[8] In a somewhat different context, Lawrence did in fact say, 'An artist is usually a damned liar. . . . The proper function of the critic is to save the tale from the artist who created it.' This dictum must seem attractive to the critic, but it is dangerously less than the whole truth.

There is another and a different kind of reason for taking Holloway: in the final section of *The Chartered Mirror* he has discussed the general critical problem of 'meaning', and he thus provides me with a convenient starting point for my own generalities, and provokes in an emphatic form the questions I wish to ask. Holloway reaffirms his allegiance to the New Criticism after several qualifications and after voicing misgivings about some of its methods. With these misgivings I am largely in sympathy. What he says needed saying; and it is said well. What happens, then, when Dr. Holloway turns to Hardy? Are his principles not sound? Has even he, who expounded these principles so clearly, failed to apply them? If so, why? Are there snags, after all, in the way of understanding Hardy?

A more general question recurs through this introductory essay: whether, if the best critics help us so little, we need this kind of criticism, interpretative criticism, at all. Two assumptions are implicit too: that the creative writer matters more than the critic, and that it is the impression of the *whole* work of art which we must respect and seek to preserve.

We shall be in a better position to deal with Hardy criticism effectively if we deal first with the general critical problem. The most noticeable thing about criticism today is that there is a lot of it. The teacher of literature must often wonder whether he or his students will ever get to the poem, the play, or the novel again, unimpeded by the surrounding growth. To the layman, puzzled as to what all these thousands of books about books can be saying, there is a short if incomplete answer: in a few pages or a few hundred most of the critical books are urging us to concentrate upon the actual work of literature, and to ignore everything else. The paradox has been noticed; but there seems no way of resolving it. At one time the university lecturer who felt constrained to publish something could spend his spare time harmlessly writing a biographical or a historical background study. 'Harmlessly', because its irrelevance was recognized, and the laziest student knew he still had to read the actual text. But now such innocuous pursuits are discredited; a critical analysis must be attempted; and a real educational problem arises. For it is one thing for a lecturer to analyse a poem (say) with his pupils, and tell them to go away and read other poems as carefully; but quite another for him to publish his readings. Our students now find on the library shelves critical analyses of almost everything. Their reading is done for them. Sometimes it is well done, sometimes not. But is it as valuable for students to read even the most brilliant exposition as to tackle the text itself? It is hardly necessary to point out that the critical analysis is not only not the same thing as the actual work of literature, it is a thing of a different kind.

The second problem is that of communication. If a poem or a novel includes everything that the sensitivity of the critic can find, and communicates only with the critic's help, is it the author's meaning we reach, or the critic's? The work of art is our finest means, 'our last hope' some might say, of communication. And the artist has no means other than the work of art itself. If the critic filters through to us, and elaborates, only what conforms to his own sense of values, telling us what to find, we accept him, instead of the artist or poet, as the 'maker', the explorer of life's values. This may be what the critic wants; but is it what we want ourselves?

Finally there is the question of language. If the critic finds meanings and implications in a poem or a novel that are just not there, and Holloway insists that this happens, the language is being blurred. A writer may of course suggest more than he says; but this does not mean that what he says can mean anything that anybody likes.

Some of these misgivings, as I have indicated, are Dr. Holloway's own. He sees that the New Critics have a penchant for complexity, and insists that a poem should be allowed to be itself; even simple, if it wants to be. Secondly, even with complex poems, he says it is important to know where to draw the line: searching indefinitely for complexities and ambiguities is absurd because 'it means that there is nothing the poet can definitely *not* say, definitely decline to say': Holloway rightly insists that by making one statement, a writer may exclude something else. Third, he blames the 'scientific' approach that was originally encouraged by I. A. Richards; he explains:

The notion that there will always be some new complexity, some new hidden interrelatedness of structure to discover, that certain methods of enquiry can be applied over and over again, and that if they yield anything, then what they yield is really there, is characteristic of what science takes as its objects; while poems are entities of another kind and (though they may contain more than their creators deliberately put into them) contain what the text offers, and emphatically do not contain what the text excludes.[9]

[9] 'The Critical Intimidation' (*The Charted Mirror*).

Holloway's remedy, then, is to let the text decide; and he speaks of a 'tact' which, if the critic has not been confused by the methods of science, will tell him where to stop. Much of this we must applaud. But in Holloway's premises about science there is an error that leads him to omit something too often brushed aside. Unless it is mentioned, this 'tact' may be no more effective in the future than it has been in the past.

First about Richards: whatever his disciples have done, Richards himself did not encourage wild interpretations. Admittedly he preferred the more complex poem, but not the more complex interpretation; nor, in his Practical Criticism lectures, did he suggest that it was just a matter of taking one's choice, that one interpretation was as good as another. He showed how our 'criticisms' could be rendered worthless by prejudices and inhibitions; he pointed out that some metaphors, taken too far, obscured the meaning, and that some poems 'worked' without metaphors or imagery. He urged us to give the poem every chance by reading it in different moods when our preoccupations did not intrude, and to avoid hasty conclusions; and he suggested that we should understand and take into account the various 'meanings' of the poem, amongst which he included the author's intention. Richards did not suggest that 'intentions' necessarily found their way into the poem, nor, if they did, that they made it good; but understanding these intentions at least prevented our own preoccupations, our own ideas of what the poet ought to be saying, from intruding and distorting. By ridding us of some of our prejudices in this way, he made our tastes more catholic.

The point to which I have been leading is now clear: Richards taught something not unlike the scientific method. But a scientist does *not* assume that if his methods 'yield anything, then what they yield is really there'. If they yield what he wants, the scientist, unlike the critic, is suspicious, and devises control tests to ensure that the results have not been determined by his own wishes and prejudices. This, then, is what must be mentioned: that a critic should take pains to recognize, and discount, his own prejudices.

It is commonly assumed that he hasn't any; that his interpretations are on a level of sensitivity, of 'tact', on which it is irrelevant to discuss literal meanings, and on which his prejudices are but part of his critical personality, his fine awareness of values. But it is just on such levels that one is most easily misled. We may concede that for the poet, interpreting life, 'what the Imagination seizes as Beauty must be Truth'; but if the critic exercises the same kind of imagination in interpreting poetry, he gives us not the poet's truth, but his own dilutions or irrelevancies; and he betrays the poet's truth, and other kinds of truth as well.

There is no new thing in the kind of misunderstanding from which Hardy suffered. A writer was always at the mercy of those who thought he ought to be saying something different. Thus Victorian critics quoted

> Old, unhappy far-off things,
> And battles long ago,

as if this were the heart of Wordsworth's poem, ignoring the real stress on:

> Or is it some more humble lay,
> Familiar matter of today?
> Some natural sorrow, loss, or pain,
> That has been, and may be again?

Because much as they liked Wordsworth they would have liked him still more had he been still more romantic. From remote places, Wordsworth brings us right back home: he says that even the nightingale to weary travellers in the desert, or the first song of spring in the wintry Hebrides, could not be more wonderful than the song he himself heard from this 'solitary reaper'. And the contrast between the romantic and remote on the one hand, and the near and real on the other, is repeated when he wonders about the song's words. A critic might indeed argue that this is only what Wordsworth *says*, but that he *betrays* by his vivid imagery a far more lively interest in 'far-off things' and places than he would admit even to himself. But this statement, masquerading as one about Wordsworth, is in reality only about the critic, to whom any mention of Arabia and nightingales and battles long ago would immediately be more convincing than 'Familiar matter of today'. Wordsworth had to refer to romantic joys in order to make his point that his own real and homely joy was just as intense. There was no other way of doing it. He is, we might say, only *conceding* the value of the romance. And this may not seem so very different from what Hardy is doing (in the *Romantic Adventures of a Milkmaid*, for instance) when he concedes the attractiveness of certain romantic and fatalistic acquiescences, while also suggesting the claims of reality. But Hardy and

Wordsworth differ too widely in other respects, in their attitudes to 'Nature' for instance, to make this type of comparison illuminating. All the same, each is facing the same problem of communication: the difficulty of getting an unromantic and unpopular point of view across. And like Hardy on many occasions, Wordsworth is defeated in this instance by those who see a part instead of the whole, those who extract a few phrases and fail to see what they are leading up to. To find the true meaning the reader has only to go back to the poem as a whole: the poise of feeling, and the quiet emphasis with which Wordsworth then brings us down on the side that for him is the right one, are controlled by the whole rhythm. But if there were any doubt, the poet's known intentions could relevantly be taken into account. They cannot be decisive, but they can help.

The critic refuses to allow this. He argues that the poem is much more than the conscious aims of the poet; that the poet's conscious 'meaning' is modified by all kinds of unconscious pressures. True. But does the critic imagine that his understanding and appreciation of the poem are not influenced in the same way by his own unconscious pressures and inhibitions? Can he be so sophisticated about the poet's unconscious and at the same time so naïve about his own? I am not suggesting the critic distorts deliberately, but that he can be unconsciously driven by his feelings when these are deeply engaged. And I need hardly say that a critic's feelings sometimes *are* deeply engaged, even when the discussion centres upon the rival claims of such abstractions as 'Nature', 'Romance' and 'Reality'.

Even Dr. Leavis can nod: arguing that Keats's desire for life was as great as his wish to 'swoon to death', he once insisted that this life-instinct was present even in the word 'rich' of the phrase 'rich to die' in the Nightingale *Ode*. This taking of a single word out of context is not uncommon in modern criticism. But it denies a basic axiom: that words only become real language, only have meaning, in context. What more emphatic way is there of denying the richness of life than to say it is 'rich to die'? Again when Leavis says Keats is 'strictly' only 'half in love with easeful Death', he is not writing 'strictly'; he is misreading the poem, where 'half in love' refers to 'many a time' in the past; now, Keats says, it is different: '*Now more than ever* seems it rich to die. . . .' This is an instance of what Holloway deplores: a critic fixing upon a meaning that the poet has taken pains to exclude. And if even Leavis can do this, the prospect of another critic's finding more than he wants to find, is bleak. It happens that I am more in sympathy with Leavis than with the values that Keats is expressing in this particular passage. But this does not affect the issue. I want Keats to be Keats; and Wordsworth to be Wordsworth. I deplore this sifting from each writer only what conforms with the prejudices and moral judgements of the critic's time. It is an insidious kind of censorship.

Dr. Holloway says we must let the poem decide. One might imagine that he means by this that the critic should stop writing. But unfortunately he does not. And his talk of 'tact' and 'drawing the line' is disquieting. Who draws the line? Clearly, Dr. Holloway. And if he disagrees with any interpretation of mine, he need only say that I am being 'uninformative' or 'insensitive', and so failing to reach his 'line', or that in defiance of 'tact' I am chasing ambiguities beyond it. I shall say the same when I disagree with Dr. Holloway. 'Tact' is clearly mere question-begging, a way of silencing the voice of disagreement. An effective way, too: for to re-establish the truth after any kind of falsehood is a labyrinthine and ridiculous task; the very prosiness of explaining the real force of a reference, or that a quotation means not that, but—in its context—this, puts one boringly in the wrong. And after all the only real context, and this is as true of a novel as of a poem, is the whole text. But this, so often re-iterated in modern criticism, can only mean that every critical exposition must distort; only the work itself can tell us anything about itself. Unfortunately even the whole work is not the same after we have read the criticism.

In the introductory chapter of *The Victorian Sage* Holloway explains how we should respond to these 'sages' whose views, he says, lose their last vestige of interest when paraphrased in literary histories: 'They provoke only bored surprise that anyone could have insisted so eagerly on half-incomprehensible dogmas or trite commonplaces.' We give our 'real assent', Holloway reminds us, to something richer and more detailed, to something the author makes us see and feel through our whole being, something in the 'whole weave of the book', in its incidents, persons, and, very important, in its figurative language. Holloway puts all this well. Itself, it 'commands assent'. But when he puts his theories into practice it seems to me that he is implying a good deal more than he is saying. He is instructing us how to read a novel: good. But he is also suggesting how we should read, assess, and assent to, something in a different dimension, namely the *critic's interpretation* of the novel, which cannot possibly be the 'whole weave'.

Take the figurative language: the figures are indeed threads in the weave. But even if each one is interpreted justly according to its context, the selection of these by the critic and the laying of them side by side will present a colour and texture quite different from the 'whole weave of the book', and different too from the colour and texture of a selection made by a reader with different preoccupations. Holloway realizes this; but says drily that the responses of some readers will prove 'of general interest, and of others not'. In short, the truth is what the critic can get away with.

But what immediately convinces, what 'catches on', is not always the truth. On the contrary, the telling phrase, the convincing analogy, the argument that 'commands assent' from the heart of the reader, is often what chimes with what we already assume, what we wish to believe, what, in short, evokes an immediate response from our prejudices, the sometimes strong doctrinaire prejudices of critical fashions. That the truth was 'what one can get away with' was indeed a view familiar enough to Hardy himself, and one that appalled him. On William James's words, 'Truth is what will work,'[10] Hardy commented, 'A worse corruption of language was never perpetrated.' For him the truth was something that had to be told,[11] but it was not easy, nor was it easily believed: a point made forcibly in the *Lausanne* poem, and indirectly implied by his feeling of helplessness when he was attacked by a critic who aimed only at being 'smart and amusing'.[12] It is the lie or the slick half-truth that only too often 'will work', and be readily accepted; Ben Jonson did well to define 'deceit' as 'the likeness of truth'; and one would have thought that one function of criticism was to prevent these counterfeits from gaining currency.

The critic who urges us to read the whole book, but who first spotlights certain quotations, is employing basically the technique of the newspaper editor who gives us the news in full, perhaps, but determines which part of it we shall notice and remember, plays on our prejudices and snobberies, and generally angles our approach, by the careful selection of one or more points in a headline. And, indeed, is there not every now and then in the tone of many critics,

[10] *Later Years*, p. 242; *Life*, p. 428. Hardy may not be fair to James, but he clearly defines his own attitude.
[11] *Vide*, *inter alia*, the first preface to *Tess*.
[12] *Later Years, p.* 7; *Life*, p. 246.

something that reminds one of the journalist or the 'ad man': a tone of superiority to those who disagree?

A novel offers limitless opportunities for the selective or imagist methods of the New Critic. If we, the public, have not read it, our approach can be angled; or if we have read it, we are unlikely to go back and check contexts. Contexts are not always checked even by critics and literary historians, for the same quotations, often provisional or half statements, minor concessions, halves of sentences, and the like, but misinterpreted and quoted as if they were deliberately formulated dogmas, crop up again and again. This is true, at least, of Hardy criticism. For example, several recent critics, desirous of convincing us that Hardy was not interested in human potentialities, have referred to his 'wish to set the emotional history of two infinitesimal lives against the background of the stellar universe', suppressing the rest of the sentence and the point to which Hardy was leading: 'and to impart to readers the sentiment that of these contrasting magnitudes the smaller might be the greater to them as men.'[13] And I have long since abandoned my count of those who quote Hardy as saying that 'happiness is but the occasional episode in a general drama of pain'. Hardy in fact says something in almost direct contradiction to this: namely that this had been the mistaken impression of Elizabeth-Jane's youth, abandoned in the 'unbroken tranquillity' of her adult life. The words come in the last sentence of *The Mayor of Casterbridge*, and are thus easily checked.

Although Hardy wished to avoid a conventional happy ending to the book, he wished to affirm that a quiet enjoyment of life was possible for a person who did not demand too much. Elizabeth-Jane expected little of life. One recalls her modest attitude on her first evening in Casterbridge. She subsequently, and consequently, found life good enough. It is a favourite theme: Boldwood, Knight, Angel, Eustacia, Wildeve, Fitzpiers . . . have all finally to adapt themselves to reality or to pay the price for not doing so. But to accommodate oneself to life instead of optimistically believing that life will accommodate itself to one's dream of what ought to be, is to find 'enough poetry in what is left in life after all the false romance has been abstracted'.[14] I am not limiting Hardy to this or to any other bald 'statement': he is saying much more in the extended 'impressions' of his books. I mention this point, nonetheless, because

---

[13] Preface to *Two on a Tower*.   [14] *Early Life*, p. 150; *Life*, p. 114.

Holloway interprets it differently. He sees, all credit to him, that Hardy is frequently contemptuous of the dreamer; but when he turns to what Hardy is advocating instead of the false 'self-generated dream' he defines this as 'Nature'. He sums up Hardy's philosophy as: 'It is right to live naturally.'

Man's roots in Nature, the essential goodness of the agricultural communities, the contempt for the deraciné, these are the pre-occupations of a generation influenced by Jung, Lawrence, Sturt and Leavis. And that Holloway, like the other critics I mentioned at the beginning of this chapter, finds Hardy pre-occupied too with these things is what we might expect. It tells us much of the modern attitude; nothing about Hardy. And that Holloway should later discover that the interpretation does not work, is also what we might expect; for he is a good critic, and has looked again at the books. But we are still some way from the truth.

With the novel, as we have said, the critic has almost limitless scope for selective misrepresentation. But with Hardy's novels the opportunities are not only numerous, they are also of a special kind, because he narrates by means of continual contrasts. These are in the very grain of his thought, the way he sees situations and people in terms of chance and change, 'flux and reflux'. It is easy, for anyone as careless or prejudiced as those who quote the half-sentence about the 'stellar universe' and ignore the rest, to select one side of the contrast and misrepresent him. I don't mean that to read him properly is difficult, however: it is easy to read on, in sequence, and see one event in relation, sometimes an ironic relation, to another.

A frequent type of contrast in the novels is between a seemingly hopeless situation and the appearance of a chance (not always taken) for effective action, between suicidal impulse and sensible calm resolve, between near-despair and renewed vigour. Swithin, when someone forestalls his 'New Astronomical Discovery', has no wish to recover from his illness, and the doctor despairs of his life: but he suddenly finds he *must* live to see the new comet.[15] Of many instances in *Far from the Madding Crowd*, I select two that I wish to return to later: Gabriel, after losing his sheep, sees the waning moon's reflection, broken in the ripples of the pond, like an 'attenuated skeleton'; but instead of accepting this invitation to suicide, he pulls himself together, and when we next meet him he possesses a

---

[15] *Two on a Tower*, IX and X. As often in Hardy there is a sharp contrast of mood between the close of one chapter and the opening of the next.

'dignified calm he had never before known' and an ability to make something out of the worst that life offers.[16] Again at the beginning of the storm scene:

. . . The moon vanished not to reappear. It was the farewell of the ambassador previous to war. The night had a haggard look, like a sick thing; and there came finally an utter expiration of air from the whole heaven in the form of a slow breeze, which might have been likened to a death.[17]

And the lightning that follows is like 'a mailed army' in the heavens.[18] Clearly no man can fight against such odds. Yet Gabriel does; and he wins. There are many such contrasts: when Jude first opens the Latin Grammar, and realizes the magnitude of the task, he despairs. No one able to advise him and lighten his load comes by, 'because nobody does': a sentence that has been quoted as revealing Hardy's pessimism at its simplest and darkest. But on the next page, which is also the beginning of a new chapter,[19] we are told that the very obstacles in the boy's way had awakened in him a heroic resolve to overcome them. Earlier critics, fairly solidly, have quoted the first part of such sequences, talked of Hardy's gloom, and failed to notice the reprieves, the rallies and the successes Hardy's men and women win after taking 'a full look at the Worst'. Several critics, for instance, suggest that a malign omnipotence mocks Troy's efforts over Fanny's grave: I do not recall one who points out that immediately after Troy has gone off utterly defeated, Bathsheba comes, quietly repairs the damage, and takes steps to prevent the accident from recurring: 'accident' (over which Hardy has several jokes in his earlier novels[20]), 'fate', the 'inevitable', the 'President of the Immortals', whatever we name the thing that too often gets the better of us, is at least partly under human control; under the control, that is, of *some* human beings: Hardy draws a distinction between people like Oak and Bathsheba, and those like Troy.

Holloway is much influenced by the older Hardy critics, but whereas they represented Hardy's men and women as frustrated by a malign fate, Holloway sees them as *controlled entirely by Nature*. To him, and to some others, Hardy's 'philosophy' is one of complete natural determinism. And it is interesting, that, within a generation, there should have been so complete a change from the reading of I. A. Richards, who saw Hardy's Nature as completely neutral. At

---

[16] *Far from the Madding Crowd*, V and VI.
[17] Ibid. XXXVI.   [18] Ibid. XXXVII.
[19] *Jude the obscure*, I-v.   [20] See below, page 45 and footnote.

all events Holloway, as much as the old-fashioned critics (with whom
I do not include Richards, of course), is interested in denying man's
freedom of action; but with this stress on the essential goodness of
'living naturally', he is even more liable than they to ignore the
relevance in Hardy's world of an effort or intelligence distinctively
human.

It is easy to show that Holloway's view is mistaken, and indeed he
has modified it himself in later essays. What is disconcerting is the
fact that his method looks so sound and his case so watertight. The
problem is to see where the gap comes: where Holloway builds on
something other than evidence, and convinces himself by means of
something different from 'tact'.

He argues that Hardy's sense of Nature is complex and pervading:
nature is no mere backcloth to human actions; it is ubiquitous, and
variously but continuously active and changing; it affects man's
life at point after point. This is true: Nature, to Hardy, is the scheme
of things, no less; the reality that man must cope with. Holloway's
references and quotations lead directly to this point. But it is not
quite the point he makes. He forces the issue further. It is true that
having summarized Hardy's point of view as 'it is right to live naturally', he explains that this acceptance 'is not nothing; human
choice can exert some influence on the course of things simply by
working with and not against it', but the context leaves this statement with little meaning. Out of context, it might mean that by
taking a 'full look at the Worst', an intelligent and honest scrutiny
of the difficulties and conditions and loopholes presented by life, man
could (and, in the sense that there is nothing else for him to do except
surrender, must) make something out of this reality. This, I believe,
is the kind of thing Hardy meant; but it is not the meaning that
Holloway finds. I should like to think that Holloway, despite what
he says about 'living naturally' and accepting nature, would agree
with me that Hardy thought it wrong for Troy to submit to the
natural elements and go off defeated; that it was right for Bathsheba
to use her intelligence and get the lead in the gargoyle deflected, thus
controlling nature; and that it was absolutely right for Gabriel to
fight *against* nature as hard as he did, not only nature in the storm,
but the natural optimism of Troy (who insisted that it wouldn't rain),
and the natural sleepiness and drunken inertia of those in the barn, and
his own natural and instinctive desire to let things take their natural

course since the odds against him were too great. I should like to get
Holloway to agree too that one of the most natural activities of a
family of Hardy's most natural people, the Durbeyfields, was
dreaming[21]: the activity that, according to Holloway himself, Hardy
most condemns. In Hardy's world, in short, man sometimes can and
should strive *against* the natural flow of things; there is a margin for
choice and action and intelligent intervention, a chance to 'bend a
digit the poise of forces, And a fair desire fulfil'.[22] The chance to act
effectively may or may not come often, but it comes. I suspect that
this was Holloway's impression; and that his statement about
'human choice' exerting 'some influence' is the remnant of this
impression, struggling gamely for survival.

Holloway does not give it a chance: references, quotations, selective imagist interpretations—all the resources of the New Criticism
—are formidably marshalled against it, along with insistent comments
from Holloway himself: 'Nature's heterogeneous things are integrated, however obscurely', he tells us, 'into a system of *rigid and un-
deviating law.*' Again, 'That human life . . . is *wholly subject to the
control of nature* is something which the people in Hardy's novels
illustrate *everywhere.*' And, 'the life of mankind . . . is moulded by it
totally and without intermission'. Again, 'A determined system of
things ultimately *controls human affairs without regard to human
wishes*'; and much more of the same kind, not just summarizing the
evidence but directing the way we should take it. So when Holloway
says that man's choice is 'not nothing', he has on the contrary
whittled it down to exactly 'nothing': Nature saying, 'Either submit, or waste your time kicking against the pricks. Heads, I win;
tails, you lose.'

It seems that Holloway glimpsed Hardy's meaning, only to push
it out of sight. His critical method proved useless in itself to tell him
or us anything about the text; it seems only to have helped to lead
him astray, to have subserved (*a*) Holloway's old-fashioned prejudices about Hardy's pessimism, and (*b*) compatible prejudices of a
more 'modern' kind.

And Holloway's quotations could be used to illustrate a quite
different case, if differently presented: for example, arguing the all-
pervasiveness and inescapable control of Hardy's nature, Holloway
mentions the sounds over Norcombe Hill, described near the

---

[21] *Tess*, see especially chapters I, III, IV.
[22] *He wonders about himself. Collected Poems*, p. 479.

beginning of *Far from the Madding Crowd*. To illustrate not this control of nature, but Hardy's humanism, I too would quote this passage. But I would add Hardy's description of the stars in the next paragraph and his suggestion that their beauty and 'poetry of motion' become significant only when reflected in the consciousness of a human being; and I should then quote the next paragraph, in which Hardy drives home his point by switching back to the sounds, contrasting the vague uncontrolled sounds in Nature with those of a significantly different kind:

Suddenly an unexpected series of sounds began to be heard in this place up against the sky. *They had a clearness which was to be found nowhere in the wind, and a sequence which was to be found nowhere in Nature.* They were the notes of Farmer Oak's flute.[23]

Hardy has thus been describing the pervasiveness of nature only to notice where man is different, where he can be, indeed must be, independent. 'The notes of Farmer Oak's flute' represent 'man' beginning, as Arnold put it, 'where Nature ends'. But there are several stages to this proposition in *Far from the Madding Crowd*. Once, 'Nature ends' by destroying Oak's sheep. After that he does not trust the flow of nature to its 'end', but tries to intervene. And very effectively, for the most part, with the fire, with Bathsheba's sheep, with the storm, does Oak begin *before* Nature ends, replacing Nature's amorality and lack of law by human intelligence and morality.

None of Holloway's distortions is large; but all are in the same direction of denying a margin for the exercise of human intelligence or freedom, till finally we are led well out of sight of the truth. Amongst the unpractical dreamers, Holloway includes Swithin: 'the country lad', he mocks, 'who wants to be Astronomer Royal'. But this scorn was not Hardy's: Swithin's aims were not frustated, but were pursued realistically and successfully, and Viviette's sufferings were not his fault. Again, Holloway says:

The whole plot of *The Mayor of Casterbridge* turns on Henchard's deep need for kinship and his deprivation of it.

This is not quite true. Hardy's meaning is a shade more subtle. Henchard thinks, mistakenly, he needs kinship; but he then discovers that his real need is simple human affection from a girl he

---

[23] Op. cit. chapter II. (My italics.)

loves although there is no kinship. My point is that 'Life', 'Fate'—whatever Holloway likes to call it—did indeed deprive Henchard of kinship, but not of his real needs. Love and friendship were realities and recurring possibilities in his life; he was not 'deprived' of them: he neglected and destroyed them, and even so they were slow to disappear. Even his lie to Newson provides him with a way of excusing himself: he has only to say, 'Forgive me, Elizabeth-Jane. I lied because I loved you, and could not bear to lose you.' It is as easy as that. She has time to spare, and goes with him to Grey's Bridge to say goodbye; every minute (and Hardy spins them out) is another opportunity; but though he can lose nothing by the words and will gain at least the right to return, he does not speak them. . . . In one instance after another, these human opportunities, 'chinks of possibility' as Hardy called them, are denied by Holloway altogether.

Let us pause for a moment to be explicit. Hardy was a 'pessimist' in the sense that he saw life as not too easy: no Providence will extricate us from a mess just 'because we are ourselves' or because 'it can't happen to us'.[24] But between saying, thus, that life is difficult, and saying that it is impossible, there is not a slight difference of degree, there is all the difference in the world. In the first case, there is point in exploring where the possibilities of freedom and happiness may lie—and the more remote they are, the more urgent the enquiry might be deemed. In the second case, there is no point.

But Holloway continues to reduce Hardy's writings to pointlessness, to a denial of any meaning in human choice or human effort, and perhaps none of his arguments is more calculated to convince his fellow critics than his dubbing of certain images 'proleptic'. These images, he says, 'hint at a whole determined sequence of things'. Could they not hint, equally well, at the uncertainty of the future, at untoward *contingencies*? Could they not jolt man out of too placid an acceptance, and suggest that the worst might after all 'happen to us', if we let the 'sequence' drift? If the sequence is determined, we have no choice: but isn't this where Holloway begs the question? He reminds us of something he calls a proleptic image in *Tess*:

Crick the dairyman is listening to Tess herself describe how she can daydream her mind out of her body: he 'turned to her with his mouth full, his eyes charged with enquiry, and his great knife and fork . . . *planted*

---

[24] *Desperate Remedies*, I. 5, and *Two on a Tower*, XXVIII.

erect on the table like the beginning of a gallows.' On every reading after the first, the comparison is incandescent; surely it does more than any volume of generalities to fix in us Hardy's sense of the unalterable sequence of things.

This won't do. It is Holloway, not Hardy, who is trying to 'fix in us' this 'sense of the unalterable sequence of things'; and he asks us to accept the interpretation (which is, to say the least, unproven) not instead of a 'volume of generalities' but instead of Hardy's novel. In the three hundred pages of that novel between the 'proleptic' image and the gallows (no wonder that the reader is not struck by it on first reading!) the whole rhythm and tension of our interest is controlled by the reprieves, the rallies, the second chances; by our sense of what might, even at a late stage, be done to prevent the disaster. Why do circumstances prompt Tess again and again to confess? Why does she find the letter before her marriage?[25] Why are we told she would have been spared all her later sufferings had she persisted in her plan to visit Angel's parents? Why did Hardy show her as so nearly reaching that objective?[26] Why, after Izz Huett's admission that no one could love Angel more than Tess does, is Angel shown as 'within a featherweight's turn' of going back and searching her out, and taking her with him?[27] Why does Angel tell Tess at the end that 'it might have prevented much misunderstanding and woe' had she told him of the sleepwalking?[28] At these, and other points, the 'unalterable' sequence might have been altered. And any reader with an eye for images that 'fix' the sequence of things as 'unalterable' or 'determined', cuts himself off from the full experience of *Tess* and from all Hardy's other novels, where again and again the point of the narration is to indicate not only events, but also possibilities. Why does Giles have a clue—which he neglects— that Grace still loves him?[29] Why does Grace have a hint of Fitzpiers's philandering before she marries him?[30] Why those minutes when Elizabeth-Jane accompanies Henchard to Grey's Bridge?[31] And why the marriage hitches in Hardy's stories—I can think of a dozen off-hand—where there is a reprieve and a rechoice, foolish or wise?

The New Critics will have nothing but bored contempt for my

[25] 'The incident of the letter she had jumped at as if it prevented a confession; but she knew in her conscience that it need not; there was still time.' (*Tess*, XXXIII.)
[26] Chapter XLIV.
[27] *Tess*, XL.   [28] Ibid. LVIII.   [29] *Woodlanders*, XV.
[30] Ibid. XXIV.   [31] *Mayor of Casterbridge*, XLIII.

simplicity in supposing that mere incidents can weigh in an argument against *images*—the latter being regarded as in some way more
essentially part of the book, part of its 'weave'. But Hardy has used
some images that support my contention. 'Unalterable' is an abso-
lute term; and if Hardy uses images to indicate a sequence of events
that is, quite clearly, altered, he could have had no fixed opinion that
the sequence was unalterable. Two such instances I have already
referred to as 'contrasts': the elongated skeleton of the moon seen by
Oak reflected in the pond, and, still more striking, the images of war,
disaster and death before the storm. What are these but images of
what is about to happen but what, significantly, does not happen? In
the latter case it does not happen because the means employed by
Oak (including his improvised lightning conductor) *averts* the 'determined sequence' of death and disasters. Again, when Henchard
goes to Ten Hatches with the actual intention of killing himself,
what image could be more obviously proleptic than what he saw
floating in the river:

. . . He perceived with a sense of horror that it was *himself*. Not a man
somewhat resembling him, but one in all respects his counterpart. . .[32]

But Henchard had not read Dr. Holloway, so instead of plunging in
he puts on his coat and goes home. And what of the trilobite Knight
sees on the cliff and himself recognizes as an image of extinction?
Several modern critics have referred to the first part of this incident,
where a man described as highly intelligent feels as helpless as one
of the lowest of nature's creatures, and they have implied that Hardy
deliberately reduces Knight's status thus, humbles him to an acceptance of his 'creatureliness'. This word alone (Professor Brown's)
indicates how completely Hardy's point can be missed; and from
none of these critics would the reader learn that Knight was saved
from the anticipated 'sequence of things' through the exercise of a
remarkably uncreaturely, a distinctively human, intelligence, and
the will to *resist* being 'with the small in his death'.[33]

It is now commonly assumed that Hardy was chronicling the old
agricultural way of life and its roots in nature, and regretting the
impact upon that life of new methods and machinery. It is not
clear that Hardy was doing anything of the sort,[34] and since he was

[32] *The Mayor of Casterbridge*, XLI.
[33] *A Pair of blue Eyes*, XXII.   [34] See below: 'A Note on the Machine . . .'

doing many things besides, the view is a misleading simplification at best. It is the view Holloway takes in *The Victorian Sage*, but it would be unjust to pillory him for this: in a more recent essay on 'Hardy's Major Fiction'[35] he has noticed that Hardy is, after all, sometimes *attacking* the old rural order. Unfortunately this great advance in actual observation is hampered by the same prejudice that an author—or at any rate one like Hardy who writes about the country—must in the nature of things prefer the old ways of life. He believes that this must have been Hardy's attitude and that when Hardy attacks the old, therefore, he is betraying his own values, turning against himself, denying the source of his own strength and inspiration. It was Hardy's strength, Holloway explains,

to have seen the source of life-creating strength for human beings as connected always with a certain limited context, the traditional rural order. As time passed, he lost confidence in the strength of this order to resist and survive; and in part seems more and more to have regarded the element of drabness and harshness in rural life as not a product of change and modernity, but as something in that life that was ineradicably evil. This being so, he had no position to which to retreat.

The implications of this amount to a discrediting of Hardy. But the assumptions are untrue. They rest on a misunderstanding (Hardy could not lose a confidence he never possessed), and since that misunderstanding has been made possible by fashionable literary Luddism and the equally fashionable free interpretation of quotations out of context, it may be challenged.

A small point first: Hardy certainly has little to say in favour of rural life in his last novel, and Holloway puts it well when he says Arabella belongs to a 'rooted tradition of deceit'. *Tess* is a different kind of book from *Jude*; but are its values so different? Wasn't it Tess's tragedy that Angel jumped to the conclusion that she belonged to precisely that same 'tradition of deceit'? And didn't Tess in fact invite this verdict? Her mother did belong to that tradition, and Tess, who, Hardy says, was two hundred years in advance of her parents,[36] failed to live up to the *new* standards of morality that she had learnt. Hardy takes pains to show us even in the early chapters that Tess had moral scruples against going to 'claim kin' at Trantridge that her parents were quite unable to appreciate. Later, at Talbothays farm, when it is a matter of being frank with

[35] *The Charted Mirror.*   [36] *Tess*, III.

Angel, everything—gossip on the farm,[37] Tess's sense of her own unworthiness and her loyalty to the other girls,[38] Angel's reaction to the remark of the man from Trantridge,[39] to say nothing of Tess's sense of what she owes to Angel himself—all this combines to make the moral issue quite clear to her. Even the letter from her mother urging her not to confess only reminds her of the gulf that separates her mother's sense of honour from her own ('O mother, mother!').[40] I am not degrading Tess to Arabella's level; nor is Hardy, who indeed has much to say by way of excusing Tess. But in the earlier, just as in the later book, Hardy is against the 'rooted tradition of deceit', and other traditions, though he associates these with Tess's family rather than with Tess herself. He comes out very firmly too in favour of the new: particularly a new morality.[41]

Let us see what Holloway makes of *The Mayor of Casterbridge*, for this is the book he regards as the turning point, where Hardy's loss of faith in the old way of life can first be seen. Holloway sees the movement of the book centring upon the opposition between Farfrae and Henchard; and the fact that Farfrae wins, Holloway interprets as a kind of defeatism on Hardy's part, a betrayal of values; since Hardy thought little of Farfrae. He gives little evidence for Hardy's dislike of Farfrae, taking it for granted, I suppose, that we shall all agree. It is true that on one occasion Farfrae emerges from the depths of a machine, which Henchard has rashly said will never work, and with boyish enthusiasm explains to Elizabeth-Jane and Lucetta how it does work. This may be evidence of Hardy's dislike; or, again, it may not. Douglas Brown makes a point: he reminds us that when Farfrae is singing Scots songs to the people gathered in the bar of the Three Mariners, Christopher Coney asks why a man so fond of his 'ain countree' should have left it. 'They are baffled,' Brown says, 'that a man should sing so truthlessly.' But the context shows us that this point was not Hardy's: it is Professor Brown's invention.

First, who are 'they'? Everyone in the inn was captivated by the warmth of Farfrae's singing, with the one exception of Coney, who (Hardy says) 'could get no public sympathy'. Second, part of Coney's point is to ask why Farfrae has left his 'ain countree' *for Casterbridge*,

---

[37] *Tess*, XXIX, where the actual subject of confessing before marriage crops up.
[38] Ibid. XXI, XXIII, XXXI.   [39] Ibid. XXXIII.
[40] Ibid XXXI.   [41] See especially end of XI.

the defects of whose inhabitants are discussed freely, and whose 'rogues', 'lammigers', 'wanton hussies' and 'slatterns' would be unlikely, they all agree, to inspire a song. 'I've no more love for my own country,' says Christopher Coney, 'than I have for Botany Bay'—a remark in which even Brown might fail to find any loyalty to the organic community. Third, even Coney is won over (a fact Brown omits to mention) when Farfrae sings again: 'he had completely taken possession of the hearts of the Three Mariners inmates,' Hardy says. And when it was learnt that Farfrae was not going to stay in Casterbridge, 'a general sense of regret' was felt. Of particular significance are the reactions of Elizabeth-Jane, who, with her qualities of modesty and patience, represents a kind of norm:

As she looked at Farfrae from the back of the settle she decided that his statements showed him to be no less thoughtful than his fascinating melodies revealed him to be cordial and impassioned. She admired the serious light in which he looked at serious things. He had seen no jest in ambiguities and roguery, as the Casterbridge tosspots had done; and rightly not—there was none. . . .

Henchard, too, outside in the street, has been listening to Farfrae's singing, and has been deeply attracted by the Scotsman's warmth of personality: 'How that fellow does draw me!' The whole chapter [42] effectively contradicts the suggestion that Hardy could have been representing Farfrae as cold or in any way insensitive or insincere.

I have referred to this scene because it has been absurdly misrepresented; but let us swiftly review others. Farfrae enters the story through a quite gratuitous impulse to help Henchard out of a tight corner.[43] In response to the Mayor's entreaties he gives up his plans to emigrate.[44] The dislike he arouses in the Mayor later is only jealousy: he is loved and liked as an 'understanding man' by all the townsfolk.[45] All the girls wish to dance with 'one who so thoroughly understood the poetry of motion' as he did.[46] At the hiring fair, when it seems that a young man's duties to his aged father are going to separate him from his sweetheart, Farfrae is moved to tears, intervenes, and at some financial loss to himself, offers both father and son employment so that they can stay in Casterbridge.[47] Farfrae is both generous and thoughtful in buying up and giving back

[42] *The Mayor of Casterbridge*, VIII.   [43] Ibid. VI, VII.
[44] Ibid. IX.   [45] Ibid. XV.
[46] Ibid. XVI.   [47] Ibid. XXIII.

Henchard's furniture after the bankruptcy [48] and in heading a scheme for setting him up in a seed shop.[49] He is unsympathetic and withholds some of his attention when Henchard is reading Lucetta's letters [50]: would Holloway and Brown want him more warmly sympathetic here? Here and elsewhere Farfrae shows a tact and discretion foreign to Henchard.

The true significance of Farfrae's actions lies, in fact, in something more than their warmth. I shall come to this in a moment. But even the warmth is brushed aside by Holloway. Henchard's 'generosity is true magnanimity', he says, implying that Farfrae's is false. Farfrae's singing is dismissed as mere 'social accomplishment', his kindness is 'conventional'. But if we are puzzled by this estimate, the explanation is near at hand: Farfrae, Holloway scoffs,

is an agriculturalist, but of the new kind: he prospers by chemistry, machinery, book-keeping, elementary economics.

There is the indictment: Farfrae represents the new. He is therefore the incarnation of evil; and it never occurs to Holloway that Hardy might have had a different opinion. And here is Holloway on Henchard:

Henchard still stands above the others in psychic virtue. . . . He is violent and a liar and in one sense intensely selfish, but his generosity is true magnanimity, and he has reserves of affection and humility that they quite lack.

Well . . . they are strange 'reserves' that always fail Henchard when they are most needed! But Holloway continues:

The essential is something else, though: that his whole nature, good or bad, is centred upon a deep source of vital energy. The rich stream of life still issues from life's traditional order. It does not bring success, but even so, it brings greatness and in a sense goodness.

Is this true? Henchard's vulgarity (he shows off his diamonds[51] just as Alec d'Urberville does; and a tell-tale point is that what most upsets his wife Susan and almost stops her from making herself known to him is Henchard's prosperity), his snobbishness,[52] impatience, uneasiness and self-assertiveness mark him as the parvenu. He has not the poise that would justify Holloway's words.

If we give a provisional and thoughtless consent to Holloway it is

---

[48] *The Mayor of Casterbridge*, XXXII.   [49] Ibid. XLII.
[50] Ibid, XXXIV, XXXV.   [51] Ibid. V.   [52] Ibid XX.

first because Henchard has indeed energy, and second because, simply, he is the hero of the book: it is *his* story. By comparison we see little of Farfrae's private affairs, choices and problems; though we see their effects. Farfrae's gradual, rather undramatic rise is not of great interest to us or to Hardy; its main interest is that it sets off the spectacular rise and fall of Henchard. None the less if we had discussed the book with Hardy, and talked of a 'deep source of vital energy' or 'rich stream of life' issuing from 'life's traditional order', Hardy would have been bewildered. He might even have thought the remarks—so irrelevant to Henchard—must refer to the resilience of Farfrae. I do not deny Henchard's force, his potential greatness, a rough (sometimes turning to a bullying) charm. He is a wonderful hero in that he is inescapably human; he has all our 'all-too-human' weaknesses: pride, moodiness, impulsiveness, inability to co-operate. . . . But what of the 'deep source of vital energy', 'psychic virtue', the 'rich stream of life' and 'life's traditional order'? And what about '*in a sense* goodness'? What can Holloway be referring to? His language betrays the answer: he is applying the standards and values of D. H. Lawrence in the world of another writer where such criteria can only hamper us. Henchard's energy is not 'vital': it is egocentric. His impulses are to separate himself, to compete, to survive alone. These impulses eventually destroy him, but from the first they cut him off from 'the rich stream of life', from the everyday human contacts, between free men and equals, which renew and vitalize our lives. His warmest contacts, ironically enough, are with Farfrae. Our intensest experience of reading the book is our sense of Henchard's desperate loneliness: no less deeply moving because it is self-inflicted. And the tragedy lies not just in our sense of his suffering, but in the waste of great potentialities. In his business activities, as with his personal contacts, a kind of separatism is at the base of all the trouble; little or nothing 'issues from life's traditional order': he speculates, tries to corner the market, borrows, goes bankrupt: these things destroy him, and they also endanger the community and the 'traditional order'.

Turning back to Farfrae, we can now see the point of the references given earlier. Almost everything he does helps the community: his decision not to leave Casterbridge [53] (and one might add his later decision to stay on despite Lucetta's misgivings [54]); his business methods (small profits and quick returns [55]) his employment of the

---

[53] *The Mayor of Casterbridge*, IX.   [54] Ibid XXXIV.   [55] Ibid. XXIII.

young man and his father; his endeavour to provide employment for Henchard and later to set him up in business—what do these do but keep the 'traditional order' going? Henchard's employees are only too glad to work for Farfrae for a slightly lower wage because of their far greater security.[56] And what of the symbolism of Farfrae's first impact upon the story: Henchard is endangering the life and health of the whole town by supplying bad flour, bad bread; Farfrae restores that life.[57]

There is more in the contrast still. Henchard fails to cope with circumstances, nature, the chances of changing rural conditions. Farfrae shows what can be done with exactly the same set of circumstances. But he is not just a foil. He not only *shows* Henchard, but also provides him with the means of *doing*: of fulfilling his great possibilities. Hardy is not just condemning the old (in Henchard) and advocating the new (in Farfrae), or vice versa. He was exploring the possibilities of one helping the other, and suggesting that the new might help the old to survive.[58] It is here, however, that Holloway makes a more than usually puzzling statement:

From beginning to end Henchard's course is downward. Whenever his old way of life meets the new, it is defeated.

The reader will remember that, on the contrary, Henchard's course is not just downward. With Farfrae's help, 'the great corn and hay traffic conducted by Henchard throve . . . as it had never thriven before,' Hardy tells us. 'It had formerly moved in jolts; now it went on oiled casters.'[59] Farfrae is presented as the key to Henchard's success. It is only when Henchard's way of life *rejects* the new, and continues to reject it, that it is defeated.

Holloway's main argument is that in *The Mayor of Casterbridge* we see a change in Hardy's attitude: here for the first time we see the old traditional and good being defeated by the tawdry and the new. I trust I have shown that the movement of the book does not mean quite this. But even if Hardy *were* showing the good being defeated by the common or worthless, would this mean that he was being, in any degree, defeatist? What then should a writer do? Show the good

[56] *The Mayor of Casterbridge*, XXXI.   [57] Ibid. V.
[58] A note written by Hardy in February 1881, about three years before *The Mayor of Casterbridge* was begun, reads: 'Conservatism is not estimable in itself, nor is change, or Radicalism. To conserve the existing good, to supplant the existing bad by good, is to act on a true political principle, which is neither Conservative nor Radical.'—*Early Life*, p. 191; *Life*, p. 148.   [59] Op. cit. XIV.

triumphing over the worthless? That would indeed be a reassuring display of 'poetic justice'!

Notions about 'poetic justice' never die; and it is surely some confusion over what tragedy does that lies behind Holloway's treatment of *The Return of the Native*. It is this book, published eight years before *The Mayor*, that he uses to prove how Hardy's attitude had changed; for in *The Return of the Native* Holloway finds none of the signs that so disquiet him later. 'Egdon triumphs,' he says:

The renegades have been destroyed or won over. Even if Venn had not married Thomasin, the faithful would have been in possession. The novel resolves in an assertion of the old order, its regenerative austerity, its rewarding unrewardingness.

Egdon has indeed triumphed: the Egdon of poor Susan Nunsuch and the adders: superstition, prejudice, ignorance, misunderstanding. But if Holloway—and here isn't he merely paraphrasing Lawrence?—supposes that Hardy was showing what *ought to* happen, he is missing Hardy's irony and foisting upon him a quite alien contempt for human values.

And we can go back further still, to *Far from the Madding Crowd*, written four years before *The Return of the Native*, and find—*pace* Dr. Holloway—still the same standpoint, except that here the tone is not tragic, and we find no ironic suggestion of 'unfulfilled intentions' running beneath the story; not, at least, if we read it to its conclusion. The book depicts an agricultural community that is easy-going and inefficient: the rustics cannot put out a fire unaided (Hardy calls them 'that class of society which casts its thoughts into the form of feeling, and its feelings into commotion'[60]), they get drunk when there is work to do, letters are delivered to the wrong people, the bailiff is dishonest, a farmer leaves his harvest uncovered in a storm . . . and so on. Into this community come two strangers. One is Bathsheba, whose parents were townsfolk, shopkeepers: and Hardy makes a special point of her new and unconventional approach to farming. The other is Gabriel Oak, who comes from the bleak downs of Norcombe: less distant than Farfrae's homeland but distant all the same from the comparatively lush valley of Weatherbury. Gabriel, too, comes with new skills, and new standards of conscience and conduct. Between them, these two newcomers pull the old community together and give it new life.

[60] *Far from the Madding Crowd*, VI.

And going back further still, only a naïve reader, surely, can regard some of the descriptions of the Mellstock parishioners in *Under the Greenwood Tree* as quite devoid of satire? The *tone* changes as Hardy grows older; that, no one will deny. But the values are the same; Hardy is only trying to express them (it is a sobering thought!) more emphatically.

If there were not a sorriness about the whole process of destroying an author's meaning, some of the misunderstandings would have at least an entertainment value. It is especially difficult not to be amused at Holloway's comment on the glow-worm scene in *The Return of the Native*, when he writes of Diggory Venn's luck with the dice as the 'tide of life' running with the countryman. In the previous scene in the Quiet Woman Inn, Hardy had forestalled just this interpretation, and made fun of the *mystique* about luck and the 'tide of life' in the dice. Christian Cantle—another countryman indeed, but 'almost the village idiot', as one critic has called him—makes virtually the same comment as Holloway; he congratulates himself on his luck, and the 'power' that is in him: a piece of fatuousness that is not lost on the bystanders, since the luck of the dice, the 'tide of life', has given him a gown for a wife he does not possess![61]

What is the cause of this almost total failure of communication? Has Holloway glanced only at a few pages of the novels? Is he one of those 'experts' acclaimed by Oscar Wilde who judge a vintage by 'rinsing a glassful round the mouth'? I believe he is well aware that a novel is not a vintage, and cannot be tasted in the same way. He objects to this kind of reading as much as I do; he has put forward all the arguments against it, and done so far better than I can. He is strongly in favour of reading the whole work, and has doubtless read the whole of *The Mayor* and of *The Return of the Native*, and read them attentively. The trouble is that he has read them with strong preconceptions as to what he would find there.

Perhaps this is what we all do; it may be what I have done myself, with the excuse, however, that mine is a point of view derived

---

[61] I would suggest that the real significance of the gambling scene is as follows: neither Diggory Venn nor his author believes in gambling or any other taking of unnecessary chances in the ordinary business of life. Venn does not regard it as reasonable conduct or a 'good chance'; it is, simply, the *only* chance, the one possibility of winning back Tamsin's guineas. He takes this last chance and is successful—or rather he could have been successful if he had taken reasonable care to discover the proper destination of the guineas. Luck and good intentions, even combined with Diggory's perseverance (can Hardy be suggesting?) are insufficient: his action, to borrow a phrase of Hardy's from another context, is 'without the knowledge that should really guide it'.

not from other criticism but from Hardy's books and his own protests; it is a point of view that has not had a fair hearing, and it
seeks to modify the one-sided criticism of the past. But apart from
such attempts at redressing the balance, is there any justification for
interpretative criticism? What is the critic doing, and for whom?
Between the two extremes of those who understand literature anyway, and those who cannot, are people more likely to get something
from literature by making the attempt unimpeded, or by relying on
the help of the sort of criticism we have discussed?

Against some of my contentions there is a possible argument:
namely, that there would be no point in writing an accurate account
of a poem or a novel, for this merely endorses what the author has
written, narrowing the meaning in the way that any second-hand
version, any paraphrase, must do. A misrepresentation has the
virtue (it could be argued) of a 'free interpretation', of being 'creative'. Here perhaps is the crux of the matter: it cannot be so creative,
I contend, as the work of art itself. And the more creative it sets out
to be, and the more it seeks to impose upon the reader the critic's
sensitivity, the less likely it is to send the reader back to the work of
literature itself. This is also true of those critics who represent
Hardy with patronizing tolerance as a kind of Richard Jefferies or
D. H. Lawrence manqué: these may send the reader to Jefferies or
Lawrence, warning him off Hardy or conditioning and severely
limiting his responses to this author. But even if Lawrence and
Jefferies are greater authors (as these critics seem to assume), is this
merging, this identification, what we want? Would it not be preferable to preserve distinctions and differences? Are not the critics with
their crudifications destroying the richness and variety of our
literature, and blunting our tastes?

Any critic, however good or however bad, knows that he can cover
but a fraction of the meaning or the appeal of a work of literature.
From this it follows that whatever else he does, whatever he tells us
about the work of literature, is useless unless he sends us back to
read it or re-read it for ourselves with an open mind; he must awaken
or re-awaken our interest in the work itself. This is one of the proper
functions of criticism, probably the chief.

II

A Note on the 'Machine' in
Tess of the d'Urbervilles

AS WE HAVE SEEN, the preservation of intact rural communities and 'traditional sanctities' has inspired some of Hardy's critics but seems to have concerned Hardy himself remarkably little. Indeed he said of the Dorset villagers:

They are losing their individuality, but they are widening the range of their ideas, and gaining in freedom. It is too much to expect them to remain stagnant and old-fashioned for the pleasure of romantic spectators.[1]

Hardy was much more concerned with the difficulties of man helping man 'to unify the mortal lot', difficulties of overcoming prejudice, convention, inhibition or any other of the barriers between individuals or groups that cause unnecessary suffering. Such problems sound nebulous, perhaps, but they are worked out clearly and consistently enough in the personal and social relationships in the novels.

To the solution of such problems, machines had not yet proved their relevance. Hardy did not dislike them. What he disliked was the fact that men complacently pointed to machines as if they represented real achievements of a human and moral kind. In *The Jubilee of a Magazine* [2] the point is made clearly: he concedes the mechanical inventions of fifty years,

> But if we ask, what has been done
> To unify the mortal lot. . . .
> Beyond mechanic furtherance—what
> Advance can rightness, candour, claim?
> Truth bends abashed, and answers not.

The same point is made in the biography: Hardy writes to Mrs. Henniker in 1919 deploring the lack of real progress in the world

[1] *The Dorsetshire Labourer, Longman's Magazine*, July 1883.
[2] *Collected Poems*, p. 386.

and complaining that 'All development is of a material and scientific kind'[3]; but his point is that scientific progress *should not exclude* moral progress.

That it did in practice seem to be excluding moral progress is perhaps the implication of remarks still later in his life [4]; but certainly until the war years Hardy had suspended judgement, feeling that the machine held at least possibilities for good. There is a scene in *Tess of the d'Urbervilles* (it is when Tess and Angel take the milk to the railway station at Wellbridge[5]) where he hints that the railway is bringing not only prosperity and markets to the rural farms, but health (if the milk is not too much watered!) to the people of the cities. Indeed he makes again the point [6] he made in the Preface to *Two on a Tower*, by describing the 'lamp' of the little station as 'a poor enough terrestrial star, yet in one sense of more importance to Talbothays Dairy and mankind than the celestial ones to which it stood in such humiliating contrast'. Moreover in the passage defining his 'evolutionary meliorism' in the Apology prefixed to *Late Lyrics and Earlier*, and quoted in the next Note, Hardy refers to the certain gains to be derived from scientific knowledge.

But what of the threshing machine in *Tess* [7] which has attracted the attention of the Lawrentian critics? It is true that this machine and the engineer who works it are described by Hardy with some distaste:

The isolation of [the engineman's] manner and colour lent him the appearance of a creature from Tophet, who had strayed into the pellucid smokelessness of this region of yellow grain and pale soil, with which he had nothing in common, to amaze and discompose its aborigines.

But the impact is not a major theme of the novel, which is not about the decay of the peasantry, since Hardy makes it clear that the Durbeyfields are typical of the worst, not the best of the 'peasants'. So let us forget for the moment what the passage I have quoted might have meant had it been written a few decades later, and by another writer, and see how the threshing machine fits into Hardy's novel, and Tess's story.

We remember the machine mainly because, exhausting as it is, Tess prefers to remain working with it rather than meet Alec, who is

[3] *Later Years*, p. 192; *Life*, p. 389.   [4] *Later Years*, p. 213; *Life*, pp. 405–6.
[5] *Tess*, XXX.   [6] See above p. 11.   [7] Chapters XLVII and XLVIII.

waiting for her. It is a crucial point in her life: Tess is made acutely aware of her precarious position. Can she hold out? To read these two chapters is to remember how often Hardy is concerned with the problem of time, and to realize that the machine is a symbol of accelerated time. Its time is limited, for it has to be moved on to other farms; Farmer Groby, to save expense, insists that the work shall be finished before the end of the day. The machine itself, 'whilst it was going, kept up a despotic demand' upon all those who worked with it; for Tess, we are told, 'there was no respite; for as the drum never stopped, the man who fed it could not stop, and she . . . could not stop either. . . '.

When I come to deal with Hardy's poetry, I shall have to deal more explicitly with Hardy's attitude towards time and its relation to happiness; here I must be content with reminding the reader how often Hardy returns to the subject:

It is the ongoing—i.e. the 'becoming'—of the world that produces its sadness. If the world stood still at a felicitous moment there would be no sadness in it. The sun and moon standing still on Ajalon was not a catastrophe for Israel but a type of Paradise.[8]

There Hardy touches the quick of the nineteenth-century ulcer, from Keats, trying to escape into the timeless world of the Urn, or prolonging 'for ever' the ecstacy of being 'pillowed upon' his 'fair love's ripening breast', to Schopenhauer and Arnold with their consciousness of the 'sick hurry' and 'divided aims' of civilized man. But it seemed to Hardy that there were two possible mistakes. First, one could be *too much* concerned about time, and so miss present happiness in regretting the past or worrying about the future; like little Old Father Time, absurdly unable to enjoy the flowers because he knew they would fade,[9] or like Eustacia, 'full of fears' even whilst Clym is wooing her, because 'love will evaporate like a spirit'[10]; or, again, like Giles Winterborne 'all night' thinking over 'that unsatisfactory ending of a pleasant time, forgetting the pleasant time itself'.[11] Or, second, one could be concerned with time *too little*: losing the 'gleam' of the present equally unhappily, by letting it slip by unheeded, while one is 'looking away'.[12] All Hardy's novels are, to

[8] *Early Life, p.* 265; *Life*, p. 202.   [9] *Jude*, V-v.
[10] *The Return of the Native*, III. iv.   [11] Woodlanders, XXXIX.
[12] The reference is to the last lines of *The Self Unseeing*: '. . . Blessings emblazoned that day; Everything glowed with a gleam; Yet we were looking away.'

a greater or lesser degree, about time; and there is a special irony in Tess's attempt to avoid Alec, her demand that time should stand still at this very juncture when everything seems to combine with the machine to tell her that the tyrant time cannot be stopped.

Postponement is a theme of the book. At the beginning the Durbeyfields are described as '*waiters* upon Providence', and even Tess, conscious as she is of the weaknesses of her family and anxious to do something to help the budget and pay for the loss of the horse, makes only half-hearted attempts to get 'some light occupation in the immediate neighbourhood' (VI). It is because she fails to control circumstances in time, that circumstances push her eventually in the direction of Trantridge and Alec. Even then Hardy does not describe Tess as hopelessly trapped: she has paid one visit to the d'Urbervilles, and knows, or has misgivings about, what she is in for. But even if she has had only slight misgivings about Alec after her first visit, these become definite enough when Alec fetches her for the second journey and pesters her on the road. The seduction is not a sudden one; she knows what to expect; but does nothing with the reprieve.

So too with the confession: she knows what she must do, but fails to act in time. And when she turns back from Emminster Vicarage,[13] it is with thoughts of summoning up courage for another attempt later; but the attempt is never made, though her meeting with Alec should have urged upon her the still greater necessity for it.

Angel is not free from blame on this score; he too fails to see any threat in the pressure of time, any danger in postponement: when, after his hesitation, he pushes on with his plans to go to Brazil without seeing Tess again, it is with the thought that 'he could always come back to her'; and it never occurs to him that circumstances might have changed in the meantime. Angel's first entry into the story is significant: he leaves something undone; he looks back, sees Tess, 'the pretty maiden with whom he had not danced', gazing after him. And although 'he felt he had acted stupidly', he hurried on after his brothers. One recalls Angel's negligence, too, in not writing to Tess. 'Too Late Beloved', Hardy's first title for the book, clearly refers to these failures of Angel's; but at the moment we are more concerned with the tendency to drift, to postpone, to leave things to chance, on the part of Tess herself.

[13] Op. cit. XLIV.

And here the threshing machine assumes a central position: a symbol of time's tyranny, time's pressure, amidst the comparatively easy-going seasonal rhythm of the countryside; and yet also a reprieve from Alec, the very temporariness of which is a reminder that she must do something. For all the time she knows Alec is waiting. And, ironically, the very shaking of the machine tires her out, shakes her resolution; although that same evening she also writes a long and desperate appeal to her husband.

That is all she does with her reprieve. When the other girls, less capable than Tess, leave Farmer Groby and secure better-paid and more congenial work, Tess—having had 'a vaguely-shaped hope that something would happen to render another outdoor engagement unnecessary' (XLVI)—is unemployed. Hardy's words are critical; but Tess herself had on several occasions in the past proved the value of encountering life's difficulties realistically, she had learnt to distrust 'd'Urberville air-castles' and the Durbeyfield *Compleat Fortune Teller*; so to her too 'a vaguely shaped hope that something would happen' must have seemed an inadequate basis for inaction. Hardy goes on to point his moral by describing a Lady-day encounter between the brightly painted waggon taking Marion and Izz to their new work and the unpainted 'creaking erection' on which the Durbeyfield family and furniture with its typical 'muck and muddle' is in disorganized transit to Kingsbere, where Mrs. Durbeyfield has failed to secure lodgings, so that they and their belongings have all to be dumped in the approach to the churchyard.

'Less capable than Tess': there is the irony. It is Tess's capability, her physical strength and stoical endurance, of which indeed she has already given abundant proof at Flintcomb Ash, that come out most strongly in the threshing machine scene. Farmer Groby puts Tess to work on the machine partly perhaps because he has a grudge against her, but partly because she can best do it: 'she was one of those who best combined strength with quickness in untying, and both with staying power.' Moreover, she stays at the tiring and exacting work longer than she need in her desire to escape Alec. How is it that this same girl, almost heroic in her patience and endurance, turned back so weakly at Emminster, and despite Alec's molestations, made no second attempt? Hardy may be implying something here about Tess's nature which could not be said more openly in those times without losing the sympathy of too many readers; I mean a certain compliance and weakness that were essential accompaniments of her very warmth and passionate woman-liness. But whether that is the case or not, he is clearly keen to suggest a curious mingling of strength and weakness in other parts of Tess's character, in her will; and to indicate how far Tess fell short of her considerable potentialities.

III

A Note on 'The President of the Immortals'

A REFERENCE to this phrase in my first chapter has already indicated that it can, and indeed, if we are to make sense of Hardy's books, must, be taken ironically. The phrase is part of a sentence (the manuscript shows) that Hardy added to the final paragraph of the book. I regard the insertion as unfortunate, as I shall explain later; although not the serious blunder it is sometimes taken to be. Through it, Hardy's reputation has suffered out of all proportion to its seriousness.

It is doubtful whether, at this late date, we can clear up the general misunderstanding of Hardy, without considering briefly how it has come about. In the introductory chapter, I was more concerned with recent misrepresentations, but I indicated that a major cause of misunderstanding was an early preconception about his pessimism, upon which later mistakes were grafted. When Hardy was credited with a belief in a malign force, or a malign being, that frustrated all human efforts, he protested,

As I need hardly inform any thinking reader, I do not hold, and never have held, the ludicrous opinions . . . assumed to be mine.[1]

What, then, were the opinions he did hold? On 1 January 1902—it was often his custom to write down more carefully considered opinions on New Year's Day—Hardy made a note entitled 'A Pessimist's Apology':

Pessimism (or rather what is called such) is, in brief, playing the sure game. You cannot lose at it; you may gain. It is the only view of life in which you can never be disappointed. Having reckoned what to do in the worst possible circumstances, when better arise, as they may, life becomes child's play.[2]

This optimistic assertion of the practical value of pessimism, is

---

[1] *Later Years*, p. 4, *Life*, pp. 243-4.   [2] *Later Years*, p. 91; *Life*, p. 311.

clearly related closely to the attitude we have discussed earlier: the readiness to adapt oneself to life as it is, to lower one's demands upon life, to forgo one's dreams of the bed of roses, with Cleopatra thrown in for good measure, that we feel life ought to be.

The date of the 'Pessimist's Apology', 1902, is much later than the time when many critics suppose Hardy abandoned all hope in man's betterment. But even at the end of his life, after he had been saddened by the 1914–18 war, we still find him putting forward basically the same views:

What is today, in allusions to the author's pages, alleged to be "pessimism" is, in truth, only such "questionings" in the exploration of reality, and is the first step towards the soul's betterment, and the body's also.

If I may be forgiven for quoting my own words, let me repeat what I printed in this relation more than twenty years ago, and wrote much earlier, in a poem entitled "In Tenebris":

If way to the Better there be, it exacts a full look at the Worst:

that is to say, by the exploration of reality, and its frank recognition stage by stage along the survey, with an eye to the best consummation possible: briefly, evolutionary meliorism.

And in the next paragraph we find him pleading that pain to all upon the globe

shall be kept down to a minimum by loving-kindness, operating through *scientific knowledge* [my italics] and actuated by the modicum of free will conjecturally possessed by organic life when the mighty necessitating forces—unconscious or other—that have "the balancings of the clouds", happen to be in equilibrium, which may or may not be often.[3]

The tone is less buoyant than in the 'Pessimist's Apology'; and for this, indeed, there is little wonder. But we are still a long way from the kind of pessimism critics claim to find in Hardy's novels.

I have already indicated one method of misreading Hardy: a simple failure to read on, to read the whole book, the next chapter, the next paragraph, even the last half of a sentence; an inability to see two events together and to let one throw light on the other. But sometimes we seem unable to read the actual words before us, in our impatience, our conviction that we already know what Hardy is going to say. An example of this is provided by the note:

[3] Preface to *Late Lyrics and Earlier*.

Oct. 30th, 1870. Mother's notion (and also mine)—that a figure stands in our van with arm uplifted, to knock us back from any pleasant prospect we indulge in as probable.

Critical comment, including that of the editor of Hardy's *Notebooks*, has assumed that Hardy is here stating a conviction that all man's efforts in the way of amelioration are brought to nothing by an evil and omnipotent being. If that is what Hardy means, it is not what he says. The figure does not 'knock us back' from everything pleasant, but only from those prospects we 'indulge in as probable'—those towards which we have aimed our steps too directly, too optimistically. And that this is what Hardy meant, we can see by turning to another passage written, or revised, at this very date; the words are different, but the statement is almost identical:

. . . once more in the history of human endeavour a position which it was impossible to reach by any direct attempt was come to by a seeker's swerving from the path.[4]

Faced with the fact that Hardy's note and other passages have been misread, one can only conclude that the minds of many readers move along different tracks from those favoured by Hardy himself. It is not easy to change tracks, perhaps the gauge of our thoughts, as we all know. But to say this, is merely to define prejudice. How did the prejudice first come about? The 'Pessimist's Apology', advice about taking 'a full look at the Worst', and similar remarks in the novels themselves, such as Louis's warning to Tabitha, 'We generally think we shall be lucky ourselves, though all the world before us, in the same situation, have been otherwise',[5] seem sensible and harmless. How was it, then, that this rather commonplace 'philosophy' brought upon Hardy's head all kinds of protests and misrepresentations from our Victorian and Edwardian grandfathers?

The answer is that beneath the apparent harmlessness of the 'Pessimist's Apology' and all statements of the same tendency, whether explicit or by way of narration, there lies what is in effect— and, indeed, in intention—a denial of Providence. Hardy is keen to show that no Being, or Force, is going to change the course of things for us. If we want things changed, then it is no good to let things

---

[4] *Desperate Remedies*, VI. 4. This novel was revised in the autumn of 1870.
[5] *Two on a Tower*, XXVIII. The same thought is expressed in *Desperate Remedies*, I. 5: 'There is in us an unquenchable expectation, which in the gloomiest time persists in inferring that because we are *ourselves*, there must be a special future in store for us. . . .'

drift, to trust to 'the favour of accident', or to *The Compleat Fortune-Teller*, like those 'waiters upon Providence', the Durbeyfields [6]; we must do something ourselves. Alec d'Urberville is sometimes derided as a villain of Victorian melodrama. Hardy obviously intended the likeness to be noticed, but he was making one big difference clear to his Victorian readers: Alec's seduction of Tess, 'a pure woman', was successful. A typical villain of Victorian melodrama would have been foiled by the intervention of Providence.

It is the purpose of the next chapter, on Hardy and Wilkie Collins, to discuss Hardy's ironical treatment of Providence and his adoption of an indirect method. I need hardly insist how difficult it was in the nineteenth century to write directly; nor need I remind the reader how many authors complained of the tyrannous restrictions imposed by editors and public. We may remember Hardy's heartbreaking difficulties over *Tess of the d'Urbervilles*, but his determination to find a way round the 'figure' that then stood in his van. Dr. R. L. Purdy, in his excellent bibliography, notes that certain key chapters which could not be printed in the serial form were published *in advance*, so that Hardy's more serious readers should have a chance of understanding the real book. Many other changes were made for the serial publication, and made laboriously; and then, at last, with equal labour, the text was restored and rewritten for final publication in book form. For a long time, however, Hardy had clung to the optimistic belief that people would be eager enough to understand his books, that he was voicing opinions accepted generally, but tacitly. There was a wide gap, he believed, between what 'everybody thinks' and what 'everybody says'; and the writer should address himself to those more enlightened thoughts that men habitually keep unspoken.[7] When, even in the Preface to the first edition of *Tess*, he asked,

any too genteel reader who cannot endure to have said what everybody thinks and feels, to remember a well-worn sentence of St Jerome's—'If an offence come out of the truth, better is it that the offence come than that the truth be concealed,'

He was expressing himself defensively, hoping still to win over the 'too genteel' reader, and expecting most others to endure, indeed to welcome, the saying of 'what everybody thinks and feels'.

[6] The references are to *Tess*, chapters VII, III and V respectively.
[7] *Early Life*, 102 and 211; *Life*, pp. 77 and 162.

Hardy may have been underestimating, then, the difficulties of communication. Or it may be that many of those for whom he wrote at the time understood him well enough, and saw the point of the ironic contrasts we discussed in the introductory essay. Like dramatic irony, the irony is directed not against the reader, but against some of the fictional persons, and raises questions of the type, 'why was Troy completely baffled by a problem solved at once by Bathsheba's commonsense?'[8] or 'how was it that Jack Durbeyfield could labour heroically to bury the carcase of his horse, when he was too ill or too lazy to cultivate vegetables for his family?'[9] 'Why did Barnet make no effort to revive the spark of Lucy's love for him, when he had recognized so magnificently the value of perseverance when it was a matter of reviving the spark of life in his unlovable wife?'[10] and so on. 'The President of the Immortals, in Aeschylean phrase, had ended his sport with Tess' is irony of a different kind, because it is aimed, at least partly, against the reader. But irony it is and this can easily be shown.

Coming in the very last paragraph, the sentence—if we take its meaning literally—contradicts a number of insistent stresses in the book. Tess is neither a very strong, nor a very weak character; like so many of Hardy's people, she has potentialities for a much better life than she leads. But, as critics have often noticed when they have wanted to accuse Hardy of inconsistency, she is not the victim of any supernatural power; she is the victim of man and man-made circumstances. Hardy makes little of the fact that she is Alec's victim; she should have recovered from that, and nearly did. She is much more the victim of a conventional idea of morality, of the condemnation of society coming to her through the mouth of the man she loves. And no reader who reads *Tess*, making sense of the book in ordinary good faith, can suppose that Hardy was equating the man-made conventions and man-made morality of which Tess is a victim, with Fate or anything superhuman. Hardy clearly regarded such morality as obsolescent, ready to be swept away; man-made, but belonging to the past, something that could and must be changed [11] —and, in fact, *Tess of the d'Urbervilles* did much to change it. In addition there is the whole complex of circumstance—again essentially man-made circumstance—that surrounds Tess initially: the fatal weakness of the 'shiftless house of Durbeyfield' described so

---

[8] *Far from the Madding Crowd*, XLVI.   [9] *Tess*, IV.
[10] *Fellow Townsmen*, V and IX.   [11] See, particularly, the end of chapter XI.

adequately in the first twelve chapters of the book, and the scandalous irresponsibility of Tess's mother who, 'trusting to the favour of accident', had sent Tess to Trantridge quite unprepared. Nor is it possible to excuse Tess herself who, knowing better, so often slid into the typical rural fatalistic acceptances[12]; Tess, who endured some things so bravely, yet failed to reach Angel's parents ('She knew it was all sentiment, all baseless impressibility . . .'). All through the novel Hardy is writing of human weaknesses, and pleading for just that degree of greater effort and courage, of readier sympathy and tolerance and humanity. And after all these protests against the alterable in the human situation, it is hardly sensible to take the 'President of the Immortals' literally, thus *contradicting* its whole context. Instead, the phrase must *take its meaning from* its context: 'Some people, God help them, may still suppose,' Hardy is saying, 'like Aeschylus long ago, or like Joan Durbeyfield, shifting the blame from her own shoulders, that Fate can be blamed for Tess's disaster. The reader may wish to believe this too: but surely I have shown where the real blame lies.'

A little reflection shows that this is not only the most meaningful interpretation in the context, but that it is borne out by considering the other novels. We may recall that Troy blamed Fate, and *surrendered to* it; Henchard, in his weaker moments, does the same thing: he gambles on his luck, puts himself into Fate's hands, and then blames Fate instead of himself. In *The Return of the Native* Hardy refers, quite definitely though in different words, to the same 'President of the Immortals' when he says of Eustacia: '*Instead of blaming herself for the issue* (my italics), she laid the fault upon the shoulders of some indistinct *colossal Prince of the World* who had framed her situation and ruled her lot.'[13] In blaming Eustacia thus, Hardy makes it clear that he does not himself believe in this 'colossal Prince of the World'; but that he regards this Personage as merely the invention of those who wish to shift the blame from their own shoulders, as Troy and Eustacia and Tess's mother do.

At the beginning of this note, however, I admitted that Hardy's

---

[12] Cf. 'Tess was now carried along upon the wings of the hours, without the sense of a will. . . . Her naturally bright intelligence had begun to admit the fatalistic convictions common to field-folk and those who associate more extensively with natural phenomena than with their fellow creatures; and she accordingly drifted into that passive responsiveness to all things her lover suggested, characteristic of the frame of mind' (XXXII). For a more detailed analysis of the conflict between Tess's 'naturally bright intelligence' and her tendency to lapse into 'fatalistic convictions' see chapter VII below.

[13] *Return of the Native*, IV. viii.

reference to the 'President of the Immortals' was a mistake. In the earlier chapters, and indeed through all but the final section of the book, Hardy insisted on the human causes for Tess's loss of happiness, and particularly upon the Durbeyfields' 'reckless acquiescence in chance' (XXXVII) and their willingness to blame 'nater', 'God' or accident for any mishap. He has insisted enough; and we do not need the reminder. Moreover, in the final section of the book, which Hardy calls 'Fulfilment', there is a complete change of tone, of key, comparable to the mature change that has taken place in Angel himself. For the first time, Angel loves Tess not as an idealized figure but as the woman she is, even though she may be a murderess; and for the first time he approaches life as it is, 'with an instinct as to possibilities' (LVII). Hardy's writing too, is direct, with a simple dignity befitting the denouement of the tragedy. His first instinct, it seems to me, was right; and the afterthought that prompted the additional words was mistaken; for the irony is just out of key, or any irony, I should say, in addition to the more generalized ' "Justice" was done . . . '.

There is an integrity in not explaining irony. Hardy's defence was not that he was being ironical, but simply that he was using figurative language; and the implication that in using a 'well-known trope', he was doing much less than affirming a belief in the 'President of the Immortals' must, I suppose, seem odd to many modern critics. But is there anything specially absurd in his contention? In *The Well-Beloved* there are many references, and much more consistent ones, to the Goddess of Love. The effect, however, is not to suggest that Hardy believes in her, under any of her names or manifestations. Indeed he is rejecting her, as a kind of romanticism indulged in by Pierston, the hero. I suspect that many readers are made uneasy by Hardy's classical references just for this reason: to refer to classical deities when you clearly do not believe in them, is to weaken them, to bring them into disrepute; and consciously or unconsciously, but with a kind of insistent if often somewhat affectionate irony, this seems to me just what Hardy is trying to do.

IV

Hardy Starts upon his Career
as a Novelist

THE IRONY of 'the President of the Immortals' is not typical of
Hardy, as we have seen. More usually his irony consists simply in
leaving something unstated or at least understated, in presenting an
incident which takes on its full meaning only in the light of subsequent events, or in presenting it already framed for the reader by
events that have gone before.

Hardy is not commonly credited with understating things or
leaving them unsaid, but this may be due to mistaken assumptions
as to what he intends to say. When Hardy tells us in *Tess* that the
country people shrug their shoulders and say, 'It was to be', he at the
same time shows us that it need not have been—at least, not always.
But it is not only the country people. Behind Knight's growing distrust of Elfride in *A Pair of Blue Eyes* lies the point that the distrust
is undeserved, and the pain he is about to inflict upon Elfride and
himself is unnecessary. The woman Knight rejects had once proved
her worth and her love for him by risking her life to save his,[1] a fact
of which Hardy reminds the reader later on only in the most casual
way. And yet this incident is, of course, the frame in which the
reader sees nearly all the subsequent events of the book, and realizes
what should have become of Knight and Elfride and their relationship. Knight's inexperience and folly and Elfride's foolish but understandable lack of frankness make up the 'ill-judged execution' (by
human beings, be it noted) of the 'well-judged plan of things'; an
'intention' is left 'unfulfilled'.

And Hardy's notorious 'coincidences' are 'ironical' in the same
sense. They are not statements that bad luck is inevitable. To invent
a crude instance: if I spend an evening at the roulette table betting
upon a single number and always losing, and play my last stake
and lose that; and then watch someone take my place, play on the
same number and immediately break the bank, there is nothing I can

[1] XXI, XXII.

do, or could have done, about it; and I at least have the satisfaction of having played my game to the end. This, it seems to me, is just what Hardy does not show. Those rare individuals who are determined to make use of every chance, including their last one, are usually successful (Oak, Reynard, the reformed Fitzpiers, Ethelberta, Venn, the Napoleon of the Elba escape,[2] and so on). Hardy's failures are more often those who give in just too soon, who throw away their last chance. Hardy is more likely to have shown the gambler hesitate and withdraw his last stake, to be cashed in for the fare home or to the cliff edge. The irony of seeing the next player win would not mock the gambler's complete helplessness but prompt the thought that he had been within a throw of recovering his fortune. 'To have lost is less disturbing than to wonder if we may possibly have won.'[3] When South dies, Giles does not just lose the lease: he finds he could have renewed it [4]; Barnet would have won Lucy, if he had called on her once more [5]; the mother in *A Sunday Morning Tragedy* despaired just too soon and so did the bride in *A Conversation at Dawn*. Eustacia leaves home without seeing the letter from Clym which would have changed her mind and saved her life[6]—I mention only instances that are close to my case of the gambler. But in the same way, if Tess had found the letter *after* her marriage,[7] if Troy, prostrated with grief at Fanny's grave, had known that he had done all he could for Fanny in her lifetime . . . there would be no irony in these stories; or it would be a different irony, not Hardy's.

A glance at Hardy's first approach to fiction throws light on his aims. Meredith made two suggestions when, as Chapman's reader, he discouraged Hardy from publishing *The Poor Man and the Lady*: first, that Hardy should express his views on life less directly; and, second, that he should write a novel 'with a more complicated "plot".'[8] It is always assumed that the first piece of advice referred only to Hardy's social views. But a comparison between *An Indiscretion in the Life of an Heiress* (which Rutland [9] has shown to be an extract, virtually unchanged, from *The Poor Man*) and Hardy's later novels, indicates that the advice may have been given and taken in a more general sense as well. *An Indiscretion* is oddly direct in method, and

---

[2] *Dynasts*, III. V. i.
[3] *Return of the Native*, V-v.
[4] *Woodlanders*, XIV.
[5] *Fellow Townsmen*, IX.
[6] *Return of the Native*, V. vii.
[7] *Tess*, XXXIII.
[8] *Early Life*, p. 82; *Life*, p. 62.
[9] W. R. Rutland, *Thomas Hardy, a study of his writings & their background*.

thus sets in relief the ironical narration which usually characterizes the later novels and stories. As the book is not easily accessible, I will summarize part of it.

The hero, Egbert Mayne, learns that his grandfather is to be evicted from his farm. Readers of the later novels will expect that the situation will be left until nothing can be done, so that the irony of Fate, not human dilatoriness, can be blamed; but this is not so. Egbert decides that every attempt must be made, every string pulled, to prevent the disaster. Doing all he can means not merely taking what chances come his way, but *making* those chances. Egbert contrives a meeting with Geraldine Allenville, daughter of the owner of the manor and the surrounding property, to plead his grandfather's cause. Unfortunately he falls in love with her; and the meeting becomes the first of a series of contrived 'tender waylayings'. That these 'accidents' are really under the control of the human will even becomes the point of a mild joke, significantly repeated:

He told his fair mistress at their next accidental meeting (much sophistry lay in their definition of "accidental" at this season) that he had determined to leave Tollamore . . .

And—

Meetings had latterly taken place between them *without any pretence of accident*.

But Geraldine is alarmed by Egbert's love, or by the growth of her feeling for him; and she decides to stop seeing him, and to intervene no more over his grandfather's tenancy. This drives Egbert to contrive one last meeting to reopen his plea. He still leaves as little as possible to chance:

Egbert had previously surveyed the spot and thought it suitable for the occasion, much as Wellington antecedently surveyed the field of Waterloo.

Years later, when Egbert has made a name for himself in London, he decides he must see Geraldine again. No chance offers; he makes one. Knowing that she and her father are in London, and remembering that she likes Handel, he guesses she will attend a performance of *The Messiah*:

He resolved upon doing something at a venture. The next morning he went to the ticket office and boldly asked for a place as near as possible to those taken in the name of Allenville.

Thus, under her father's very eye, messages are exchanged. But it turns out that a marriage has been arranged between Geraldine and a man of her father's choice. In despair Egbert throws up his career in London, and returns to the country.

There, in the church where the marriage is to take place a few days later, Egbert finds Geraldine. She breaks down and confesses that she still loves him. He seizes his chance to forestall the wedding and marry her himself. He foresees the possibility of many small but fatal hitches: the clergyman may know Geraldine by sight and refuse to perform the ceremony; the licence—for there is no margin —may fail to arrive in time; Geraldine may be found, and driven by her family to change her mind again. In short, there may occur any of the little mishaps which in Hardy's later novels prevent the hero or heroine from reaching 'any pleasant prospect' they have regarded as too 'probable'. He makes Geraldine lock herself into his house, while he himself sounds the clergyman (making sure he does not know Geraldine by sight, and that the identity of her name with that of the bride in the big forthcoming wedding is satisfactorily explained away). He goes himself to the surrogate and, instead of trusting the application for a licence to the post or to a messenger, takes it himself. True the story ends unhappily: Geraldine, now married, goes to obtain her father's forgiveness and, in the midst of his recrimina- tions, bursts a blood vessel, and soon afterwards dies. But there is none of the usual irony here: Egbert has done everything possible; Geraldine's death is but a way of ending the story with a Parthian shot at the inhumanity of the upper classes.

So in what remains of his first story we find Hardy insisting that 'where there's a will there's a way', by showing Egbert contriving, anticipating, leaving nothing to chance, and getting the wife of his choice despite every difficulty, in contrast to the indirect method of the later books where Hardy suggests the same thing—that, to be effective, human efforts must be unremitting—by showing people failing to exert themselves in time, trusting fate or chance or Provi- dence, or not caring enough to have the minor 'accidents' under their control.[10]

The change can indeed be shown from the next novel Hardy wrote, *Desperate Remedies*, where Springrove, unlike Egbert,

[10] Jokes about 'accidental' lover's meetings occur also in *Desperate Remedies* (I. 1, III. 1, and III. 2) and at times too in the later novels. In *A Laodicean* Paula has a gaily dis- ingenuous explanation of an 'accident' she has neatly arranged (I. xii), and in *The Return of the Native* (III. iii) Mrs. Yeobright has much contempt for the 'accidents' that bring Clym and Eustacia together on the Heath.

arrives just *too late* to prevent Cytherea's unfortunate marriage.[11] A more literal illustration of Sainte Beuve's dictum that nothing resembles a hollow so much as a swelling would be hard to find. A few positive figures like Egbert do indeed occur in some of the later books. Gabriel Oak is one; and another is Stephen Reynard, husband of the 'First Countess of Wessex' in the story of that name. Each conquers difficulties notably greater and more real than those that dishearten most of Hardy's heroes. But usually, like Donald Farfrae, these successful people act as foils to reveal the weaknesses of more fully developed and more interesting characters.

It does not need saying that through the 'irony of fate' and 'unfulfilled intentions' Hardy found better opportunities for exploring the scope and limitations of the human will, and for touching upon the moral implications of success or failure; the tragic vein, indeed, proved the richest to Hardy, whether he owed the suggestion to Meredith or not.

A good case has been made out for the assumption that when Hardy came to consider Meredith's second piece of advice, to write a novel 'with a more complicated "plot"', he turned to Wilkie Collins in search of a model. To read *The Woman in White* and then *Desperate Remedies*, the first novel written after the Meredith interview, is to see the force of this suggestion. But the similarities commonly noticed—a mistaken identity, a disastrous fire, a guilty secret, an illegitimate child, a confession in which obscure points in a crime are clarified—are not my concern. Such parallels in mere incident do not obscure, indeed they only underline, fundamental differences of attitude in the two writers.

The first sentence of *The Woman in White* declares it to be the 'story of what a Woman's patience can endure, and what a Man's resolution can achieve'. But the reader quickly finds that patience and resolution would be useless without the aid of Providence. That events are really part of the 'design' of Providence we are continually reminded. For instance, when Laura is cruelly treated by the villainous Sir Percival Glyde, her half-sister Marian is comforted by a dream: Walter Hartright, the poor but worthy hero who is in love with Laura but who, when she married Sir Percival, exiled himself to tropical America, appears to Marian in this vision and declares himself to be the

[11] *Desperate Remedies*, XIII. 3.

'*instrument of a Design* [my italics] that is yet unseen. . . . I am still walking on the dark road which leads me, and you, and the sister of your love and mine, to the unknown Retribution and the inevitable End.'

Later, Walter arrives back in England and is told that Laura is dead. He goes at once to Limmeridge, in Cumberland, to her grave. There at her graveside he meets Laura herself: it is not she who is buried there, but Anne Catherick her double. Laura has escaped from the asylum where she has been confined under Anne's name, and having tried unsuccessfully to establish her identity at her home, she and Marian are on their way back to the station. It is odd that they should revisit the graveyard, and encounter Walter, but this is part of the 'Design', for, as Collins says, 'the hand of God was pointing their way'.

'The hand of God' is seen again in the terrible death of Sir Percival. By 'chance' the church vestry, where he is destroying the evidence of his crime, is full of packing cases and inflammable shavings; by another 'chance' one door is permanently locked; by a third, the remaining door easily jams if locked on the inside. Thus when Sir Percival, by a fourth chance, sets fire to the shavings, he is inevitably burnt to death before he can be rescued. Walter has long dreamt of meeting Sir Percival face to face; but, as Collins says, 'the visitation of God ruled it' that he should encounter only Sir Percival's corpse. Thus the 'chances' were not accidents, but factors in the design of Providence.

Walter marries Laura; and we realize that the design is more intricate than we had imagined. At the beginning it had been assumed by all parties (with a propriety significantly lacking in Hardy's story!) that the 'poor man', Walter, could not marry Laura, the 'lady'. Providence has brought about the desired end in an ingenious way; first by making Laura marry and be unhappy with Sir Percival, then by killing him, and by temporarily depriving Laura of identity—of name, family and fortune. But lest we should protest that Providence, however ingenious, was inhumanly cruel and wasteful to inflict pain upon the innocent Laura and the long-suffering Anne, we are told that this is merely the sins of the father being visited upon the children: not only Laura and Marian, by their mother, but also Laura and Anne, by their father, turn out to be half-sisters; and in begetting the illegitimate Anne, their father had sinned.

Divine control, the reader will remember, is again in evidence at the end of the book. Walter needs certain information which he can buy only by allowing Fosco a chance of escape. But he comforts himself by thinking that the Providence that brought Sir Percival Glyde to a terrible end will surely not spare Fosco; and so indeed it turns out.

That these providentially convenient interventions, coincidences and chances differ from those in Hardy's books requires no arguing. Hardy's are often ironically *un*providential. He deliberately denies the world—is it not the world of most Victorian fiction?—in which Providence can be counted on to come to our aid, and in which seeming misfortune turns out to be the disguised ministration of a beneficent God. I have already mentioned that no Providence rescued Tess: after commenting on this, Hardy goes on—though it was many years since he had read Wilkie Collins—to reject also the idea of divine retribution such as that which visited the sins of their father upon Anne and Laura:

But, might some say, where was Tess's guardian angel? where was the providence of her simple faith? Perhaps, like that other god of whom the ironical Tishbite spoke, he was talking, or he was pursuing, or he was in a journey, or peradventure he was sleeping and not to be awaked. . . . One may, indeed, admit the possibility of a retribution lurking in the present catastrophe. Doubtless some of Tess d'Urberville's mailed ancestors rollicking home from a fray had dealt the same measure even more ruthlessly towards peasant girls of their time. But though to visit the sins of the fathers upon the children may be a morality good enough for divinities, it is scorned by average human nature.[12]

But even in *Desperate Remedies*, Hardy makes the difference of his attitude clear:

'. . . The Lord must be a neglectful party at heart, or he'd never permit such overbearen goings-on!' [13]

complains the coachman about Miss Aldcliffe's household. And later the village gossips moralize:

'. . . Well. . . . I trust Providence will settle it all for the best, as he always do.'

'Ay, ay, Elizabeth,' rejoined Mrs. Crickett . . . 'good people like you may say so, but I've always found Providence a different sort of feller.'[14]

[12] *Tess*, end of chapter XI.   [13] *Desperate Remedies*, V. I.   [14] Ibid. IX. 4.

Compared with the irony of *Tess*, the touch is light and humorous; but it is clear that in a world where Wilkie Collins's beliefs were accepted, and when he was asked to write in Collins's manner, Hardy was resolved to make his Providence 'a different sort of feller' altogether.

But other differences too are significant. Collins takes care to disguise some of the improbabilities, to explain them away. We hardly notice that the mathematical chances against such convenient happenings are almost infinite. And if we do, the answer that Providence is the agent, is final. Hardy, on the other hand, underlines the fact that some things will happen by chance; and he seeks to analyse the factors that make up chance, and with irony gentler than when he talked explicitly of Egbert's and Geraldine's 'definition of accident', shows that human intentions or omissions or imprudences materially affect chances. Many of Hardy's chances, unlike Collins's divine interventions, are those that are bound to happen, in time, in a confined community. If a thing does not happen today, or tomorrow, or the next day, Hardy's people seem to infer that it can never happen at all. This pattern is often misunderstood: critics complain that Hardy makes things happen in the way that is most awkward to all concerned, whereas what he is often doing is showing that if nothing is done to forestall an accident, or to control the way it happens, it is more and more likely, as time goes on, to happen in a way that is not convenient.

We must not oversimplify, however; it is true enough that the awkwardness is sometimes a part of Hardy's purpose; the most awkward coincidences do occur, and at times—it seems—quite fortuitously. One of the strangest is that Margery Tucker, who has promised to go to the Baron von Xanten if he should ever request it, receives an invitation to go on the very morning of her wedding.[15] But we are not to see this as a solemn statement on Hardy's part that this is how things always happen, so much as an exploration of how this 'romantic milkmaid', faced with this awkward choice, is going to act.[16] Will she honour her romantic promise to the Baron, or her realistic one to Jim? She goes to the Baron—who, knowing that her only real chance of happiness is with Jim, is horrified to learn what she has done, and rushes her home in the hope that she

[15] *Romantic Adventures of a Milkmaid*, VIII.
[16] Thus the focus is always on the human being, and his or her reaction. This is doubtless what Hardy meant when he remarked that the story should be exceptional, but that the strangeness should lie in the events and not in the human beings.

will be in time for the ceremony. Again she has a choice: will she act quickly, make her excuses and patch things up? or will she allow things to take their course? When we recall only the bare outline of the story, we fall perhaps into naïve assumptions about Hardy's fatal coincidences', but if we re-read it, we discover that my earlier point holds good: Margery admittedly does not make the coincidences occur; but she allows them to affect her. Had she fully and finally committed herself to Jim, the dilemma would not have arisen —or at least the difficulties could quickly have been overcome with his help.

And this is true of Hardy's world in general. Coincidences may occur, but they will have little power to hurt those who are honestly and realistically committed to a course. Accidents will affect the undecided, those who seek to deny the past not by frankly admitting its mistakes and making their present and future intentions clear, but by nursing secrets and allowing misunderstandings to develop. Thus Henchard, by suppressing the secret of Elizabeth-Jane's birth makes himself especially vulnerable; so too with Tess, and with Elfride; so too with the way that Clym, Eustacia and Mrs. Yeobright allow misunderstandings to multiply. The chances of a serious accident, sooner or later, begin to increase.

All readers of Hardy's novels experience this sense of something impending before it actually happens. After a prolonged and precarious equilibrium, the disaster seems pre-arranged. But only in this sense—that the reader expects it—is there a 'pattern'. There is no 'design' in Wilkie Collins's sense: what happens conforms neither to man's sense of justice nor to the dictates of any imaginable Providence. It is blind: the result of things left to themselves. The real design is the other side of this dual pattern: the garden as it should be, weeded and cultivated; the 'unfulfilled intention' (in the reader's imagination) tended and fulfilled, the course of events as it could have been directed by timely intervention or by a better-judged 'execution', not by Providence, but by man. Beside the pattern of what happens runs that other pattern, clearly visible to every reader, of what ought to be happening. *The Return of the Native* is not the bare tale of terrible mistakes and estrangements, but also the story of working compromises and reconciliations that remained, to borrow a phrase that Hardy uses elsewhere, 'for ever hidden in the darkness of the unfulfilled.' This is true even of the climax of the book: it is one of the most painful incidents in all fiction [17] for the very reason that it might so easily have been prevented. The closing in of the forces [18] is logical enough and, given the unfortunate chances, Mrs. Yeobright's retreat from Clym's and Eustacia's cottage was only too probable. But it might also be said that Mrs. Yeobright had brought the 'closed door'[19] all across the Heath with her; that something unfortunate was bound to happen—if not Eustacia's face at the window, then something else—for Mrs. Yeobright to misconstrue. It was not better 'luck' that would have saved the situation (though this is what Eustacia habitually relies upon),[20] but good faith and a determined and intelligent effort to oppose the unfortunate drift of circumstance. 'Unfortunate drift': the chances are not represented as evil, so much as absurdly haphazard, those of an undirected 'Vast Imbecility'[21] that was at last gathering a little momentum since the human beings on the Heath seemed so little interested in intervening.

I have a powerful ally here, although an unwitting one, in Frank Chapman, who, in an early *Scrutiny* article, approaches Hardy with the usual prejudices about his defeatist pessimism but notices that mishap after mishap occurs in *The Return of the Native*, and yet the final disaster, foreseen by every reader, is delayed. For a long time, each mishap adds a little fuel to the inflammable situation of suspicion and misunderstanding, but fails to ignite it. From this Chapman decides that Hardy is finding 'difficulty in bringing his tragedy about'; whereas in fact Hardy is showing exactly what Chapman is finding: that the tragedy is not inevitable, that man has reprieves he fails to make use of. Indeed, even after the tragic death of Mrs. Yeobright, there are forces—not merely Venn's efforts to protect Tamsin, but Clym's love for Eustacia and desire to forgive her, and Eustacia's half-hearted wish for a reconciliation and her vague hope 'that something should happen to thwart her own intention' to elope (V. vi and V. vii)—which seem at one point likely to prevent any extension of the tragedy. Some of the characters, at least, know what they ought to do; but they delay: 'Yeobright

[17] Like many incidents in Hardy's novels, it is equally painful to reread. Could the temptation to skip (one wonders) be a cause of some of the critical misreadings?
[18] See Hardy's definition of a 'Tragedy', written while he was at work on *The Return of the Native* : *Early Life*, p. 157; *Life*, p. 120.
[19] Op. cit. IV-vi ('The Closed Door' is the title of the fourth book of the novel).
[20] Later, when the situation is even worse, Eustacia knows she must try to explain matters to Clym but she decides on Wildeve's advice, to postpone and to 'trust to chance'. Op. cit. V-i.   [21] *Nature's Questioning.*

thought he would send for his mother; and then he thought he would not' (IV. ii); ' "I will wait for a day or two longer . . . and if (Eustacia) does not send to me in that time I will indeed send to her" ' (V. vi); and the most culpable delays are Mrs. Yeobright's. That a similar period, when the 'mighty necessitating forces . . . are in equilibrium', occurs, and often for some time persists, in every one of Hardy's novels, would have been noticed long since and its meaning realized, if we did not approach Hardy with prejudices about his defeatism, and decide that he did not know what he was doing, was 'experiencing difficulty in bringing his tragedy about', was being 'illogical' and 'failing to integrate his themes'—strictures familiar to us all.

Perhaps it is in *The Mayor of Casterbridge* that the unfulfilled pattern persists most clearly and persists longest—even though what Henchard might salvage from his life becomes less and less. But *some* chance of recovery recurs again and again. So too in *The Woodlanders*: we noticed already that Giles need not have lost his leases; but even when he has lost them and faces comparative poverty he need not have lost Grace: she gives him a clue that she still loves him, and he fails to follow it up (XV).

I have mentioned already some of the many moments in *Tess* when the far-from-inevitable sequence of things might have been broken. There is Angel's first encounter with Tess, who is not just the girl he meets too late; he meets her before her troubles have begun, and notices her, 'the pretty *maiden* [my italics] with whom he had not danced', but he hurries on after his brothers, in order to read with them *A Counterblast to Agnosticism* (II). Then there are the kindly impulses that Angel represses in the early days of their estrangement (XXXV, XXXVI); and then, after Izz Huett's admission ' "Nobody could love 'ee more than Tess did! . . . she would have laid down her life for 'ee. I could do no more," ' there is Angel's hesitation:

. . . that evening he was within a featherweight's turn of abandoning his road to the nearest station and driving across that elevated dorsal line of South Wessex which separated him from Tess's home (XL).

There are the scruples that prevented Tess from telling Angel of the sleepwalking ("Why didn't you tell me next day? . . ." '—LVIII), and Tess's failure to meet Angel's parents ('the greatest misfortune of her life was this feminine loss of courage at this last and critical moment . . .'—XLIV), and the fact that she makes no second attempt, though Alec dares her to . . . (LI). The reader will, I think, agree that Hardy indicates clearly enough what ought to be happening, but he may well object that Hardy's method is too explicit to be called 'irony'; and it might be better to define it as the irony not of what is left unsaid, but of what is left undone.

At all events, the dual pattern—the recurring possibility of what is left undone, beneath the grossly imperfect pattern of what is actually done—is characteristic of Hardy's novels and stories. And the tension between the two patterns is what controls the reader's interest and the rhythm of the narrative. It may properly be said that his tragedies are not so much about unhappiness, as about happiness missed.

But to see this method, in terms of a single incident, and at its simplest, we may return to *Desperate Remedies*, and consider Mr. Springrove's heap of couch-grass:

By eleven, everybody in the house was asleep. It truly seemed as if the treacherous element knew there had arisen a grand opportunity for devastation.

At a quarter past eleven a slight stealthy crackle made itself heard amid the increasing moans of the night wind; the heap glowed brighter still, and burst into flame; the flame sank, another breeze entered it, sustained it, and it grew to be first continuous and weak, then continuous and strong.

At twenty minutes past eleven a blast of wind carried an airy bit of ignited fern several yards forward, in a direction parallel to the houses and inn, and there deposited it on the ground.

Five minutes later another puff of wind carried a similar piece to a distance of five-and-twenty yards, where it was dropped softly on the ground.

Still the wind did not blow in the direction of the houses, and even now to a casual observer they would have appeared safe. But Nature does few things directly. A minute later yet, an ignited fragment fell upon the straw covering of a long thatched heap or 'grave' of mangel-wurzel, lying in a direction at right angles to the house, and down toward the hedge. There the fragment faded into darkness.

A short time subsequent to this, after many intermediate deposits and seemingly baffled attempts, another fragment fell on the mangel-wurzel grave, and continued to glow; the glow was increased by the wind; the straw caught fire and burst into flame. It was inevitable that the flame should run along the ridge of the thatch towards a piggery at the end. Yet had the piggery been tiled, the time-honoured hostel would even now at this last moment have been safe; but it was constructed as piggeries are mostly constructed, of wood and thatch. The hurdles and straw roof of the frail erection became ignited in their turn, and abutting, as the shed did, on the back of the inn, flamed up to the eaves of the main roof in less than thirty seconds.[22]

The passage, we must recall, describes only half-an-hour of a process which had been going on for three days. On the first day Springrove had noticed the danger; but on the third evening, lulled by the uneventfulness of the preceding days, he examined the smouldering heap with less care; later that night, the railway porter noticed the glow:

If those cottages had been his, he thought, he should not care to have a fire so near them as that—and the wind rising.

Indeed we must regard the fire as but a part of a much longer process in which Springrove allows misfortune to overtake him; for it turns out that he has failed to renew the insurance. We thus see that at several points before the outbreak of the fire human intervention was possible, and would have prevented disaster. But the fire itself, as Hardy takes pains to describe it, was a slow, natural, and gradual process; indeed it is best described as *halting* ('. . . the flame sank. . . . there the fragment faded to darkness . . . after many intermediate deposits and seemingly baffled attempts . . .'). And Hardy's exact notes on the time ('Five minutes later . . . a minute later yet . . .') carry the same insistent message: that at any time, until the last few seconds, a person alert to the danger could easily have prevented the houses catching fire. Mill's essay on Nature [23] which was later to affect Hardy profoundly was not yet published, but in the *System of Logic* he had argued that no effect was inevitable unless the causes tending to produce it were left uncontrolled; and if Hardy had tried to devise an illustration of Mill's argument, a train of events which seems to await human intervention, he could hardly have written more effectively.

And no greater contrast can be imagined than the fire in *The Woman in White*. Many people keen to extinguish the fire, or at least to rescue Sir Percival, are at hand, but can do nothing. Yet Hardy, not Collins, is labelled a determinist! The charge must have seemed to him too perverse to need denying. Yet he did deny it, explicitly when provoked, and implicitly by repeating the general pattern of

[22] Op. cit. X. 2.   [23] See below, pp. 92–3.

Springrove's fire in more general situations and trains of events so blatantly without 'design' that they are clearly waiting—while 'the mighty necessitating forces' remain 'in equilibrium'—for an alert and intelligent human being to stamp a design upon them.

And by returning occasionally to the direct method of *An Indiscretion* Hardy actually depicts such intelligent intervention. Thus, unlike the porter who thought Springrove's smouldering couchgrass was none of his business, Gabriel Oak is quick to notice the fire at Weatherbury, to fight it, and to organize others to bring it under control so that it does not spread to the other ricks on Bathsheba's farm.[24] It is a common criticism that Hardy's interest in chance led him to ignore character; but the truth is that he often defines character *in terms of chance*, in terms of a man's ability to stamp a design upon the neutral chances that touch his life. An extreme instance of this we have referred to already: the way that the same chances and conditions of life serve to define Henchard's character and Farfrae's, the same circumstances providing the one man with the means of life and success, and the other only with the opportunities for self-destruction.

There is a sense, however, in which 'character' meant little to Hardy; and again we can invoke the help of Wilkie Collins. In *The Woman in White* there are several brilliantly depicted characters quite outside Hardy's range; the chief of these are Mr. Fairlie and Count Fosco. But these are not witnesses to their author's interest in psychology; they are *actual conditions of the plot*: unless the reader is convinced by Fosco and Fairlie, he will (as I shall explain) dismiss the whole plot as absurd.

We have seen that Collins's denouement proceeds through Providential coincidences, but equally improbable are the initial complications. I pass over Anne Catherick's accidental encounter with Walter in London and her subsequent visit to Limmeridge hundreds of miles from her home—quite by chance—the very week that Laura's betrothal to Sir Percival is announced: these coincidences are necessary to make Walter suspect Sir Percival and arouse his curiosity about Anne. My concern is rather with psychological absurdities. Laura is marrying Sir Percival only out of respect for her dead father's wishes; not even the family lawyer is happy about it, but at least he intends to guard her financial interests. Surprisingly

[24] *Far from the Madding Crowd*, VI.

however, he visits Limmeridge in her absence, and on instructions from Mr. Fairlie, her guardian, proceeds to commit her to a marriage settlement that is utterly iniquitous. But there are still stranger improbabilities. Sir Percival hates and fears Anne; it is unlikely, therefore, that he would marry Laura, Anne's double, unless she were the last heiress in England. Even if he overcomes his repugnance, he would scarcely risk marrying anyone acquainted with Anne; for Anne, he thinks, knows the secret of his crime, and he has no thought yet of that other crime—of exploiting the likeness between the two women. In fine, we should reject the chain of circumstance by which Laura comes to marry Sir Percival as ludicrously weak, were it not for two monstrous improbabilities that dwarf the rest but are so skilfully handled by Collins that we accept them without a murmur: Mr. Fairlie's acceptance of the terms of his ward's marriage settlement, and his refusal, later, to verify her identity. The characterization of Mr. Fairlie, which the inexperienced reader has taken earlier for a digression included because the author cannot resist describing human eccentricities, turns out to be the pivot on which the whole improbable action turns. The Mr. Fairlie whom Collins describes to us would indeed have accepted those terms for his ward; and no one, real or fictional, except Mr. Fairlie. And no one but he would have refused to identify Laura later on. He was created for the particular purpose of performing those two inherently impossible actions, and making them seem probable.

So too with Fosco. How improbable that so ruthless and intelligent a criminal should allow Walter so much rope! How improbable that so cultured a man could tolerate the company of Sir Percival, even for gain! But these and other unlikely twists in the story depend upon his character and seem plausible and even inevitable. Like Fairlie, Fosco is a flat character; our knowledge of his accomplishments, his whims, his manners, his pets, is extensive; if we met him we should recognize him at once, and know exactly how he would act. Yet we know nothing personal, nothing of the inner springs of his actions.

Such characterization is a conjuring trick. Collins is not creating a plot in which 'character is destiny': Fairlie and Fosco do not choose and act as real people, as agents, and so map out their destinies; they act as they must, as parts of Collins's machinery, his design, to determine the destinies *of others*. Thus the whole world of Wilkie Collins, first through his Providence and second through

his fixed characters, takes on a deterministic chain quality, created—
like Sartre's paper knife—for a limited purpose.

Even many of Hardy's minor characters have a greater reality. We
know less of them than we do of Fosco, less perhaps than of Walter
Hartright; but what we know is not static. We know what they fail
to do, or choose not to do, as well as what they actually do. Understanding their hesitation and misgivings, knowing what it cost them
to make one choice and not another, we become interested not just
in their characters, but in their potentialities, as Hardy intended.
His only fixed characters of importance are the more earthy of his
rustics, but, although Hardy sometimes uses them as parts of his
machinery, making the action turn on them, they differ from Collins's
figures in representing a more or less constant factor in the environment, as Hardy sees it, of man generally. They symbolize the inertia
of Nature, which the free man has to contend with, inside himself,
and around him. And the rustics' fixity, their rootedness, sets in
relief the free actions, or attempts to achieve free action, made by
those upon whom Hardy focuses our attention. Even of a partly
fixed character such as Marty South, we are told,

The fingers which clasped the heavy ash haft might have skilfully guided
the pencil or swept the string, had they been set to do it in good time.[25]

But there is still 'good time', when we meet most of Hardy's main
characters, for them to steer a new course. The lives they have so far
realized represent a fraction of their scope. When we first meet
Henchard, he is fretting to be more than a haytrusser; Farfrae is
going abroad to seek his fortune, but abandons the resolve; Clym
Yeobright is a diamond merchant, yet longs to be a teacher; the boy
Jude may be doomed to the frustrations of a self-taught scholar, or
to the degradation of a cottage with Arabella, or he may realize his
dream of working, perhaps studying, in Christminster; Grace is to
marry Giles, or to travel abroad with Mrs. Charmond—but does
neither; Angel is to take holy orders, but he stops to dance with the
village girls at Marlott, and we next hear he has taken up farming—
but examples would fill several pages: it seems specially characteristic of Hardy's characters that they should reject or relinquish their
environments, their ready-made destinies.

[25] *Woodlanders*, II.

This is a strange realization, and seems to clash at first with our
sense that these people belong to a vividly depicted Wessex scene.
The Roman roads and earth-works, the barrows and chalk downs
around Casterbridge and Melchester; the farms of Blackmoor vale
and the Froom valley; Yall'ham Woods and Egdon; and the coast
from the Isle of Slingers round to Havenpool and Sandbourne—we
are familiar with them all, down to such details as gargoyles, bridges,
weirs and thatched piggeries. We can recall few of Hardy's men and
women without thinking of some particular vivid scene, the corner
of a field, a fir plantation, the shape of ricks against the sky. But,
except for the rustic choruses, they are not bounded by these settings; they are unrooted; and their independence is a measure of
their life. Even Oak is not a native of Weatherbury, and in the pen-
ultimate chapter he is thinking of going to California! A few of these
people are actual misfits—notably Eustacia on Egdon Heath; but
to a lesser degree are not Clym, Damon and Captain Vye misfits on
Egdon too? Even Venn abandons reddling to become a dairy farmer.
A nomadic quality has rightly been noticed in Hardy's characters, as
well as a 'crusoeistic' tendency to subtract themselves from their
contexts. Admittedly this is not always a sign of freedom; it is
occasionally a foolish escapism: even some of Tess's actions, and
Sue's, are fugitive rather than nomadic. But the point remains:
nearly all Hardy's heroes and heroines have a humanity unbounded
by their setting.

Hence perhaps arises the embarrassment of Dorset people when
foreigners arrive and wish to photograph a reddleman or a wall
with a red-painted text. What is all the fuss about? the native asks.
And other regional writers, with richer local colour, are produced
for our approbation. Apart from the absurdity of honouring a pro-
phet in his own country, the native is right. Hardy goes far beyond
what a local patriot demands. He is more than a regional novelist,
and Wessex more than a region. It is conception of man: man in
relation to other men and women, but in small enough groups to
make certain issues clear; man in relation to chance and time, nature
and the universe; man conscious of the past and its traditions, yet
adapting himself, with uneven success, to the present and the future.

V

Far from the Madding Crowd as an Introduction to Hardy's Novels

THIS NOVEL is more typical of Hardy than a casual reading and a simplifying memory might indicate. The end, for example, is emphatically not a romantic happy-ever-after affair. We need not take Joseph Poorgrass's final 'it might have been worse' at quite its long-face value; and we can see the title of the final chapter ('A Foggy Night and Morning') as perhaps Hardy's way of touching wood: there is, indeed, a suppressed and sober, but none the less noticeable, elation about the tone of the end; but the fact remains that Gabriel is no Prince Charming for a girl of three- or four-and-twenty. Ahead of Gabriel and Bathsheba is no romance, but a reality that Hardy represents as more valuable, a reality of hard and good work on the two farms:

He accompanied her up the hill, explaining to her the details of his forthcoming tenure of the other farm. They spoke very little of their mutual feelings; pretty phrases and warm expressions being probably unnecessary between such tried friends. Theirs was that substantial affection which arises (if any arises at all) when the two who are thrown together begin first by knowing the rougher sides of each other's character, and not the best till further on, the romance growing up in the interstices of a mass of hard prosaic reality . . . (LVI).

The trend of thought should by this time be familiar enough; but the passage also illustrates Hardy's 'hard prosaic'—sometimes awkward—way of thinking and writing, born of a conviction that the truth must be told, even if it cannot always be told attractively.

The distinction Hardy draws between romance and reality does not appear only at the end of the book; it is worked into the scheme of the whole. In contrast to Gabriel Oak, the two other main male characters, Troy and Boldwood, one actively and the other passively, represent aspects of romantic unreality. Boldwood is the dreamer himself, and the unreality is in the way he approaches Bathsheba, seeing in her not a woman of flesh and blood, but a romantic dream. Troy, on the other hand, approaches Bathsheba realistically enough; but he is approached romantically *by her*: he seems to her a romantic figure and, initially, an escape from a dilemma into which the circumstances of her real everyday life have thrown her. Boldwood, for Bathsheba, has represented a certain social goal: propriety and respectability. For a short time, while he seems inaccessible, these things seem attractive to her; and it is these values that he tries to insist upon: the formal rightness of her keeping her 'promise', her duty to reciprocate the love she has aroused in him. There is cruelty in Boldwood's romanticism, in the way he insists that she shall adhere to his idea of her (as there is cruelty in Angel's romanticism, and Knight's and Clym's); but Boldwood suffers more than he makes Bathsheba suffer, and the wildness and unhappiness of his love is conditioned by his dream and his distance from reality:

The great aids to idealization in love were present here: occasional observation of her from a distance, and the absence of social intercourse with her . . . the pettinesses that enter so largely into all earthy living and doing were disguised by the accident of lover and loved-one not being on visiting terms; and there was hardly awakened a thought in Boldwood that sorry household realities appertained to her . . . (XIX).

But Boldwood remains just as blind to realities when he gets to know her. After the disappearance of Troy, he again nourishes his love, but

almost shunned the contemplation of it in earnest, lest facts should reveal the wildness of the dream (XLIX).

It is a 'fond madness': and the anticlimax is the discovery (while Boldwood is in prison, awaiting trial) of all the jewellery and clothing labelled 'Bathsheba Boldwood', bought for a woman who had never promised to marry him (LV).

Hardy is disparaging romance, the dream and the dreamer. He is suggesting, instead, that one should live—not in accordance with nature—but in accordance with reality. And this point is made clearly by the three choices open to Bathsheba: Oak, Boldwood, and Troy. Boldwood, of course, ceases to attract her as soon as he forces his attentions on her: and there is a gentle irony in the fact that she sees in Troy, who has taken her away from Boldwood, something of what Boldwood has seen in her: a figure of romance, someone from

another world. But it is not only Troy's glamour; it is also that 'arch-
-dissembler'[1] Nature that prompts Bathsheba to love Troy. She
goes to meet him, hesitates, and then surrenders her heart, in the
chapter called 'The Hollow amid the Ferns'. The scene is one of
great natural beauty, of lush growth:

. . . tall thickets of brake fern, plump and diaphanous from recent rapid
growth, and radiant in hues of clear and untainted green.

At eight o'clock this midsummer evening, whilst the bristling ball of
gold in the west still swept the tips of the ferns with its long, luxuriant
rays, a soft brushing-by of garments might have been heard among them,
and Bathsheba appeared in their midst, their soft, feathery arms caressing
her up to her shoulders. She paused, turned, went back . . . (XXVIII).

But again she changes her mind, and goes on to the meeting place, a
hollow where the fern

grew nearly to the bottom of the slope and then abruptly ceased. The
middle within the belt of verdure was floored with a thick flossy carpet of
moss and grass intermingled, so yielding that the foot was half-buried
within it.

Nature is softly inviting and reassuring her. She surrenders to
Nature as much as to her lover,—to her own natural womanliness
which, Hardy tells us, she normally had too much sense to be quite
governed by (XXIX). The treatment of this theme is more subtle,
perhaps, and certainly more extended, in *Tess*; but it is effective in
Far from the Madding Crowd, all the same.

Bathsheba's third possibility is Oak; whose name at least cannot
be made to suggest *compliance* with nature, but rather sturdy resistance, hard use and endurance. The distinction Hardy draws at the
beginning of the novel (II) between the intermingling sounds of one
vast integrated body of Nature over Norcombe Hill, and the 'clearness' and 'sequence' of the 'notes of Farmer Oak's flute',[2] runs right
through the book. Gabriel Oak is not a part of Nature. He may be a
countryman, but he is always a human being, fully conscious of his
human responsibility, always ready to modify, to deflect, to improve,
Nature's workings; always, that is, after his first setback. A
'natural' sequence of events destroys his sheep; but he does not see
himself as a victim of fate—as Troy would have done, or Henchard
('I am to suffer, I perceive'). He realizes he is ruined, and that, not

---

[1] *Early Life*, p. 231; *Life*, p. 176.
[2] See p. 16 above.

having insured his sheep, he himself is to blame. And his second thought is that things would be even worse if Bathsheba had married him:

'Thank God I am not married: what would she have done in the poverty now coming upon me?'

Thereafter he intervenes in the natural sequence of events in as timely a fashion as he can. He prevents the fire from spreading to the ricks and buildings of Bathsheba's farm (VI); he cures the poisoned sheep (XXI); he saves Bathsheba's harvest from the storm (XXXVI, XXXVII); and he tries to intervene, but unsuccessfully, before Boldwood's optimistic dreams lead to disaster (LII, iii and vi), and before Bathsheba gives way to her infatuation for Troy:

'. . . But since we don't exactly know what he is, why not behave as if he *might* be bad, simply for your own safety? Don't trust him, mistress . . .' (XXIX).

—Gabriel's version of Hardy's own advice to take 'a full look at the Worst'. But Oak's attitude towards Nature is best seen in the account of the storm, because here Nature appears in her two aspects: creator and destroyer. She is prepared, but for Gabriel, to destroy the harvest she has bounteously created; and it is Gabriel's appreciation of the bounty, his sense of its meaning in terms of human life and sustenance, that makes him put forth all his strength to save the bounty from the destruction and to pit himself against the whole scheme of things, the whole trend of circumstance at that time. He fights not only against elemental nature, but against 'nature's' hold on the humanity around him: Troy's insidiously easy-going ways (' "Mr Troy says it will not rain, and he cannot stop to talk to you about such fidgets" '), the only too natural sleepiness and inertia of the drunken workfolk in the barn, and his own natural fears when the threat of the lightning becomes too great. The critics who suppose that Hardy shared and advocated the philosophic resignation of some of his rustics should read again the thirty-sixth and thirty-seventh chapters of *Far from the Madding Crowd*: if ever a man had the excuse of surrendering, of saying 'It was to be', Oak has the excuse on the night of the storm. Instead, he fights.

Yet throughout his fight, there remains a sense in which Nature's opposition is 'neutral'; nothing is purposely aimed against Oak. The chances mount against him; but they are still chances. And he seeks to keep ahead of them; he gets a lightning conductor improvised. Had there been any malicious purpose, an earlier flash of lightning would have struck him down. It is a fight between a man intelligently directing his efforts and 'senseless circumstance'. Oak persists; and he wins. He is not quite alone; in the latter part of the night he is helped by Bathsheba. The scene is one of many in the novels that vividly suggest the need of the human pair for each other, the individual's comparative—sometimes complete—helplessness alone.

There is another side to Gabriel's feeling for Nature: he fights her successfully because he understands and can sympathetically interpret the doings not only of his sheep, but also of Nature's smaller creatures—slug, spiders and toad (XXXVI). He seeks to learn from Nature; for instance, from the sprig of ivy that has grown across the door of the church tower, proving that Troy has *not* been in the habit of entering here modestly and unobserved (as Bathsheba too readily believes), and that Troy is, therefore, a liar (XXIX). Nature is one of Gabriel's resources; but he is never controlled by her, nor, in any Wordsworthian sense, does he ever trust her. The essential thing about Gabriel is not that he is in contact with Nature, but that he is in contact with reality. He neither evades it nor resigns himself to it; he makes something out of it.

This point is effectively made by a metaphor embodied in an incident early in the book, just at the turning point of Oak's fortunes, when he has proved he can survive even the worst that life has to offer and when his luck (if such a word can be used) is at last on the mend. He is drinking cider in the Malthouse, and has just endeared himself to the Weatherbury folk by refusing the luxury of a clean cup:

'And here's a mouthful of bread and bacon that mis'ess have sent, shepherd. The cider will go down better with a bit of victuals. Don't ye chaw quite close, shepherd, for I let the bacon fall in the road outside as I was bringing it along, and may be 'tis rather gritty. There, 'tis clane dirt; and we all know what that is, as you say, and you bain't a particular man we see, shepherd.'

'True, true—not at all,' said the friendly Oak.

'Don't let your teeth quite meet, and you won't feel the sandiness at all. Ah! 'tis wonderful what can be done by contrivance!'

'My own mind exactly, neighbour.' (VIII).

The incident is a precise metaphor of what Oak has been doing in the wider sphere of his life: he has had his share of 'unpalatable reality', but by contrivance he has managed to find life's grittiness not so 'unpalatable' after all.

Hardy's attitudes and themes in this novel are, indeed, typical; what is not typical is the method: he is presenting his main theme— the value of pessimism as a practical policy ('. . . You cannot lose at it, you may gain . . .') through a pessimist, a central character who is successful. He is presenting it, that is, positively, instead of through the failure of a hero who is too optimistic or unrealistic. The total pattern, however, is not so different: there are unrealistic people (as we have seen) who are foils to Oak, just as in the other novels there are realists, like Farfrae, who are foils to the unsuccessful heroes. An advantage of *Far from the Madding Crowd* as an introduction to Hardy's novels is just that it *is* positive, and provides a basis for understanding the irony of most of the others.

Despite Meredith's advice that he should avoid the direct and positive method, Hardy has given us, in Gabriel Oak, as positive a model—after one or two initial overconfident slips—as Egbert Mayne. I see this as not without significance: Hardy wished, without doubt, to clarify the values for his readers. The fire in *Desperate Remedies* [3] that seems to proceed haltingly, and to wait every now and then— but quite in vain—for some intelligent intervention, becomes the fire Oak sees at Weatherbury (VI): it has already reached the stage of accelerated climax; but, even so, a man like Oak who can act promptly and courageously, is able to intervene, and to organize the fire-fighting, and he is just in time to prevent the spread of the flames to the farm buildings and to other ricks.

But the Weatherbury fire can serve as an illustration of Hardy's development in a more important respect. The point of the incident is not only to show how the courage and intelligence of a superior man can help the ordinary community when by itself that community is helpless; but also to show how that man gets a job. Oak has failed to get work at the hiring fair, and he is in desperate straits; but through the fire, and his ability to swallow his pride even when he discovers that the owner of the farm is Bathsheba, the woman who once rejected him, he gets the employment he needs. Hardy here embodies in action and incident what in *Desperate Remedies* had to be expressed in an explicit statement. What Edward Springrove reminds Cytherea, '. . . that the fame of Sir Christopher Wren himself

---

[3] See above, pp. 53 ff.

depended upon the accident of a fire in Pudding Lane',[4] is transposed from the key of the young architect to that of the countryman, and presented not in words, but in action. And there are other examples. We have already remarked that Hardy's note about the 'figure' that 'stands in our van with arm uplifted, to knock us back from any pleasant prospect we indulge in as probable' is paraphrased in *Desperate Remedies*, Hardy explaining that 'a position which it was impossible to reach by any direct attempt was come to by a seeker's swerving from the path'. Less than four years later, this does not have to be phrased at all. It becomes the sequence of events at the beginning of *Far from the Madding Crowd*: Gabriel, indulging in the 'pleasant prospect' of success as a sheep-farmer, and even at one point accepting as 'probable' his marriage with Bathsheba, is 'knocked back'. He is ruined. At Casterbridge hiring fair, subsequently, he fails to get a job as bailiff or even as shepherd. But then, 'swerving from his path', he gradually contrives to reach all his original objectives, one by one: he becomes a shepherd, a bailiff, the owner of Boldwood's farm, and eventually Bathsheba's husband.

Let us now consider such of Hardy's favourite narrative devices as may be illustrated from *Far from the Madding Crowd*, beginning with two of the most important: the highly-charged expressionistic incidents that have been called 'grotesques', and his contrasts. These ironical contrasts, discussed on earlier pages of this book, may be partly accounted for by Hardy's modest wish—expressed indeed at this very period of his life—'to be considered a good hand at a serial'.[5] But this is certainly not the whole truth. Hardy's belief in the eternal possibility of change was something fundamental; and some of the contrasts he suggests are far more elaborate than anything required by the suspenses and sequels of a magazine serial story. In *Far from the Madding Crowd* it happens that one of the most extraordinary of Hardy's 'grotesques' has an important place in one of his series of ironical contrasts; we shall therefore be able to discuss them together. But first a word about the 'grotesques', since they have proved to be critical stumbling blocks: Hardy risked the sleepwalking scene in *Tess*, and the trilobite and cliff rescue in *A Pair of Blue Eyes*, and other such scenes, because he saw their function as transcending their awkwardness and lack of realism. And they may fulfil their function not despite their awkwardness, but because of it. Read in their full contexts, they set chords vibrating through the whole novel.

[4] *Desperate Remedies*, III, 2.   [5] *Early Life*, p. 131; *Life*, p. 100.

The sleep-walking scene, with its central incident of Angel carrying Tess precariously along the plank above the flooded waters of the Froom, reminds us of Tess's complete helplessness in Angel's care; and of Tess's responsibility too, since a false move on her part will be fatal; above all, the precariousness is a reminder that the happiness of both is in the balance; Angel's placing of Tess in the coffin powerfully suggests that he is killing his love for her; and, behind the mere fact of the sleepwalking, is the hint that Angel does not know where he is going. It is Tess, indeed, who finally takes control, leading Angel back to safety; this is an indication that the salvation may be in Tess's own hands. Through the very incident—if she tells Angel about it—she may help him to clarify his feelings. The cliff scene in *A Pair of Blue Eyes* is less complex; but this too might be taken primarily as an indication of the deep need of Elfride and Knight for each other, while subsidiary details suggest the completeness with which Elfride has renounced all thought of marrying Stephen. These are but suggestions; with the most interesting expressionistic scene in *Far from the Madding Crowd* I will try to give the implications a little more fully: it is the scene where the grotesque gurgoyle spouts water over Fanny's grave and undoes all that Troy's remorseful labour has accomplished.

The first irony is Troy's astonishment. He feels he has turned over a new leaf and made a virtuous show of remorse; but finds that

. . . Providence, far from helping him into a new course, or showing any wish that he might adopt one, actually jeered his first trembling and critical attempt in that kind . . . (XLVI).

But Hardy, in the preceding chapter, 'Troy's Romanticism', had shown Troy's activities in a different light. After a long and tiring day, in which he had walked to Casterbridge and back, arranged for a headstone to be inscribed and dispatched, and finally toiled at the grave late into the night, planting flowers by the light of a lantern, Troy had taken shelter in the church porch, and fallen asleep. 'Troy', Hardy remarks, 'had no perception that in the futility of these romantic doings, dictated by remorseful reaction from previous indifference, there was any element of absurdity.' Here, then, is another and a greater irony: in the contrast between the immense trouble that Troy takes, to prove his love for Fanny now she is dead, and his neglect of her during her lifetime. Seen in this light, the gurgoyle's mockery is but a picturesque projection, an image, of Hardy's own feelings about Troy. But even if we share Troy's view [6] that Fate cruelly prevents him from adequately displaying his remorse, we certainly cannot suppose it was Fate that had stopped him from marrying Fanny: it was injured pride. And is not this the explanation of his present defeat? His pride is hurt; the approving pat on the back that he expects from Providence has not come. If he had been thinking, not of the hurt to himself, but simply of what could be done to repair the damage, he could have done it; and with a quarter of the effort he had spent toiling by lantern-light the night before. Hardy pushes this point home, as there is no need to remind the reader, by showing Bathsheba doing simply and easily what Troy thinks it is useless to attempt: gathering up the flowers and replanting them, cleaning up the headstone, and arranging for the pipe in the gurgoyle's mouth to be deflected. For Troy such actions are impossible:

He slowly withdrew from the grave. He did not attempt to fill up the hole, replace the flowers, or do anything at all. He simply threw up his cards, and foreswore his game for that time and always . . . Shortly afterwards he had gone from the village.

He has no intention of returning to Bathsheba's farm; and surely the greatest irony of all is that in his remorse for the past, he is neglecting the present. He regrets having neglected Fanny when she was alive; but, repeating the same pattern, he is neglecting the woman—in every way Fanny's superior—whom he has actually married.

Indeed, as one contemplates the situation, the ironies seem to multiply. There is the fact that Troy, of all people, should not be surprised at what the rain can do: only a few weeks before, the storm he confidently predicted would not happen, did happen, and would have ruined him and Bathsheba but for Oak's courage. Then he had blamed the rain for all the money he had lost at the Budmouth races. And this reminds us that the money he spent on Fanny's grave, like that he lost on the horses, was not even his own; it was Bathsheba's. And again the realization is forced upon us that from the rain and the gurgoyle Troy had suffered no tangible harm; his ego was hurt, his gesture spoilt: nothing else. But the world of *Far*

---

[6] Shaw once complained that his critics always agreed with his sentimental heroines; one might say with equal truth that Hardy's critics always agree with his fatalists. It is odd that Troy gets little sympathy from the critics, *except at this point*—where he gets no sympathy from Hardy.

from the Madding Crowd is, after all, one where more is at stake, sometimes, than the success of a gesture; and beyond the ironies of what Troy had left undone, and still leaves undone, there is the further ironic contrast between the way Troy is immediately and utterly defeated by the mere *appearance* of disaster and difficulty, and the way Oak has fought against what might have been a real disaster and at the real risk of his life. Many facets of Troy's character are recalled as we ponder over the incident; and in particular his weakness for display: a small point is the splendid impossibility of the lie about his modestly entering the church in such a way as to avoid being seen, and the blindness of Bathsheba in believing him.[7]

The occasional importance of images in Hardy's narrative method is not likely to be overlooked. Discussion of these has proved easy, and sometimes uninformative. When Bathsheba first meets Troy, the gimp on her dress is caught in one of his spurs, and as Troy seeks to disentangle it, the lantern throws their shadows against the trees of the fir plantation so that 'each dusky shape' becomes 'distorted and mangled till it wasted to nothing' (XXIV). It is easy to see this as a 'proleptic image', a hint of the trouble in store for them when their lives become entangled. But why 'when'? Why not '*if* their lives become entangled'? Why should Bathsheba ignore a danger that almost everyone else in Weatherbury sees clearly? There is no need to repeat what I have already stressed [8]: that far more striking images—such as those which predict death and disaster for Gabriel before the storm—indicate not a determined future, but undetermined possible dangers that can be averted.

But there is one image in *Far from the Madding Crowd* on which it is necessary to comment, since it has escaped the notice of other critics. Gabriel is investigating an unfamiliar light (II), and finds that it comes from a shed set into the hillside. He peers through a hole in the roof, and finds himself looking down upon a young woman whom he at first does not recognize, seeing her 'in a bird's eye view, *as Milton's Satan first saw Paradise*'. There are ways of dealing with things as awkward as this: some critics may say that Hardy does not know what he is doing; that he is writing here without inner conviction; others may ridicule Hardy's attempt to display his book knowledge. But there is only one way of reading this in good faith: to

[7] It is possible that Hardy got the hint for Troy's lie from an inscription in Puddletown ('Weatherbury') Church which reads: 'Huc ades non videri sed audire et precari.'

[8] See pages 12–13 and 19 above.

assume that Hardy meant what he said. And Hardy is not parading his own book knowledge: *Paradise Lost* was one of Gabriel Oak's books, we discover later (VIII); and we are following *Gabriel's* eyes, *his* impressions, *his* slight feeling of guilt, as he peers into the hut. There is nothing satanic about Gabriel; and indeed there is something very unsatanic about his name; all the same, he would like to intrude, and does in fact later intrude, upon this girl's life. The function of the image is, indeed, clear: it strikingly raises the question whether the intruder is always evil, or whether he can be—as Gabriel turns out to be, by and large—a good angel.

It is through this image, in fact, that we approach the social theme of the book—in so far as it has one: the strengthening of a rather backward, pleasant, easy-going rural community by two newcomers, two intruders. The Weatherbury folk are too close to nature; ignorant, lazy, rather irresponsible, and superstitious: it is significant that when Bathsheba, against her better judgement and under Liddy's persuasion, consults the 'Sortes Sanctorum', a rusty patch on the page indicates how often the Bible has been used before for this purpose. In all kinds of small ways the country people show that they are not adapting themselves for survival under new conditions of life, and weaknesses are creeping in. They need someone like Bathsheba, an unconventional woman, whose parents were townsfolk, to come and take a personal interest in the farm, to sack the dishonest bailiff, and take full responsibility herself. The workfolk are capable enough, but they are useless in an emergency: they get flustered or they are tipsy; and they have none of the new skills and scientific knowledge that enable Gabriel Oak to operate upon the sheep that have poisoned themselves in the young clover. But more than this, they need Oak's new conscientiousness, his firmness, his readiness, his refusal to let personal griefs affect his actions (he is contrasted strikingly in this respect with Boldwood, whose preoccupation with grief—as we learn when Gabriel meets him the morning after the storm—has caused him to neglect his harvest). Neither Oak's new skills nor the qualities of his character were learnt from the Weatherbury community; he brings them—as Bathsheba brings her vitality and unconventionality—from outside. They are strangers in a sense that even Troy is not; Troy slips only too readily into the easy-going country morality. Gabriel and Bathsheba have all the strength of newcomers, outsiders, who revitalize the old stock.

I have mentioned the fact that Bathsheba allows herself to be influenced by the irresponsible and romantic Liddy in the Sortes Sanctorum scene and the sending of the valentine. This does not contradict my argument: it is a lapse on Bathsheba's part, and she pays dearly for it. And every detail of the episode is interesting as revealing that Bathsheba is all the time aware of the more sensible course; for instance she reverses the conditions of the toss because she thinks the book is more likely to fall open:

'. . . Open Boldwood—shut, Teddy. No; it's more likely to fall open: Open, Teddy—shut, Boldwood' (XIII).

It falls shut. And Bathsheba, who knows perfectly well what she wants to do, and what she ought to do, acts instead as she is directed by chance. It is an interesting illustration of the fact that human beings who are capable enough of acting independently of chance, and more intelligently, sometimes choose to put themselves in chance's hands. The relevance of this point to incidents in the other novels (for instance, Elfride's decision that her horse shall choose her direction for her) needs no emphasis; nor need we stress the irony with which Hardy links Bathsheba's foolish and, indeed, disastrous action with the Sortes Sanctorum and tossing of a hymn book, and so, by ironic implication, with the workings of Providence.

So often is Hardy's attitude to chance misunderstood, that it is perhaps worth adding that chances, in his books, are not always disastrous ones; and there is an instance in *Far from the Madding Crowd* of a singularly fortunate chance: Bathsheba happens to pass near Gabriel's hut and to notice that both ventilators are closed. Her chance discovery saves Gabriel's life:

'How did you find me?'
'I heard your dog howling and scratching at the door of the hut when I came to the milking (it was so lucky, Daisy's milking is almost over for the season, and I shall not come here after this week or the next). The dog saw me, and jumped over to me, and laid hold of my skirt. I came across and looked round the hut the very first thing to see if the slides were closed. My uncle has a hut like this one, and I have heard him tell his shepherd not to go to sleep without leaving a slide open . . .' (III).

But there is more to it than the lucky chance of Daisy's milking not being quite over: the event is nearly a disaster; and the disaster is prevented only because the person happening to come by was—by

Wessex standards—remarkably responsible, and intelligently alert to the worst contingencies.

A final point: Hardy was much interested in what one may call the psychology of the 'object': the distress and sudden weakness felt by someone—often a woman—when she discovers she is being talked about, and has thus become an object in the eyes of others. Tess's 'feminine loss of courage' at Emminster is caused by over-hearing Angel's brothers talking about her [9]; Sue cannot ignore the gossip she overhears about herself and Jude [10]; Elfride is horrified to find that Knight is writing an article about her [11]; even Ethelberta is disconcerted at overhearing some gossip about her own future [12]; and, as we might expect, Hardy explicitly theorizes about this human weakness in *Desperate Remedies*.[13] Bathsheba is vexed that Gabriel has seen her unconventional behaviour on horseback; and she is indignant at his tactlessness in letting her know. None the less, the fact that she knows he has seen her, and is critical of her conduct, makes her a little dependent on him; she finds herself sounding him as to what others are saying about her, and seeking Gabriel's good opinion. Her self-justifications and confidences are not just a narrative device: Hardy is doing more than conveying to us a few facts we should otherwise not know—Bathsheba's doings in Bath, for instance—he is showing her becoming more and more dependent upon Gabriel and Gabriel's approval. At the same time Gabriel himself is be-coming more and more the controlling centre of all the activity on the two farms; and from looking *to* him, Bathsheba gradually finds herself looking *up* to him.

Romantic Westerners are sometimes a bit surprised that Bathsheba marries Oak; but between the man we meet in the opening pages, pleasant and unassuming but tactless and just a shade too confident, and the Gabriel Oak of the last chapters, there are many subtle differences; and perhaps her choice is not so surprising. In the East, feelings are reversed: surprise is sometimes felt that *he* could have brought himself to marry *her*. She had slighted him, as Japanese and Chinese readers point out, and she was not an easily controllable woman. Not many English people react in this way because, I suppose, we share Gabriel's liking for a woman who is exceptional.

[9] *Tess*, XLIV.   [10] *Jude*, V. vi.
[11] *A Pair of Blue Eyes*, XVIII.   [12] *The Hand of Ethelberta*, XXV.
[13] '... We do not much mind what men think of us ... provided that each thinks and acts thereupon in isolation. It is the exchange of ideas about us that we dread ...' (*Desperate Remedies*, I. 5).

And also, surely, because we have learnt to understand his great merits; first, he leaves pride and pique to fools like Troy, and second, we feel he can cope even with Bathsheba: there has been nothing so far that he has failed to cope with. We have learnt to accept, as one of the greatest of qualities, Oak's adaptability; and, at the end of the book, we take Hardy's point that it is a special sort of goodness to arrange to go to California, if that seems best, and then to be able, equally easily, to cancel such plans when, at the last moment, the factors in the situation change, and he can marry Bathsheba after all.

VI

The Dynasts

THE DYNASTS has a curious position on the list of Hardy's books. Few people read it; but many uproot from it—or cull from other critical books—quotations about the 'Immanent Will' which they use to explain Hardy's pessimism. The poem, they believe, is a final formulation of his 'philosophy' and provides the key to understanding the novels. 'What finally became explicit', says S. C. Chew, 'had always been implicit.' And the same view is strongly argued in *The History of the English Novel* by Baker, who feels that Hardy had always been groping towards a conception of the universe which should give coherence to his impressions, and that he reached it at last in *The Dynasts*.

Baker's reaction has to be taken seriously because, first, he seems to start with some sympathy for Hardy; second, he pursues his argument to a conclusion which, if his premises were correct, would damn Hardy completely; and, third, he quotes many other authorities, and thus seems to have a weight of critical opinion on his side. He is following, and to some extent commenting on, the verdicts of others; and a little reflection will, I think, confirm the impression that even when critics are less explanatory than Chew and Baker, they none the less habitually rely on *The Dynasts* and the 'Will' for the language of their interpretation of Hardy. Thus Chapman attacks Hardy's phrase about 'the President of the Immortals' on the grounds that Hardy here deserts his 'own conception' of the Immanent Will—ignoring the fact that he did not formulate that conception until years later, and, in the actual sense understood by this critic, never formulated it; and many others make the same mistake of assuming that the 'Will' was something much more than a part of the mythological framework of *The Dynasts*, that it had for long been a real belief of Hardy's, a basic conception underlying the novels.

That Hardy should have written the novels without being fully conscious of their 'meaning' is not, in itself, absurd; what *is* absurd is the fact that a questionable interpretation of *The Dynasts* should be used, not to make the novels more coherent, but to destroy any coherence they seemed previously to possess. Baker himself follows his statement that Hardy's determinism gives coherence to the novels, by saying it cripples their tragic force; whereas, surely, whatever cripples their tragic force cannot give them more coherence. 'Where is the tragic conflict when Tess, Jude, Sue and their fellow combatants are reduced to mere automata?' he asks. Where, indeed? If this complete fatalistic determinism were Hardy's brand of pessimism we could all agree to ignore him. But it is not; and Baker himself gives away his whole case by admitting that until the novels are read in the 'full light' of this determinism, the tragic figures seem to have a measure of freedom; as of course they do. And when Baker goes further and includes Gabriel Oak among the victims of Fate (Oak, who so signally proves himself more than Fate's match!) the flimsiness of his theory is shown. It may be that when we *recall* Hardy's novels, a deterministic interpretation can be made to seem plausible; but it is very different when we read or re-read them.

At all events, the purpose of this chapter is not just to question the propriety of using *The Dynasts* as a key to the novels, when all that the key has done is to jam the lock. It is, in part, to use our reading of the novels to help elucidate *The Dynasts*; to throw doubt, at least, upon the usual superficial interpretations; to ask whether the human beings in the poem are depicted as always and necessarily puppets of the Will, or whether there is any suggestion that they ought to have, and could have, a measure of freedom. Do not some of the people succeed in acting more effectively than others? Surely if some men lose battles, others must—sometimes—win? Would it not be almost beyond the bounds of possibility for Hardy to depict the Will as frustrating equally the endeavours of *all* men, and *all* types of human activity?

The fact that such obvious and basic questions are seldom asked is itself significant: for from many casual critical references, we might infer that *The Dynasts* had nothing to do with human beings at all.

It was once a commonplace of criticism to point to the two scales employed by Hardy: first he showed human beings seemingly dwarfed against a vast universal background; second, he showed

these 'smaller' figures close up, insisting upon their greater significance; imparting 'to readers the sentiment that the smaller might
be the greater to them as men'. It is very unlikely that Hardy would
have reversed his procedure in *The Dynasts*, or that we shall reach
his intention by concentrating upon the Will and the aerial choruses
and ignoring the human beings completely.

It is upon the humans, then, that we shall concentrate. But first a
word about the Will and puppetry. While Hardy was still writing
The Dynasts, he began a poem, published much later, in which he
said he could forgive all mankind's follies and wickednesses, save the
one absurdity of their

> Acting like puppets
> Under Time's buffets . . .[1]

An early note foreshadowing *The Dynasts*, moreover, shows that
Hardy intended to

Write a history of human automatism, or impulsion—viz., an account of
human action in spite of human knowledge, showing how far conduct lags
behind the knowledge that should really guide it.[2]

Hardy blames man, in short, for *choosing* to be a puppet: the Will
does not make him so. Even in some of the most hackneyed passages
in the Fore Scene, the real subject appears to be not the Will Itself,
but Its remoteness, Its irrelevance, Its 'mindlessness of earthly
woes'. When the Spirit of the Pities suggests that

> . . . though Its consciousness
> May be estranged, engrossed afar, or sealed,
> Sublunar shocks may wake Its watch anon?

The Spirit of the Years replies,

> Nay . . .
> The Will has woven with an absent heed
> Since life first was; and ever will so weave.

The Will, as First Cause, started life going; but it does not now
intervene to comfort, to guide, to set things straight. Man's one
hope, Hardy thought, was to realize this fact, and to rely on himself.
The Pities' description of the Will, 'Its consciousness . . . estranged,
engrossed afar, or sealed . . .' is an unmistakable paraphrase of

[1] *Thoughts at Midnight*, published posthumously in *Winter Words*.
[2] *Early Life*, p. 197; *Life*, p. 152.

Hardy's ironical description of 'the Providence of Tess's humble faith' that was 'talking, or pursuing, or in a journey, or sleeping and not to be awaked' when she desperately needed some protection.[3] It is clear that although at the end of *The Dynasts* Hardy is faintly mythopoeic, writing of the Will as if It might one day conceivably develop a mind or a conscience, Hardy's usual references to It are mythoclastic: It is Something that, literally, isn't there. Even his more definite references—before the After Scene—depersonalize the Will; they describe It as so amorphous that everyone is a part of It. Hardy is presenting Something which cannot be relied upon for help: It can help you only if you help yourself.

Hardy once remarked that classical philosophers made the mistake of assuming that the world had been created as 'a comfortable place for man'.[4] It is interesting to note that an orthodox philosopher, Professor John Laird,[5] makes precisely this assumption even about the world Hardy shows us in *The Dynasts*. It is not surprising that, with this view of Hardy's intentions, he should decide that the poem is a failure. He attacks it for inconsistency and because, as he says, it offers but

. . . a troubled perspective to every serious reader who is eager for a clue and a philosophy.

It does not occur to him that Hardy might be *trying* to give the reader a 'troubled perspective', that he might be *refusing* to hand out a 'clue and a philosophy'. In the Preface Hardy says the doctrines of the 'supernatural spectators' are

. . . advanced with little eye to a systematised philosophy warranted to lift 'the burthen of the mystery' of this unintelligible world.

When Hardy quotes Wordsworth it is more often than not to dissociate himself; at all events, he is gently doing so here. He had no sympathy for the Wordsworth who found in Nature a 'holy plan' protecting the Blind Highland Boy and the Idiot Boy better than their friends or parents could. To Hardy, human care and effort were never superfluous; for humans to bear the 'burthen' bravely alone was always better than to wait for Someone or Something to lift it from their shoulders.   The world is not made comfortable *for*

---

[3] *Tess*, chapter XI. See above, p. 48.
[4] *Early Life*, p. 234, *Life*, p. 179.
[5] *Philosophical Incursions into English Literature*, 1946.

man. Too often, however, 'man makes life worse than it need be'—
as Hardy once remarked to William Archer.

Let us see what man makes of the chances left him in *The Dynasts*.
For the most part we are not, as in the novels, in the sphere of individual freedom, exploring man's loss or gain of love or happiness;
we are in that of social, political and military manoeuvring, exploring
actions that win or lose battles, win or lose empires. But we are still
concerned with human beings.

Few of Hardy's humans, however, are exactly 'heroic'. Even in
the scenes leading up to the battle of Waterloo, we are reminded
continually of the sufferings of the common soldiers, even of the
women and children camp-followers. Even the leaders, amidst
their desperate efforts and anxieties, are men rather than dramatic
heroes or history-book figures. Blücher, for instance, has been wounded, and has risen from a sickbed to lead his forces. His army has
marched since five in the morning, but he leads it on, checking the
rumour of a French interception post before advancing across the
Lasne valley, exhorting his troops on, encouraging them, but also
insisting on strict discipline, and keeping the whole army together
(III. VII. iii). All this reminds one of Gabriel Oak rather than a
warrior hero. But if there is an absence of the 'heroic', there is also
an absence of the mockery that often goes with the word: only
rarely and tragically do the soldiers appear less than men. Even in
the most sordid and unheroic scene in the drama (II. III. i), during
the Peninsula retreat, where the demoralized deserters, men and
women, half-naked, some wounded and dying, some dead-drunk,
hide in the wine cellar, we find Hardy still asserting their humanity.
The Spirit Ironic exclaims, seemingly with justice,

> Quaint Poesy, and real romance of war!

But he is reproved by the Spirit of the Pities:

> Mock on, Shade, if thou wilt! But others find
> Poesy ever lurk where pitpats poor mankind.

Hardy is determined, even here, that we shall not forget the importance of mankind.[6]

[6] Douglas Brown, listing the 'themes uppermost in Hardy's mind' when he came
to compose *The Dynasts*, gives most emphasis to the theme 'that human values are
meaningless'!

But *The Dynasts* is not just about man's plight: it is also about what man can do, and how and when. We shall postpone the question of the comparative helplessness of 'the Managed' in the hands of 'the Managers', and see the subordinates, even common soldiers, as sharing the aims of commanders and rulers, and wishing to contribute loyally to those aims, although not always succeeding.

One condition of effective action may most easily be explained by recalling something we noticed in the novels: Bathsheba loses something of her independence when she realizes she has been seen and judged by Gabriel Oak; Tess's resolution is fatally weakened when she sees herself in the eyes of Angel's brothers. . . .[7] Free and effective action always becomes more difficult if a person allows an image of himself to come between him and what has to be done. The most striking instance in *The Dynasts* is that of Villeneuve. Napoleon plans to invade England; he can do this only if the English fleet is kept out of the channel. He orders Villeneuve to engage them. Villeneuve need not win: if he fights and loses, that will suffice to keep the English fleet occupied. But Villeneuve does not like the idea of being beaten: his ships are rotten, crews are rebellious, and on board two ships there is fever. Perhaps he does not want Napoleon to know how bad things are; at all events, to save his navy's prestige, and his own, he refuses to give battle. He bows to 'the inevitable' as Decrès says, trying to excuse him. The whole invasion plan has been wrecked to save Villeneuve's face; and Napoleon, who sees the excuse of 'the inevitable' for what it is, is justifiably bitter about

> This traitor—
> Of whom I asked no more than fight and lose,
> Provided he detained the enemy . . . (I. III. i).

Later, Villeneuve tries to redeem himself from disgrace by fighting the English at Trafalgar. He is hopelessly defeated. Previously, in the Channel, a defeat for Villeneuve would have meant a conquest for France. But at Trafalgar it was unnecessary and wasteful for the French to fight. Better to have kept the fleet intact, even than to have gained a victory. Napoleon sees the real meaning of Villeneuve's second mistake as easily as he saw through his earlier excuses:

> Thuswise Villeneuve, poor craven, quitted him!
> Thus are my projects for the navy dammed . . . (I. VI. i).

Villeneuve's unconscious motive was to prove that he was not a

[7] See above, p. 71.

coward. Concern for this image of himself, in his own and others' eyes, destroyed his ability to act freely and effectively in the service of France.

Early in *The Dynasts*, the Will is said to be on Napoleon's side: a metaphorical way of saying he has the secret of effective action. Hardy does not explain, but he none the less clearly shows, how the secret is lost: when Napoleon starts to regard himself as a 'man of destiny', his power is on the wane:

> Some force within me, baffling mine intent,
> Harries me onward . . . (II. I. viii).

This seems, at least in part, Napoleon's excuse to Queen Louisa for doing what he wants to do; but such references become more insistent in Part III, and Napoleon's actions become less and less effective. Instead of *doing*, he becomes conscious of *being*. He becomes preoccupied with himself, his importance, his family affairs. Begetting an heir changes his attitude to the whole war, at least for a time. Bad news from Spain evokes protests from him, and the remark,

> O well—no matter:
> Why should I linger on these haps of war
> Now that I have a son! (II. VI. iii)

And the chorus, 'The Will itself is slave to him', follows immediately, sung by the Spirits *Ironic*. Later, this son's portrait is displayed 'to cheer the hearts' of his troops before Moscow (III. I. iv), and they all parade before it: a pathetic egocentric lapse just before the whole tide of the disastrous Russian campaign turns against him.

It is just this kind of personal weakness that Napoleon is quick to see in others; indeed he has just blamed Marmont for losing a battle at Salamanca, because he had

> . . . forced a conflict to cull laurel crowns
> Before King Joseph should arrive to share them.
> (Ibid.)

And what had angered him about Villeneuve was a comparable preoccupation with kudos. At that earlier stage, however, Napoleon's own conduct had been in marked contrast: he had even accepted Decrès's excuses in his impatience to get back to practical policy:

> Well, have it so!—What are we going to do?
> My brain has only one wish—to succeed! (I. III. i)

And succeed he does: until his objective political aims give way before the image of himself.

For the second mode of effective action I shall use Napoleon's own word 'contrivance'. The Napoleon of the earlier part of the poem is essentially a contriving man. He has a clear idea of his ultimate objective, and he is prepared to reach it by any method, however roundabout or unorthodox. He can look ahead, allow for contingencies, adapt himself to changed circumstances, and, above all, he knows the importance of timing.

Hearing of Villeneuve's failure to engage the English fleet, he abandons the invasion boats, and adopts another plan:

> Instead of crossing, thitherward I tour
> By roundabout contrivance not less sure, (I. III. i)

he says: and marches quickly east to surprise the Austrians at Ulm, and defeat them. Even after Trafalgar he still retains his aim of beating the English sea-power, but by still more 'roundabout contrivance'. Asked to explain how 'ships can be wrecked by land', he says he will prevent other nations from trading with England, and so

> . . . slowly starve
> Her bloated revenues and monstrous trade,
> Till all her hulls lie sodden in their docks,
> And her grey island eyes in vain shall seek
> One jack of hers upon the ocean plains! (I. VI. i)

It is Napoleon's unorthodox contrivance which upsets General Mack:

> The accursed cunning of our adversary
> Confounds all codes of honourable war,
> Which ever have held as granted that the track
> Of armies bearing hither from the Rhine—
> Whether in peace or strenuous invasion—
> Should pierce through Schwarzwald, and through Memmingen
> And meet us in our front. But he must wind
> And corkscrew meanly round, where foot of man
> Can scarce find pathway, stealing up to us
> Thiefwise, by our back door! (I. IV. iii)

It is the sort of comically pathetic protest an old-fashioned wrestler might make if his opponent used jiu-jitsu. Indeed 'jiu-jitsu' is an accurate name for Napoleon's tactics in many later battles: he directs and times his attacks according to his enemies' decisions, and turns the mistakes and weight of the enemy against that enemy himself.

Before Austerlitz (I. VI. i) Napoleon's whole approach is marked by flexibility. He does not commit himself to a definite course; the French position is described rather as '*Rich in chance* for opportune attack'; and he announces not a definite plan, but what he will do in this or that contingency. Once the battle has begun (I. VI. iii) he concentrates upon timing, holding back his forces until the moment comes:

> Leave them alone! Nor stick nor stone we'll stir
> To interrupt them. Nought that we can scheme
> Will help us like their own stark sightlessness!

At Jena too (II. I. iv) when the soldiery are impatient to attack, Napoleon says,

> Nay, caution, men! 'Tis mine to time your deeds
> By light of long experience; yours to do them.

The reader can trace in the poem a definite evolution of such tactics —a new resourcefulness and timely contrivance replacing the old methods of fighting. 'Being taught' by Napoleon, they 'return to plague the inventor'. Indeed the supreme instance of such unorthodox resourcefulness is the firing of Moscow (III. I. vi-viii).

Wellington's fortifications known as 'the lines of Torres Vedras' anger and disconcert Massena partly by their unorthodoxy and partly for another reason. He sneers at such 'prim ponderosities'; and Loison explains:

> They are Lord Wellington's select device,
> And like him, heavy, slow, laborious, sure. (II. VI. ii)

A third type of action Hardy regards as effective is here exemplified: action taken without reliance upon good luck, but, on the contrary, after a laborious 'full look at the Worst' that could happen. Hardy's successful generals are all realists or 'pessimists' in this sense.

Moore, dying at Corunna, replies to a suggestion of Hope's that the English would have won, if they had been lucky enough to induce the French to give battle at Lugo:

> Yes . . . Yes—But it has never been my lot
> To owe much to good luck; nor was it then.
> Good fortune has been mine, but (*bitterly*) mostly so
> By the exhaustion of all shapes of bad. (II. III. iii)

Napoleon says,

> Things that verge nigh, my simple Joséphine,
> Are not shoved off by wilful winking at,
> Better quiz evils with too strained an eye
> Than have them leap from disregarded lairs.
>
> (II. II. vi)

Wellington, too, praises Brunswick particularly because

> He is of those brave men who danger see,
> And seeing front it,—not of those, less brave
> But counted more, who face it sightlessly.
>
> (III. VI. ii)

The lines of Torres Vedras were the fruit of this attitude in Wellington himself. They were his guarantee against another retreat and evacuation as disastrous as that which ended with Corunna.[8]

Corunna, however, could have been worse. Moore's success in covering the evacuation of his troops reminds us of the type of action to which Hardy gives, perhaps, final emphasis: simple dogged persistence, in which every individual is prepared to give his last effort. Corunna is a 'last shot' stand. At the start of the battle, Hardy shows us two stragglers, full of excuses, about to desert. But somehow they do not. They pull themselves together, and again enter the fight. They are not heroes, but they are men (II. III. iii). Hardy seems to show, thus, that a stiffening in the whole army's resistance was due to the decision taken by such men—as individuals. A similar emphasis upon '. . . every man . . .' reinvests Nelson's Trafalgar signal with meaning (I. V. i). At Albuera, too, the battle is going against the British—even the weather (a characteristic touch of Hardy's!) seems against them. A fatalist would certainly assume that the 'Will' was against Beresford and his harassed, almost defeated army; but they are not defeated, simply because they refuse to accept defeat (II. VI. iv).

This doggedness Hardy seems to regard as an especially English

---

[8] A note that is somewhat puzzling at first-sight—'Courage has been idealized; why not Fear? . . .' (*Later Years*, p. 17; *Life* p. 253)—takes on meaning in this context.

virtue. In many battles the French gain an initial tactical advantage which they gradually lose, and the final issue is decided by simple endurance. This, much elaborated, is the pattern of the Waterloo scenes. Napoleon has an advantage, and fails to maintain it. Manoeuvres give way to more primitive fighting. As Wellington says,

> Manoeuvring does not seem to animate
> Napoleon's methods now. Forward he comes,
> And pounds away on us in the ancient style;
> Till he is beaten back in the ancient style;
> And so the see-saw sways! (III. VII. vii)

Ney attacks the English key position again and again, and is repulsed; all units are desperate and are calling for reinforcements for the deciding phase of the battle. Neither Napoleon nor Wellington has a single reserve, and Wellington, asked by Kempt's Aide for more men, can only advise that

> . . . Those he has left him, be they many or few,
> Fight till they fall, like others on the field.
> (Ibid.)

Hill, with a 'full look at the Worst', asks Wellington for his last commands in case Wellington himself is shot, and is told,

> These simply: to hold out unto the last,
> As long as one man stands on one lame leg
> With one ball in his pouch!—then end as I.
> (Ibid.)

Again Wellington receives a plea for reinforcements: the Aide is told:

> Inform your General
> That his proposal asks the impossible!
> That he, I, every Englishman afield,
> Must fall upon the spot we occupy,
> Our wounds in front. (Ibid.)

The final impression is that simple endurance was the most important factor at Waterloo. Victory is made possible only by desperate and heart-breaking stands and struggles, the squares holding out, fighting for time, until all the various forces, including the belated armies under von Bülow and Blücher, can be brought into action.

But endurance is not the only factor: the main contrast between Napoleon and Wellington is that Napoleon tries to keep up his men's morale by false optimism, by deceiving them into thinking that Blücher's army, seen in the distance, are French troops under Grouchy. Ney protests in vain; and the truth, when it finally becomes known, breaks the French. Wellington gives *his* men a 'full look at the Worst', and still relies on them 'to fight till they fall'. He gives them no false hopes. Indeed he keeps an actual asset, a Guards regiment, hidden; and throws these into the attack when the soldiers of both sides are nearing exhaustion; and their effect is decisive in breaking the French attack, and giving the English cavalry its chance. Thus, careful timing and realistic or 'pessimistic' fact-facing cannot easily be separated from the endurance that finally wins battles.

Hardy's *Dynasts* certainly does not present us with a world in which human endeavour counts for nothing. The value of discipline, co-operation, and carefully timed effort is recognized clearly. It is a world, too, in which individual decisions count. At Wagram (II. IV. iii) despite careful manoeuvring and desperate tactics, Napoleon only just turns the scales to victory, and only because the Archduke John, arriving in time, but not realizing how even is 'the poise of forces', turns tail instead of attacking. Hardy again and again makes a special effort to show the component parts—even individual parts —of any success or failure, of any movement of the 'Will', which is indeed only 'the will of all conjunctively' (III. I. v).

When we speak of 'discipline' and 'co-operation', we are, indeed, talking of individuals, of 'every man doing his duty'. The stand at Corunna—we noticed how Hardy tells the story of the two stragglers—was made possible by the resolves of individuals:

This harassed force now appears as if composed of quite other than the men observed in the Retreat insubordinately straggling along like vagabonds. Yet they are the same men, suddenly stiffened and grown amenable to discipline by the satisfaction of standing to the enemy at last . . .

                                                              (II. III. iii)

But the most striking evidence of the potentiality of the individual occurs earlier in that same Retreat, when the English were fleeing from the French in Spain. That even the most wretched creatures of that demoralized rout could have done something, is shown by the success of such platoons as did periodically rally, and fire, and hold up the enemy advance (II. III. i). And, most significant of all, two deserters who managed to escape discovery by the British officer in the same scene, found themselves, in the next scene, still hidden beneath straw in the cellar, within point-blank range of Napoleon himself! Had they not thrown away their arms, they could have shot him!

Here, as often with most effect, Hardy points his moral ironically and negatively: unpreparedness showing the value of remaining prepared. But he uses the positive method too: Napoleon has a single night when it may be possible to escape from Elba—if only the wind rises. He waits till long after others would have given up hope; the wind comes just in time, and he gets away (III. V. i).

That one man who is prepared to take any stray chance that comes his way is able to divert the whole course of the 'Will' is also shown in *The Peasant's Confession*. This poem, though published separately, derives from Hardy's Waterloo research. It tells how a messenger from Napoleon with detailed instructions to Grouchy about engaging the Prussian troops and preventing their coming to Wellington's aid, was murdered. It will be remembered that the messenger's disappearance, with the consequent uncertainty over Grouchy's movements, causes Napoleon and his generals much anxiety in *The Dynasts*. It is worth noting in passing, however, that Hardy does not make Napoleon so foolish as to blame chance or fate; he blames negligence. When Soult gives him his personal assurance that a messenger has been sent, Napoleon exclaims,

> A messenger! Had my poor Berthier been here
> Six would have insufficed . . . III. VII. ii

The Peasant's Confession tells how the peasant is told of the messenger's mission, calculates that a battle between Grouchy and Blücher would destroy his crops, and so misdirects the messenger and kills him. The main point of the poem, undeniably, lies in the Peasant's remorse; but it is also undeniable that the earlier part of the poem reflects something of the excitement of possessing, and using, the power to change the course of history.

We are told in the Fore Scene of *The Dynasts* that the Will has no aim. That we imagine It to have an aim is a pathetic fallacy, or an inescapable weakness in our language. The Will is but a neutral 'consequence': the sum of all the causes and wills, conscious and unconscious, in the web of organic life. And, as Hardy wrote to

Edward Wright, 'Whenever it happens that all the rest of the Great Will is in equilibrium' then even 'the minute portion of it called one person's will is free'.[9] Even this one person's 'share in the sum of sources' can 'Bend a digit the poise of forces, And a fair desire fulfil'. In the world of *The Dynasts* Hardy shows us many occasions when opposing forces are evenly matched, or when there is otherwise scope for the contrivers, the plodders, the careful watchers. And traitor and coward, as well as loyal supporters, have their effect upon the outcome.

Hardy makes, however, another and different point about the individual. There are larger aims, the aims of common humanity, which cut across national and dynastic interests. Just as in some of the later novels, Hardy suggests that common humanity has to contend with an unsympathetic universe *and also* with an unsympathetic man-made structure of convention and society, so too in *The Dynasts*, common humanity, 'the Managed' (III. VII. viii), have pathetically less freedom than 'the Managers' for whom the war is plied:

>   . . . On earth below
> Are men—unnatured and mechanic-drawn—
> Mixt nationalities in row and row,
>   Wheeling them to and fro
> In moves dissociate from their souls' demand,
> For dynasts' ends that few even understand.
>   (II. VI. iv)

The 'souls' demand' of ordinary human beings is shown by the way the rank and file of opposing armies, between engagements, drink together and shake hands across a brook (II. IV. v); and when the Spirit Ironic laughs at this 'spectacle of [the Will's] instruments, set to riddle one another through', drinking 'together in peace and concord', the Spirit Sinister replies:

Come, Sprite, don't carry your ironies too far, or you may wake up the Unconscious Itself, and tempt it to let all the gory clockwork of the show run down to spite me!

Unhappily humanity does not always behave thus. The impotent rage of a defeated army and the vindictive plundering of the victorious, 'driven to demonry by the Immanent Unrecking' (III. VII. viii) after a battle, are sorrier but equally true aspects of common humanity. But it is in some such context that we must take Hardy's

[9] *Later Years*, p. 125; *Life*, p. 335.

suggestion at the very close of the poem that the Will may one day develop a mind, events may 'wake up the Unconscious Itself': even mass man may develop something like a mass conscience, a sense of restraint, a mind. It seems almost as though Hardy imagined temporarily—and uncharacteristically—that human nature itself might change. More usually he conveys the impression that human nature, as it is, would be good enough if only its potentialities were properly used.

'War is doomed' Hardy had told William Archer,[10] about the time he was writing *The Dynasts*, explaining that men were becoming too civilized to resort to this absurd way of settling differences. The Great War and the Treaty of Versailles disillusioned Hardy, and he then regretted having given the end of *The Dynasts* this optimistic turn. But let us be clear that what Hardy regretted was having suggested that there might be an improvement in the Will itself—something automatic and independent of human effort. The more characteristic belief that a way through all the difficulties that beset us might still exist, if we regarded those difficulties honestly and courageously, he never retracted: a belief in—

> The fact of life with dependence placed
> On the human heart's resource alone,
> In brotherhood bonded close and graced
>
> With loving-kindness fully blown,
> And visioned help unsought, unknown.[11]

[10] *Real Conversations*, William Archer, 1904.   [11] *A Plaint to Man.*

VII

Hardy's 'Evolutionary Meliorism': Nature, the Garden and 'God's Gardener'

MANY YEARS ago I. A. Richards adapted Hardy's own words and spoke of the 'neutrality of nature' in his writings. The meaning was clear; but it has since been obscured by those who have sought to enlist Hardy in the ranks of those who believe in 'Nature's holy plan'. Perhaps Wordsworthian nature-worship seems so normal to us that we turn in dismay or incredulity from the quite different attitude of Hardy:

An object or mark raised or made by man on a scene is worth ten times any such formed by unconscious Nature. Hence clouds, mists, and mountains are unimportant beside the wear on a threshold, or the print of a hand.[1]

At about the same date Hardy wrote the famous description of the figure on the top of Rainbarrow:

There the form stood, motionless as the hill beneath. Above the plain rose the hill, above the hill rose the barrow, and above the barrow rose the figure. Above the figure was nothing that could be mapped elsewhere than on a celestial globe.

Such a perfect, delicate, and necessary finish did the figure give to the dark pile of hills that it seemed to be the only justification for their out-line. . . .[2]

Hardy makes his point: Nature should be justified by 'her last work', humanity. Modern man should dominate nature, as even his ancestors did, who once made the barrow. But the implied promise, at the start of the book, is not fulfilled. There is no need to follow Lawrence, and suggest that Nature must always win, man always fail. Hardy's irony (as we have seen) is that man fails through neglecting chances of success.

[1] *Early Life*, p. 153; *Life*, p. 116. Note dated September 28th, 1877.
[2] *The Return of the Native*, I. ii.

In *Tess of the d'Urbervilles*, which seems to me Hardy's greatest novel, his attitude is not very different from the one revealed in *Far from the Madding Crowd* and *The Return of the Native*; but his method—if one may use so cold a word for the warmth of sympathy he shows for Tess—is more elaborate and more effective. There is less contrasting of types—Oak the practical realist with Boldwood the romantic idealist, and so forth—and much more analysis of Tess herself as a type of womanhood or humanity, with its weaknesses and its possibilities. The ironical contrasts are still there, but they are all in her: she is the old order and the new education; moved sometimes by instinct, led at others by her conscience and intelligence; she is passionate and yet scrupulous; brave and long-suffering, yet at times absurdly weak; a murderess and an adulteress, yet a 'pure woman'; she loves only Angel, yet she deceives and betrays him. . . . And in particular, the contrasting significances of Nature, the creator and the destroyer, are shown in Tess herself, in what is perhaps the most striking of Hardy's narrative contrasts.

The ground is first prepared by an elaborate series of impressions of the 'natural' life of the Durbeyfields in Marlott. First we have a splendid picture of 'Sir John', alias Jack Durbeyfield, 'luxuriously stretched . . . out upon a bank among the daisies'. Then we have glimpses of the 'muck and muddle' of the home life of these 'waiters upon Providence'. Their life-aims are supplied by *The Compleat Fortune Teller*, and their resource, 'to get up their strength' in time of trouble, is a visit to Rolliver's pub. That this shiftless, tipsy existence is 'man in a state of nature', a mockery of the Wordsworthian theme, Hardy tells us by referring bitterly to it as 'Nature's holy plan'.[3] Tess is to some extent outside this, and at times angrily critical; none the less, she is part of it too, and at times acquiesces in her family's plans 'with calm abandonment' just as she later 'abandons herself to impulse' at Trantridge. There, at Trantridge, Tess finds other children of nature, hardly more reliable than her own family:

. . . They followed the road with a sensation that they were soaring along in a supporting medium, possessed of original and profound thoughts, *themselves and surrounding nature forming an organism of which all the parts*

[3] Chapter III. This chapter also contains Tess's protest against the visits to Rolliver's and a revealing preliminary analysis of Joan's character:
  '. . . Going to hunt up her shiftless husband at the inn was one of Mrs. Durbeyfield's still extant enjoyments in the muck and muddle of rearing children . . . to sit there for an hour or two by his side and dismiss all thought and care of the children. . . .'

harmoniously and joyously interpenetrated each other. They were as sublime as the moon and stars above them, and the moon and stars were as ardent as they.[4]

These people, on whom Tess is relying to see her home, are drunk; instead of their helping her, she soon has to be 'rescued' from them by Alec d'Urberville. They go their way, their oneness with nature described in an ironical (notice the haloes!) but even more brilliantly lovely passage:

. . . As they went there moved onward with them, around the shadow of each one's head, a circle of opalized light, formed by the moon's rays upon the glistening sheet of dew. Each pedestrian could see no halo but his or her own, which never deserted the head-shadow, whatever its vulgar unsteadiness might be; but adhered to it, and persistently beautified it; till the erratic motions seemed an inherent part of the irradiation, and the fumes of their breathing a component of the night's mist; and the spirit of the scene, and of the moonlight, and of Nature seemed harmoniously to mingle with the spirit of wine.[5]

The climax is the seduction, introduced by a few lines describing Nature in her most reassuring mood, serenely indifferent to Tess's danger:

Darkness and silence ruled everywhere around. Above them rose the primeval yews and oaks of The Chase, in which there poised gentle roosting birds in their last nap; and about them stole the hopping rabbits and hares. But, might some say, where was Tess's guardian angel? . . .[6]

And the anticlimax is Tess's mother's remark when she learns that through her own vanity and irresponsibility in sending Tess to Trantridge her daughter is pregnant: ''Tis nater, after all, and what do please God!'[7] It is Hardy's irony at its bitterest, and we might well judge from these early chapters that Hardy was opposed to Nature and all her promptings.

But in the chapters that follow, Tess rallies. 'The irresistible, universal, automatic tendency to find sweet pleasure somewhere, which pervades all life . . . had at length mastered Tess.' In many moving passages, Hardy makes it clear that Tess's beauty, and her 'rally' in Blackmoor vale were part of all Nature's abundance and

---

[4] Chapter X.   [5] Chapter X.
[6] Chapter XI. The continuation is given on page 48, above. The seduction scene was one of the parts published separately before the mutilated serial version of the story, and it was entitled 'Saturday Night in Arcady'!
[7] Last sentence of Chapter XII.

creativity. And from these chapters it would be easy to assume that Hardy worshipped Nature. But the real meaning—the synthesis of these two attitudes—is still to come.

'A particularly fine spring came round, and the stir of germination was almost audible in the buds; it moved her, as it moved the wild animals, and made her passionate to go' (XV). But Tess has achieved a balance: strong in the gift of nature, she is also strong in her resolve that 'there should be no more d'Urberville aircastles in the dream and deeds of her new life' (XV); and this additional strength is not 'natural', but human and intelligent. She is conscious of past mistakes, and determined to avoid them in future. The change comes not because she falls in love with Angel but because, having done so, she fails to use her 'naturally bright intelligence' (XXXII) and the conscience which she, alone of her family, possesses. Her resolve to confess weakens, drifts into postponements, and choosing not to choose. She begins to accept 'the fatalistic convictions common to field folk and those who associate more extensively with natural phenomena' (XXXII), convictions that have hitherto characterized her family more than herself. Between these two states, before resolve begins to turn to drift, comes that notable paragraph describing Tess in the unweeded garden listening to Angel playing the harp, the weeds and blights staining her dress and sliming her skin (XIX). It has impressed critics; it is even said to be of crucial importance for the understanding of Hardy; yet no one, I think, has explained the symbolism, and the time may have come to be more explicit.

The garden powerfully suggests Tess's nature, or better perhaps an untended emotional part of it, and the weeds are those natural impulses over which she is about to lose control. The next paragraph runs:

Tess was conscious of neither time nor space. The exaltation which she had described as being producible at will by gazing on a star, came now without any determination of hers. She undulated upon the thin notes of the second-hand harp, and their harmonies passed like breezes through her, bringing tears into her eyes. The floating pollen seemed to be his notes made visible, and the dampness of the garden the weeping of the garden's sensibility. Though near nightfall, the rank-smelling weed-flowers glowed as if they would not close for intentness, and the waves of colour mixed with the waves of sound.

The rhythm of the prose combines with the meaning to recall the passages I have already quoted describing the ecstacy of the drunken

Trantridge villagers; and a notable thing, again, is that Tess's sense of contact with nature coincides with a complete *loss* of contact with reality. The passage reminds us that Hardy could write 'beautifully' on occasion; but that such 'beauty'[8] was suspect for him, seductive, deceptive—too often the attribute of that 'arch-dissembler' Nature.

The interpretation is sanctioned not only by the context in the book itself, but also by the fact that Hardy had twice used the same symbolism before: the meeting in the ferny hollow near Bathsheba's farm and a more striking parallel that I want to quote later. Meanwhile it is interesting to note that the unweeded garden was used as a symbol of nature by T. H. Huxley and J. S. Mill. Hardy was greatly influenced by Mill, as we know, and once wrote [9] of having known his 'treatise *On Liberty* . . . almost by heart'; but Mill's essay on *Nature* seems to have influenced him at least equally. Mill insisted, as Hardy was to insist—explicitly in the Maeterlinck letter and elsewhere [10] and implicitly so often in the novels—that Nature cannot be regarded as both omnipotent and benevolent:

Whatsoever in nature gives indication of beneficent design proves this beneficence to be armed only with limited power; and the duty of man is to co-operate with the beneficent power, not by imitating but by perpetually striving to amend the course of nature. . . .[11]

But this, from an earlier paragraph, is still closer to the grain of Hardy's thought:

From [nature] he must wrest, by force and ingenuity, what little he can for his own use, and deserves to be applauded when that little is rather more than might be expected from his physical weakness in comparison to those gigantic powers.

And here is the metaphor of the garden:

If it be said that there must be germs of all these virtues in human nature . . . I am ready . . . to admit the fact. But the weeds that dispute the ground

---

[8] It is hardly necessary to refer here to Hardy's plea for the claims of a starker beauty, 'Haggard Egdon', 'spots like Iceland', or 'the sand dunes of Scheveningen': 'Men have oftener suffered from the mockery of a place too smiling for their reason than from the oppression of surroundings oversadly tinged' (*The Return of the Native*, I-i).

[9] *Later Years*, p. 119; *Life*, p. 330. Many years earlier Hardy had singled out for special praise chapter III of the treatise (*Early Life*, p. 76; *Life*, p. 58). It is in this chapter that Mill discusses the inevitable deterioration of a homogeneous culture and the vital importance of the individual who makes his own choices, the eccentric, and the intruder.

[10] The letter disagreeing with Maeterlinck is printed in *Later Years*, VII. See also the correspondence with the Rev. A. B. Grosart, *Early Life*, XVI.

[11] From the last paragraph of Mill's final summary.

with these beneficent germs are themselves not germs but rankly luxuriant growths and would . . . entirely stifle and destroy the former.

There, it may be thought, Mill overstates his case. As a younger man, in the chapter of *Liberty* that Hardy greatly admired, he expressed himself in a way that perhaps carried greater conviction:

. . . desires and impulses are as much a part of a perfect human being as beliefs and restraints; and strong impulses are only perilous when not properly balanced. . . . It is not because men's desires are strong that they act ill; it is because their consciences are weak. . . [12]

That, surely, is what Hardy conveys to us in his account of Tess in the early chapters and indeed throughout the book, and what, with especial appropriateness at this turning—or surrendering—point of her life, he embodies in the metaphor of the garden. From the start of the book to the part entitled 'The Rally' he is not suggesting that Tess is any the worse for the warmth of her impulses, only for failing to control them with her conscience and her 'bright intelligence'.

There is another passage I should like to quote from Mill's essay on *Nature*, this time because of a more general reference to Hardy:

Nature means the sum of all phenomena together with all the causes which produce them, including not only all that happens but all that is capable of happening, the unused capabilities of causes being as much a part of the idea of nature as those which take effect.

Whether it was this particular passage that set Hardy thinking and exploring the implications is of no account. Mill has others pointing the same way. In the treatise *On Liberty*, for instance, Mill argues that a man is only partly limited by time and place: he is free to 'use and interpret experience in his own way',[13] to cultivate some things in his past and in his environment, and weed out others. And in the *System of Logic* (Book VI) he points out that when, as often, there are many factors in a situation, many potential causes, from which one of many different effects is possible, a man may choose which of these shall take effect: 'Any given effect is only necessary provided that the causes tending to produce it are not controlled.' In each passage the thought is much the same. It is most powerfully

---

[12] *On Liberty*, III.   [13] *Ibid*. Hardy underlined these words in his own copy.

expressed, perhaps, in the *Nature* extract, but any of these might have suggested ideas and impressions with which Hardy has made us familiar: the 'unfulfilled intentions',[14] the plurality of 'First Causes',[15] Hardy's faith in the 'unknowable' and in the 'persistence of the unforeseen'[16] his sense of things pending 'in equilibrium',[17] a 'poise of forces',[18] and most of all the sense, throughout his narratives, that something quite different might have been made to happen.

It is, moreover, in terms of this vast store of 'unused capabilities of causes' that one can explain—and Hardy did explain—his 'evolutionary meliorism'. That he had also read and accepted Darwin's views, presents no difficulty; Mill's views and Darwin's are easily reconcilable: nature's 'unused capabilities' being the wastage upon which 'natural selection' works.

Elsewhere[19] I have worked out in some detail the parallels between Hardy's 'pessimism' and evolutionary techniques of survival, as a way of suggesting that Hardy's description of himself as an 'evolutionary meliorist' has a remarkable appropriateness. Since this is not often realized, and indeed is often denied, a brief summary of my main points may be permissible here.

Until recently it sometimes puzzled people that evolution did not produce uniformity of adaptation; in fact it tends to produce differences: it is largely a matter of each species finding and exploiting an 'ecological niche', having a tiny monopoly of some source of food, some set of survival tactics, and generally being able to utilize resources and chances neglected by others. Now, although Hardy is often vague and inaccurate about the names of species, and little interested in many of the things that delighted the typical Victorian naturalist,[20] his sense of ecological relationships is remarkably keen. Who but he would have thought of the effect of Waterloo upon the creatures—rabbits, moles, insects, worms—that lived on or near the surface of the battlefield?[21] It seems to me that he had a natural way

---

[14] *The Woodlanders*, VII, and *A Laodicean* V. III.

[15] *Later Years*, p. 219; *Life*, p. 410.

[16] *The Mayor of Casterbridge*, last paragraph; and the last lines of *The Darkling Thrush*.

[17] Preface to *Late Lyrics and Earlier*, and letter to Edward Wright, *Later Years*, p. 125; *Life*, p. 335.

[18] *He wonders about himself.*

[19] *Review of English Literature*, III. 1.

[20] He is unusually accurate and specific, however, in the matter of sounds. The opening paragraph of *Under the Greenwood Tree* is a good example—and it is one of many.   [21] *The Dynasts*, III. VI. viii.

of thinking about nature, men, contingencies and evolutionary inter-relationships that enabled him to follow up any hints he may have got from Darwin.

To the evolutionist, nature seems to use an inexhaustible variety of survival tactics; it appears as though every conceivable device is being 'tried out'; for any single trick, however perfect, would soon be learnt by hungry enemies. If all butterflies resembled the Leaf Butterfly, they would be easier, not more difficult, for insectivorous birds to find. The vast variety of disguises gives greater protection, widely and generally as well as to individual species. And more effective than any disguise may be vigilance, speed, skill in dodging, or energy and endurance when pursued. Second, there is none of the taking of unnecessary risks, the assumption that luck or Providence will be on one's side, that 'we shall be lucky ourselves',[22] which in Hardy's view endangers the lives and happiness of humans. On the contrary it is as if every species is a 'pessimist', toning up the effectiveness of its defences by 'imagining' its enemies to be even more vigilant and voracious than they are. Third, where much is at stake extra precautions are taken. If a species of bird builds an open nest and all the sitting is done by the hen, she is drabber and much less conspicuous than the cock. And with many insects too the gaudiness of the male may draw the fire from the dull-coloured female whose longer survival for the sometimes slow business of egg-laying is essential for the survival of the species. Fourth, there is an intimate connection between Time and Chance. This appears from my last example; but it may also be seen in the way that a succession of disguises may be used—in the larval life of an insect, for instance—by a single species, almost as if each disguise must be changed before the enemy 'gets his eye in', as if Fate must not be tempted too long, and there must be no slipping into a false sense of security. Fifth, once one gets to know it, there seems nothing static in the 'design' of nature; one finds instead, in Hardy's phrase, flux and reflux: a restless movement in which innumerable factors are losing and gaining small advantages and the equilibrium is being continually adjusted. Occasionally and locally, adjustments may be big, as when a road is cut through a forest, a wood is cleared, or there is a flood or fire: all such changes, big and small, will be met by some creatures taking advantage of new conditions ('. . . the accident of a fire in Pudding Lane') and others failing to do so. Gradually, the 'optimistic' species

---

[22] *Two on a Tower*, XXVIII.

—those that assume, or behave as if they assume, that no adaptation is necessary, that luck will go on favouring them, that their one good trick will work for ever whatever the change in conditions—will be eliminated. And the 'pessimists'—those that seem to imagine that even the best trick may be bettered, that enemies will increase in number and experience, and that they must try every 'chink of possibility' (this significant phrase is Hardy's [23]), every trick that might elude the watchfulness of that 'figure' that 'stands in our van'—will survive.

In nature there is indeed no 'philosophic resignation', no deciding that nothing need be attempted beyond 'what do please God'; there is no throwing away one's last round of ammunition or one's last chance.[24] I am following the anthropomorphic tracks of language deliberately, for it is only proper to do so if we are going to draw inferences from evolution and apply them to the conduct of human individuals. A creature does not consciously try to survive, but it survives; it does not consciously search for a loophole, but it finds one. This does not mean that if it did search consciously, it would not find one more quickly. The 'philosophers' who interpret the 'mechanism' of evolution and its absence of conscious intention as meaning that a man who makes every effort, in a 'steady handling of any means to bring about any end necessary to happiness',[25] has no more chance of succeeding than one who resigns all effort and trusts 'to the favour of accident' are blurring the distinction between man and the lower animals, denying the faculty which is man's most valuable asset in the evolutionary process, and quite misunderstanding that process. Knight hangs desperately to the cliff-face; but what saves him is not just this instinctive behaviour, but human intelligence, unconventional inventiveness, and—at the last when his muscles are almost seizing-up with strain—the intelligent caution with which he tells Elfride to test every knot in the 'rope'.[26] Hardy's intellectual pretensions are sometimes derided; but he at least respected the intellect, and took no part in the romantic betrayal. He made no mistake about the inferences to be drawn from evolution. I

[23] *Early Life*, p. 279; *Life*, p. 213. Characteristically, Hardy's 'chink' is for the possibility of happiness, not survival.
[24] See references to *The Dynasts*, pp. 82 ff. above.
[25] *Desperate Remedies*, I. 5 (s.f.). Hardy is defining 'Wisdom'.
[26] The details of Knight's difficulties, and his means of overcoming them, are dealt with as carefully as the contrivances used by Oak in his battle against the storm in *Far from the Madding Crowd*. One knot, as Elfride tests the 'rope', slips: 'Oh think! it would have broken but for your forethought', she says.

am not ignoring the moral problems involved; Hardy warned us against modelling our 'conduct upon Nature's apparent conduct as Nietzsche would have taught'[27] and I have avoided such aspects of 'Nature red in tooth and claw' as Hardy was then rejecting, and referred to Nature's smaller creatures whose survival problems are mainly defensive.

The drastic changes brought by 'progress' in Hardy's Wessex— 'roads through the forest' changing the whole balance of life—have perhaps been exaggerated. But Hardy was clearly aware of the implications of such things not only in the world of people but also in the natural scene:

When trees and underwood are cut down, and the ground bared, three crops of flowers follow. First a sheet of yellow; they are primroses. Then a sheet of blue; they are wild hyacinths, or as we call them, graegles. Then a sheet of red; they are ragged-robins, or as they are called here, robin-hoods. What have these plants been doing through the scores of years before the trees were felled, and how did they come there?[28]

Adaptation to a changing world is certainly a problem of Hardy's individuals, if not of the community. It is a world that demands resilience, patience and contrivance, but also provides opportunities for new efforts. And in the success of Oak and Bathsheba, and (temporarily) Knight, we see the lesson of evolution clearly enough. Oak, particularly after his initial failure, is a model of readiness and adaptability to the demands of life; and it is perhaps true to say that the simpler aspects of 'evolutionary meliorism' preoccupied Hardy most at this early period—at about the time of *Far from the Madding Crowd*. In the first chapter of his next novel, Ethelberta watches a duck dodging a marsh-harrier, first across the open heath, then diving beneath the surface of a pool:

The diver was far too experienced in the rough humour of the buzzard family to come up twice near the same spot, unaccountably emerging from opposite sides of the pool in succession, and bobbing again by the time its adversary reached each place, so that at length the hawk gave up the contest and flew away, a satanic moodiness being almost perceptible in the motion of its wings.

This is not merely a piece of nature description. The duck is a

<hr/>

[27] *Later Years*, p. 98; *Life*, p. 315.
[28] Note dated February 1884; *Early Life*, pp. 214-15; *Life*, p. 164.

symbol of Ethelberta herself, eluding the men and circumstances that will beset her. Finally she is caught; but, like Oak, once she faces reality, in the person of Mountclere, she masters it.

More typically the advantages of taking 'a full look at the Worst' are presented not through the success of some contriving hero or heroine like Ethelberta, but through the too sanguine and unadaptable person's failure. Hardy became interested too in the moral question: is success easier for the opportunist? Is failure sometimes a sign of scrupulousness, of sensitiveness? But then, in this world of 'flux and reflux—the rhythm of change', are there not changes and chances of which even the most scrupulous person may take advantage? Granted that Tess was right not to use tears, or the attraction of her sex, to move Angel to reverse his decision to leave her, was she not wrong to turn back without calling upon his parents? At this point her 'sensitiveness' was not a matter of scruple, but simple cowardice.

The other point about this incident I have stressed already: that Tess turned back at the most crucial moment of her life, when she most needed courage; but at other times, strange to say, she showed she was by no means lacking in courage and fortitude. And this brings me back to the evolutionary point which might, perhaps, have been stressed more clearly: that on occasions of special need, or when much is at stake, extra 'effort' appears to be exerted, or some more-than-usually efficient device is called into play. Thus a creeper which depends for its survival upon its rapid climb from the dark undergrowth to the light and air above, may possess an extraordinary hook for thrusting and grappling its way upward through other vegetation. Once its objective is reached, however, the plant ceases to produce this implement, which was in fact simply a leaf or shoot greatly modified: the plant has simply utilized, in a special way, and in time of special need, something which all plants possess. In the same way Hardy is not suggesting that for the achievement of happiness we must look forward to a change in human nature, but rather use resources we already possess. If 'Sir John' Durbeyfield, even with his fatty heart, had the energy to bury the carcase of his horse, he could have dug the ground to grow vegetables for his family; if Tess could bring herself to write the letter of confession, she could have made sure Angel received it; if she could endure hardships and humiliations at Flintcomb Ash, she could have risked a snub from Angel's father; if Troy spent half the night toiling at Fanny's grave, he could have spent a little time by daylight in repairing the damage; if Springrove cleared his overgrown field with such conscientious labour, he could have checked the smouldering heap of weed with more care—more especially as the buildings were no longer insured, and so much depended on their safety; for it is, after all, in the nature of fires to burn, and winds to blow and to change direction.

But the irony of this simple contrast between what these people can do and what, even when much is at stake, they fail to do, is sometimes only a part of Hardy's purpose. At other times he is drawing an important distinction between action that is persistent enough but purely instinctive, and that which is directed humanly and intelligently. Fanny Robin, throwing snowballs at the barracks window, is undeterred by her poor marksmanship: she goes on, just like Nature herself, careless of wastage.[29] When this hit-or-miss technique won't work, and she must take intelligent care to hit first time, she misses, and gets to the wrong church.[30] Eustacia, in *The Return of the Native*, is far more complex: in piling her grandfather's fuel on the bonfire, her persistence is like Fanny's; or like that of a male cicada whose song continues automatically until he is successful —like Eustacia, he is calling for a mate. But to catch Clym she uses not only persistence but also ingenuity: furthering Wildeve's marriage to get Tamsin out of Clym's way. Eustacia's instincts thus drive her to an activity that is rational and intelligent, and that need not, therefore, ebb and flow with the human animal's moods. But it does ebb, unfortunately: she uses none of that intelligence, although it would have required but a fraction, to understand and make friends with Mrs. Yeobright and save her marriage with Clym. We are back again at Tess's problem: her conscience and her 'bright intelligence' need not have been destroyed by her love for Angel, but might have helped her to win him back. It is persistence aided by these more human qualities that may—

> Bend a digit the poise of forces,
> And a fair desire fulfil.

Hardy had apparently not read *The Descent of Man*; for it was as a modification of Darwin's theory that he put forward the value of co-operation: '. . . certain cells destroy other cells; but others assist and combine.'[31] That men might achieve much in 'brotherhood bonded close' was his firm belief. Knight on the cliff-face is intensely aware

[29] *Far from the Madding Crowd*, XI.   [30] Ibid. XVI.
[31] *Later Years*, p. 25; *Life*, p. 259.

of his loneliness, and knows that alone he can do nothing: even his determination and intelligence are useless without the ingenuity and courage of Elfride. Oak's victory over the elements was not won alone: Bathsheba helped ably. In *The Return of the Native* the point of the fatal misunderstandings is reinforced by successive images of loneliness: Eustacia, the lonely figure on Rainbarrow; Mrs. Yeobright, alone in her moral aloofness; Tamsin, setting out across the Heath to be married, unaccompanied by those who claimed that they loved her, '. . . diminishing far up the valley—a pale-blue spot in a vast field of neutral brown, solitary and undefended except by the power of her own hope'[32] . . . and finally the pathetic and lonely figure of Clym preaching at the end. Loneliness, misunderstanding, the failure to communicate: Hardy often puts these at the root of man's suffering. And if love symbolizes happiness, it stands also for the co-operation and understanding that Hardy sees all men and women longing for in 'this cold world' that in itself 'shows no sympathy'.[33]

Oak, going home in the dark on the night of the storm, kicked against a toad, found it uninjured, and carefully placed it in safety at the side of the road. With this incident in mind, and thinking also of Oak's care of his lambs, some too-sensitive readers feel that it is 'out of character' for Gabriel in an early chapter to kill the young dog, 'George's son'. This animal—

under the impression that since he was kept for running after sheep, the more he ran after them the better . . . had given them momentum enough to break down a portion of the rotten railing, and so hurled them over the edge.

George's son had done his work so thoroughly that he was considered too good a workman to live, and was in fact taken and tragically shot at twelve o'clock that same day—another instance of the untoward fate which so often attends dogs and other philosophers who follow out a train of reasoning to its logical conclusion, and attempt perfectly consistent conduct in a world made up so largely of compromise.[34]

---

[32] Op. cit. II. viii.

[33] *Later Years*, p. 17; *Life*, p. 253: '. . . How strange it is that we should talk so glibly of "this cold world which shows no sympathy", when this is the feeling of so many components of this same world—probably a majority—and nearly everyone's neighbour is waiting to give and receive sympathy.'
Some of Hardy's rough drafts for stories he never finished have recently been published and several hinged on the sufferings of two people in deep sympathy, perhaps love, with each other, but too shy to speak. For a similar point, see *An Imaginative Woman* (*Wessex Tales*), to which, however, Hardy added another twist.

[34] *Far from the Madding Crowd*, V. Cf. p. 76 above.

But no good shepherd could have spared 'George's son's' life, and it seems to me that Oak's action was consistent with the general attitude in *Far from the Madding Crowd* that nature must be controlled; the garden—to use the metaphor in *Tess*—must be kept weeded. And there is no one to weed it but man—whom, in *Jude the Obscure*, Hardy calls 'God's gardener'.

The question remains, however, as to whether Hardy in his later years would have handled the dog incident in quite the same way. The pig-killing scene in Jude comes to mind; one remembers Hardy's frequent references to animals in his later years, the complaints of Max Gate visitors that the dog Wessex was absurdly spoilt, and the deliberate affirmation in the *Late Lyrics and Earlier* 'Apology' that '. . . pain to all upon [the globe] . . . shall be kept down to a minimum by loving kindness'—these 'all' explicitly including the 'dumb' as well as the 'tongued', and 'kindred animal races' as well as the 'human'. We may recall another incident in *Jude*: the boy Jude's concern that the rooks were 'living in a world that did not want them':

'Poor little dears!' said Jude, aloud. 'You *shall* have some dinner—you shall. There is enough for us all. Farmer Troutham can afford to let you have some. Eat, then, my dear little birdies, and make a good meal!'

They stayed and ate, inky spots on the nut-brown soil, and Jude enjoyed their appetite. A magic thread of fellow-feeling united his own life with theirs. . . .

It is not surprising that the farmer, coming upon the boy unawares, beats him and sacks him:

Though Farmer Troutham had just hurt him, he was a boy who could not himself hurt anything. He had never brought home a nest of young birds without lying awake in misery half the night after, and often reinstating them and the nest in the same place next morning. He could scarcely bear to see trees cut down or lopped, from a fancy that it hurt them; and late pruning, when the sap was up and the tree bled profusely, had been a positive grief to him in his infancy. This weakness of character, as it may be called, suggested that he was the sort of man who was born to ache a good deal before the fall of the curtain upon his unnecessary life should signify that all was well with him again. He carefully picked his way on tiptoe among the earthworms, without killing a single one.

Not quite all Hardy's sympathy is with Jude, perhaps: but most of it is. And it is Hardy, not Jude, who perceives 'the flaw in the terrestrial scheme, by which *what was good for God's birds was bad for God's gardener*.'[35]

Does this reflect a significant change in Hardy's attitude?

First, it must be recognized that the 'unweeded garden' image in *Tess* was deliberate. Hardy had used the same image before for exactly the same purpose, to indicate the encroachment of nature, of the sexual instinct, upon a woman's will, and the weakening of her power to resist. In *Desperate Remedies*, Manston and Cytherea are standing by the ruins of a mill, the running water hidden beneath 'rank broad leaves' which—adumbrating the lush ferns that caress Bathsheba on her way to meet Troy—Hardy calls 'the *sensuous natures* of the vegetable world'. Cytherea is to some extent fascinated by Manston, but she dislikes him, and she is determined at this stage to resist him. Manston, however, takes her hand—

. . . Should she withdraw her hand? She would think whether she would. Thinking, and hesitating, she looked as far as the autumnal haze on the marshy ground would allow her to see distinctly. There was a fragment of a hedge—all that remained of a 'wet old garden'—standing in the middle of the mead, without a definite beginning or ending, purposeless and valueless. It was overgrown, and choked with mandrakes, and she could almost fancy she could hear their shrieks. . . . Should she withdraw her hand? No, she could not withdraw it now; it was too late, the act would not imply refusal. She felt as one in a boat without oars, drifting with closed eyes down a river—she knew not whither.[36]

Are we to assume that from *Desperate Remedies* to *Tess*, during the period spanned by this image, Hardy believed that the garden should be weeded? And to understand that in *Jude*, or from *Jude* onwards, Hardy saw the weeds as posing impossible moral problems? That thenceforward Hardy is questioning the right of God's gardener, mere man, to decide that he shall live and have food, while 'God's birds' shall starve, and God's weeds 'bleed' and die?

These assumptions seem to me mistaken. Long before *Jude* we find Hardy doubting the wisdom or possibility of 'God's gardener' acting consistently and logically 'in a world made up so largely of compromise'. Long after *Jude*, we find Hardy voicing many positive and hopeful statements. And the boy Jude himself, be it noticed, is not arguing that either the birds or the humans should starve, but

---

[35] All three quotations from *Jude the Obscure*, I. ii.
[36] The exceptional interest of this passage (*Desperate Remedies*, XII. 6) is not, of course, limited to the garden image. I have commented upon it in a later chapter.

that 'there is enough for us all'. We may take the greater 'pessimism' of *Jude the Obscure*—such as it is—either as reflecting temporary misgivings and darker moods increasing, perhaps, as Hardy grew older, or as something stressed deliberately as of particular relevance to this book. Perhaps both explanations are true in part. The biography provides ample evidence of fluctuations in Hardy's moods, and so do the poems; and some readers might judge that only someone who himself knew fits of depression could so successfully describe such moods in people as different as Edward Springrove, Oak, Swithin, Eustacia and Henchard.[37] But it is also true that Hardy had a special purpose in the early chapters of *Jude the Obscure*: he is here attacking complacent assumptions about the poor and the weak (weak, and therefore 'unfit to survive'); he is enlisting, with success, our sympathy for Jude, the obscure, the unwanted, by insisting upon the arbitrariness of the whole 'order' of 'wanted' and 'unwanted' beings. Hardy is indeed skilfully balancing the maximum sympathy for Jude's weakness and unwantedness against hints that he possesses a certain resilience and remains a free agent. We don't exactly admire Jude's weakness; his sense of the sufferings of the 'little birdies' is disproportionate; and it is just this kind of weakness that Hardy exaggerates and parodies, with a strange mixture of pity and mockery, in Jude's son, 'little old Father Time'. There are tougher fibres in Jude. His learning Latin and Greek is but one of many rallies; consider, for example, what follows his dismissal by the farmer and his aunt's scolding (the italics, of course, are mine):

... As you got older ... you were seized with a sort of shuddering, he perceived. All around you there seemed to be something glaring, garish, rattling, and the noises and glares hit upon the little cell called your life, and shook it and warped it.

If he could only prevent himself growing up! He did not want to be a man.

Then, like a natural boy, he forgot his despondency and sprang up. During the remainder of the morning he helped his aunt, and in the afternoon, when there was nothing more to be done, he went into the village. Here he asked a man whereabouts Christminster lay. (I. ii)

And he goes up the hill, it will be remembered, through the very field where he has been told never to show himself again; and just before sunset, as the mist clears, he sees his vision of the 'heavenly

---

[37] Henchard describes these moods to Farfrae (*The Mayor of Casterbridge*, XII). And similar but briefer confidences are made by Swithin and Edward.

Jerusalem'. This, briefly and oversimply, is Jude's story. Not the book's story: for Sue counts for a good deal more in the book than just a source of happiness and unhappiness for Jude. But Jude himself is a study of loneliness and unwantedness, redeemed by brief periods of happiness and continual rallies, and by visions of 'the heavenly Jerusalem'—the possibilities that Hardy felt ought to exist even for the obscure and unwanted of the earth.

VIII

Remorse and Memorials: Romance or Reality

IN THE MOONLIGHT, the last of the 'Satires of Circumstance' illustrates a characteristic irony of Hardy's with unusual completeness: a workman, standing alone in a graveyard and staring at a grave, is accosted by a stranger:

> ". . . If your great gaunt eyes so importune
> Her soul by the shine of this corpse-cold moon,
> Maybe you'll raise her phantom soon!"
>
> "Why, fool, it is what I would rather see
> Than all the living folk there be;
> But alas, there is no such joy for me!"
>
> "Ah—she was one you loved, no doubt,
> Through good and evil, through rain and drought,
> And when she passed, all your sun went out?"
>
> "Nay: she was the woman I did not love,
> Whom all the others were ranked above,
> Whom during her life I thought nothing of."

If we except the 'corpse-cold moon', which is hardly more than a stock counter of Hardy's to indicate the coldness and remoteness of Nature, there is virtually no imagery in the poem. It relies for its effect almost entirely upon its ironic statement. But this is not to ignore the artistry that lies in its very bareness, the perfect control and modulation of tone.

The dryness underlines the irony. It is not the simple irony of *The Self-Unseeing*:

> Everything glowed with a gleam;
> Yet we were looking away.[1]

[1] *Collected Poems*, p. 152.

It is the double irony of Troy in the churchyard bemoaning the loss of Fanny, whom in her lifetime he had neglected, and again in the actual present, neglecting Bathsheba, the far greater prize he had actually won. Whether the 'workman' in the poem is being equally foolish, we do not know; but we do know that he is neglecting such present possibilities as he has. A strain of similar irony, tinged with self-criticism, gives peculiar poignancy to *After a Journey* and some of the other poems Hardy wrote in memory of his first wife. And it is the absence of such irony—the complete and surprising lack of any kind of remorse or regret—that gives serenity to such poems as *Regret not me* and *Julie Jane*.

Hardy was not contemptuous of feeling, but often suspicious and critical of too much display. Many instances, apart from Troy's remorse, will spring to mind. One is Rings-Hill Tower:

Over the door was a stone tablet, bearing, apparently, letters or words; but the inscription, whatever it was, had been smoothed over with a plaster of lichen.

Here stood this aspiring piece of masonry, erected as the most conspicuous and ineffaceable reminder of a man that could be thought of; and yet the whole aspect of the memorial betokened forgetfulness. Probably not a dozen people within the district knew the name of the person commemorated.[2]

Another is the frank criticism voiced by the country-folk of the way Lord Luxellian mourns for his wife:

'Sich wonderful black rims as they letters had—half an inch wide, at the very least.'

'Too much,' observed Martin. 'In short, 'tis out of the question that a human being can be so mournful as black edges half-an-inch wide. I'm sure people don't feel more than a very narrow border when they feels most of all.'[3]

This is not the voice of cynicism, but simply a reminder of the vanity of trying to find an appearance, a display, that can properly represent reality. For the other side of the picture, genuine feeling that makes itself felt despite the tawdriness or incompleteness of appearances, we may turn to the burial of Tess's child:

. . . In spite of the untoward surroundings, however, Tess bravely made a little cross of two laths and a piece of string, and having bound it with

---

[2] *Two on a Tower*, I.   [3] *A Pair of Blue Eyes*, XXVI.

flowers, she stuck it up at the head of the grave one evening when she could enter the churchyard without being seen, putting at the foot also a bunch of the same flowers in a little jar of water to keep them alive. What matter was it that on the outside of the jar the eye of mere observation noted the words 'Keelwell's Marmalade'? The eye of maternal affection did not see them in its vision of higher things.[4]

Tess's child is hardly mentioned again, and only once is Tess described as returning to the grave. Her grief is simple, largely temporary—but real. No exaggerated gestures, such as Troy indulged in, or Tess's father, when he buried the horse in the garden, could make it more so. And in significant contrast to Tess, whose warmth and living reality her author depicted so well, the one character in Hardy's novels who is described as a perpetual visitor of graves is also one of his few sinister and evil characters: Mrs. Jethway 'appeared to spend her life in journeyings between Endelstow churchyard'— where her son was buried—'and that of a village near Southampton, where her father and mother were laid'.[5] And Hardy not only depicts her as unhappy, and gives her a terrible and violent death, he also shows her nature, preoccupied in this way with the dead past, as turning to evil and malice.

From all angles, Hardy returns to this favourite subject: reality. It is sometimes contrasted, thus, with the dead past; more often with romance or appearance. The theme recurs repeatedly. But in *Tess of the d'Urbervilles* it can hardly be said to 'recur': it is always present in the weave of the book, and is never forgotten. In the very first chapter there are the romantic dreams Tess's father has about his ancestry buried in 'coats of mail and jewels' in the 'city' of Kingsbere ("Tisn't a city," Fred interrupts him;"leastwise 'twaddn when I was there—'Twas a little one-eyed, blinking sort o' place."): dreams that not only conflict with reality but effectively absolve him from coping with the real needs of his family. These are quickly followed by his wife Joan's dreams of Tess's future as a 'lady', dreams into which Tess is betrayed in spite of herself,[6] though she resolutely puts them aside when she goes to Talbothays: 'There should be no more air-castles. . . . She would be the dairymaid Tess, and nothing else.'[7] Above all there are the dreams of that complicated

---

[4] *Tess of the d'Urbervilles*, XIV.   [5] *A Pair of Blue Eyes*, XIX.

[6] The accident to the Durbeyfield waggon, which Tess is taking to Casterbridge with the bee-hives (IV), happens when Tess is asleep; but it is perhaps significant that she has first fallen into a reverie about her future, induced by the foolish talk of her family.

[7] *Tess*, XV.

self-deluder, Angel, who comes to farming in search of reality, and is not content with the gem of reality he finds, but has to romanticize it:

He called her Artemis, Demeter, and other fanciful names half-teasingly, which she did not like because she did not understand them.

'Call me Tess,' she would say askance. . . .[8]

The irony of Angel's disillusionment over Tess is just that there is no need for it. The feeling and trend of the whole book show what Hardy puts explicitly elsewhere:

There is enough poetry in what is left in life, after all the false romance has been abstracted, to make a sweet pattern.[9]

What 'has been abstracted' from Angel's life, Hardy shows, is a worthless and meaningless idea, a conventional notion about womanhood; and what is left is enormously valuable:

In considering what Tess was not, he overlooked what she was, and forgot that the defective can be more than the entire.[10]

A fragment of dream about 'purity' has been lost; a sweet and loving wife—and, in essence, a pure one—has been gained; and Angel is so little in touch with reality that, until much later, he does not realize this. Well might Tess protest:

'I thought, Angel, that you loved me—me, my very self! If it is I you do love, O how can it be that you look and speak so? It frightens me! Having begun to love you, I love you forever—in all changes, in all disgraces, because you are yourself. I ask no more.'[11]

And well might Hardy, with all this in mind when he had just revised *Tess* for publication in book form, reflect,

It is the incompleteness that is loved when love is sterling and true. This is what differentiates the real one from the imaginary, the practicable from the impossible, the Love who returns the kiss from the Vision that melts away. A Man sees the Diana or the Venus in his Beloved, but what he loves is the difference.[12]

[8] *Tess.* XX.   [9] *Early Life*, p. 150; *Life*, p. 114.   [10] *Tess*, XXXIX.   [11] *Tess*, XXXV.
[12] *Early Life*, p. 314; *Life*, p. 239. The note is dated 28 October, 1891, and so may have been written with Angel and Tess in mind. Angel, like the 'man' in the note, uses the names of classical goddesses, but unlike the 'man', cannot accept the 'difference', the real woman. Hardy later raises the very question as to whether, with more 'animalism', Angel would have been the better man (XXXVI), indicating the irony, perhaps, in Angel's name. Then there is the passion with which Tess 'returns' Angel's kiss (XXX s.f.), showing her love for him but also her experience as a woman—for which (Hardy insists) she was none the worse.

In so far as Angel could not love the 'difference', he was, for all his idealism and sensitivity, less than a man.

Eustacia, in *The Return of the Native*, may be a person of a different kind, but she has many of the same weaknesses. She is not real enough: she was 'the raw material of a divinity' and had 'the passions and instincts which make a model goddess, that is, those which make not quite a model woman'. Nor is she sufficiently realistic: towards the end of the same chapter (I. vii) she is criticized for lacking 'the homely zest for doing' what lies within an ordinary human's reach. Before she had met Clym, she was already 'half in love with a vision' (II. iii), much as Boldwood was with Bathsheba, and the similarity of her passions to Madame Bovary's has more than once been noticed.[13]

It may seem that I have strayed far from 'Remorse and Memorials,' but Hardy takes pains to show that there is in fact a close connection between remorse and the sort of idealization that involves a dangerous escape from reality.

I wish to discuss some special instances of this. But first I should like to investigate further the opposition between fact and idea, reality and dream; and I think it should be admitted that, contemptuous as Hardy often is of the dreamer, there are times when he seems to waver, to wonder whether there is not a level at which make-believe is justifiable and even good. Hardy wrote a letter in 1901[14] in which he talks of 'an Idealism of Fancy':

... that is, an idealism in which fancy is no longer tricked out and made to masquerade as belief, but is frankly and honestly accepted as an imaginative solace. . . .

He is writing, it is true, of religious beliefs; and the similarity between Hardy's views and those of Arnold and some of his other contemporaries is clear. None the less, the same idea, on a different level, crops up in the novels. Jude, for instance, beginning to be disillusioned in Arabella, 'kept up a fictitious belief in her. His idea of her was the thing of most consequence, not Arabella herself, he

---

These points seemed of importance to Hardy, for they were adumbrated earlier: in *A Pair of Blue Eyes* there is some discussion on the clumsiness of inexperienced kisses; and Knight is blamed—as in effect Angel is blamed—for being too sensitive, and lacking a necessary alloy of coarseness (XXX).

[13] See especially the excellent article by M. A. Goldberg in *Essays in Criticism*, 1957.
[14] *Later Years*, p. 90; *Life*, p. 310.

sometimes said laconically'.[15] Some such 'fictitious belief'—honestly
accepted as such—might be the answer if it does not conflict too
much with reality. We may doubt if it could have helped Jude, while
feeling it might have been brought successfully to the aid of Angel.
And a faintly comparable 'fictitious belief' was successfully invoked
to keep romance alive in the 'wicked heart' of Bathsheba Everdene's
father—at least if we are to believe Jan Coggan:

'. . . "Coggan," he said, "I could never wish for a handsomer woman than
I've got, but feeling she's ticketed as my lawful wife, I can't help my
wicked heart wandering, do what I will." But at last I believe he cured it
by making her take off her wedding-ring and calling her by her maiden
name as they sat together after the shop was shut, and so 'a would get to
fancy she was only his sweetheart, and not married to him at all. And as
soon as he could thoroughly fancy he was doing wrong and committing
the seventh, 'a got to like her as well as ever, and they lived on a perfect
picture of mutel love.'[16]

'A most ungodly remedy', as the pious Joseph Poorgrass says; but a
sensible one, if it is adopted, as we may suppose it was by Mr.
Everdene, with an eye to reality: after all, the fact that his wife was a
handsome woman was real enough—he 'could never wish for a
handsomer'. The only thing wrong was the label: she was 'ticketed
as his lawful wife'. More often Hardy's characters adopt a romantic
illusion or a 'fictitious belief' which, instead of preserving the reality
of their lives, seems bound to destroy it. Margery's romantic dream
of the Baron von Xanten almost destroys her: it is only by the
utmost effort on his part that she is brought to accept life again.[17]
This is often the main pattern of Hardy's stories, or the pattern of
their concluding chapters: the hero or heroine rejects the illusion,
and learns to accept reality. Tragically, like Angel Clare or Henry
Knight, he may learn the lesson too late. But Oak (who learns the
lesson early), Bathsheba, Fitzpiers and many others learn in time
that satisfaction and fulfilment lie in reality: not in surrendering to
it, but in accepting it as the raw material of life, out of which something must and can be made. Some, like little Baptista Heddegan in
A Mere Interlude,[18] face a reality whose harshness causes them temporary despair; but it is despair with life on its far side; and many of

15 *Jude*, I. ix.
16 *Far from the Madding Crowd*, VIII.
17 *The Romantic Adventures of a Milkmaid.*
18 *A Changed Man & other Tales.*

Hardy's stories and poems have the point that happiness is by no means unattainable, for those who 'ask no ill-advised reward'.[19]

But those who are 'looking away' from reality are only too success-ful in making themselves miserable. One of these is Timothy Petrick, the central figure in *Squire Petrick's Lady*.[20] The 'lady' her-self is the most shadowy of the 'noble Dames', since she dies at the beginning of the story, having made a deathbed 'confession' to her husband: her baby son, a few days old, is not his (she tells him) but the child of a Wessex nobleman. Timothy, not unnaturally, is dis-concerted. He has promised his wife to look after the child, so he provides him with a nurse; but he takes no interest in the baby's up-bringing, seldom sees him, and indeed takes steps to prevent his inheriting the family property. Timothy then lives a lonely and dis-appointed life. Gradually, however, meeting the child occasionally by accident, he takes more and more notice of him. Neither the idea of a 'son', nor the pride of having a legal heir, matters to Timothy as much as he had supposed. The important reality to him is the need to give and to receive human affection. He grows to love the boy, and to take an interest in his welfare and development. Unfor-tunately, out of this deep reality of love, germinates another false idea—a pride in the boy's aristocratic blood; it becomes a greater and greater satisfaction to him that the boy does not come from Timothy's own plebeian stock. He takes to reading up the family history of the boy's noble father, and to 'examine young Rupert's face for the un-folding of those historic curves and shades that the painters Vandyke and Lely had perpetuated on canvas.'

Then, after a chance talk with the doctor who had been his wife's family physician before her marriage comes the revelation expected by the reader: the women of the family sometimes suffered from delusions at times of illness or emotional stress, or experienced dreams which they firmly believed to be realities. With this hint to go on, Timothy makes enquiries, and quickly discovers that Rupert's supposed father was living abroad for more than a year before the baby's birth. Absurdly enough, the discovery that he is the real father of the boy he has grown to love quite unmans Timothy. It makes him as thoroughly miserable as he had once been made by his

---

[19] In *Epitaph*, Life addresses the dead man and praises him because:
    'Thou didst ask no ill-advised reward,
    Nor sought in me much more than thou couldst find.'
                         (*Collected Poems*, p. 657)

[20] *A Group of Noble Dames.*

wife's disclosure. The story is a simple but effective exploration of the human weakness of allowing an idea to obscure reality. The delusion of Rupert's mother, with which the story opens, gives the theme; Timothy's sufferings provide the development and variations. Throughout Timothy's story, reality remains the same: 'the human necessity to love,' Hardy calls it; the father's need for the child, the child's for the father—whether he is legally or literally the father or not.[21] This reality is first pushed aside by what Timothy persuades himself, in the name of convention and social morality, he ought to feel; and then, later, by some curious snobbery about the aristocracy, about 'blood'. Professor Guerard, who admires the story and praises its economy, takes Timothy's snobbery, his sense of his own family inferiority, to be its theme. But snobbery is only a part of the theme, one of several ways Timothy Petrick allowed ideas to destroy human realities.

Death, that makes young widows, often makes them 'protest too much'. Hardy has a poem [22] about a widow so prostrated by grief that she had inscribed her own name as well as her husband's on his memorial tablet—for she had hoped to be buried one day in the same tomb—and had, in the same inscription, protested her undying love, and implored prayers for the souls of her husband and herself. She feels she forgoes heaven if she marries again; and yet she cannot resist the claims of a new love. . . . A humorous treatment of this same theme occurs in the story, *Fellow Townsmen* [23]; though the main action is ironical and tragic. Barnet, the hero, has been foolish enough to allow a misunderstanding to separate him from Lucy, whom he claims he loves, and to marry, for the sake of her wealth and social pretensions, a woman who comes to despise him. Again we see an idea, and again a snobbish and ambitious idea, crowding out reality. In course of time, Barnet's 'fellow townsman', Downe, loses his wife, and Barnet persuades him to employ Lucy as a governess for his now motherless children. Barnet is out to help Downe, and also to help Lucy; but he also wishes to prevent her from emigrating, as there seems a chance of her doing: for he cannot bear to think of never seeing her again. At the back of his mind is the possibility that he may one day be free again to marry Lucy; for his wife, who has in any case now deserted him, is not in good health. At last he hears of

[21] A similar theme, it will be recalled, is worked out in *The Mayor of Casterbridge*.
[22] *The Inscription.*   [23] *Wessex Tales.*

his wife's death; but his freedom comes just too late: he hears at the same time that Lucy has agreed to marry Downe.

We have claimed that the irony of Hardy's coincidences lies in the fact that a message *need not* have been sent too late, a meeting or discovery *could* have occurred in time. Tess—and we all understand her reluctance in speaking to Angel—could have put her letter into his hands. But even as it was, she was virtually certain the very next morning that he had not received it: the search she made six days later, when she found what had happened to the letter, could have been made that morning; and she could have left herself plenty of time, instead of barely time, to confess. Even when things do happen 'just too late' apparently by accident, in Hardy's books, we are usually well enough aware that they could have been *made* to happen in time, if people had been quick to realize the contingencies. And so it was with Barnet and the news of his wife's death and of Lucy's marriage. Could he not have guessed (as we readers guessed) that Lucy's marriage with Downe was a possible development? And might not a word from him, a former lover, have delayed the marriage and made Lucy think twice? Lucy's and Downe's turned out to be a happy marriage: but it was in part, at least, a marriage of convenience, with Downe's children a major factor in the situation. It was not a passionate love affair; and what might not Barnet have done, even with the virtuous Lucy, to revive in her a spark of her previous love?

These are not just idle questions, the result of 'reading into' the story. Hardy has suggested the questions, and given the answers. Barnet does in fact have a clue to the change in Downe's feelings; he has it in good time, and he neglects it. The clue is this: Downe had been prostrated by his wife's death, and had ordered a magnificent tomb. He had refused to listen to advice from friends or from the architect; and, indeed, the extravagance of his grief had led to disagreement with the architect over what was suitable and what was not, and to some delay. Meanwhile Lucy has been employed in the Downe household. The next that Barnet hears is that Downe himself has come round to the notion of a more sensible tomb, 'a more modest memorial even than had been suggested by the architect' (VII). Finally, months later, and just before Barnet hears news of his own wife's death, and learns that his freedom has come too late, he hears that Downe 'reduced design after design . . . till in the end it has become a common headstone'! (VIII) Barnet could

9

hardly have had clearer hints of what was happening to his friend's feelings.

There is a good deal more to this interesting story [24]; but I am concerned here only with Mrs. Downe's memorial; its tragic significance as a missed clue, an unfulfilled possibility in Barnet's life, and its ironical significance in Downe's. Downe's genuine love of his first wife had yielded to fictitious exaggeration, something almost inevitably false, since the memorial referred to something past. The problem of reality and self-deception is, as often with Hardy, related to Time and Change [25]; for an idea can remain fixed, but reality is changing and alive, so that discrepancies and falsification quickly arise.

Another interesting story, more centrally concerned with this question of reality, and again worked out in terms of 'remorse and memorials', is *Barbara of the House of Grebe*.[26] It has the additional interest of having horrified several eminent critics. It is a fable; less shocking than many fairy tales. If it seems more horrible, this is because it has a realistic setting. We all know the stories in which the kind and handsome youth has his courage and good faith put to the extreme test: he suddenly finds that, to fulfil a promise or repay an obligation, he must marry an old crone; or the beautiful princess finds she must marry a toad or some other loathsome creature. They put a good face on it, and go through with it graciously, and the toad turns out to be a bewitched prince and the old crone, a beautiful princess. The main difference is that Barbara Grebe cannot go through with it.

At the beginning of the story, Barbara elopes with Edmund Willowes, a poor but strikingly handsome youth who lives in a nearby town. Sir John and Lady Grebe are rich landowners, and they had every intention of marrying Barbara to Lord Uplandtowers. They are shocked by the marriage, but make the best of a bad job, and eventually forgive Barbara and her husband. They are, indeed, a little won over by his handsome appearance and pleasantly modest manner. They decide to send Willowes abroad for a year with a

[24] The story centres upon one of Hardy's ironical contrasts. Barnet's wife is thought to be drowned; but despite his wish to be free to marry Lucy, and despite the doctors' decision that his wife is actually dead, he continues artificial respiration and at last revives her. That the spark of love might be revived too is the obvious lesson. And when, years later, Barnett returns and finds Lucy a widow, he does in fact revive the spark of love in her. But he does not realize this, and goes off discouraged after a single call at her house.

[25] 'I am more than ever convinced that persons are successively various persons. . . .'—*Early Life*, p. 301; *Life*, p. 230.

[26] *A Group of Noble Dames*.

tutor, so that he can acquire the culture that befits Barbara's husband. He will then return to England and to Barbara, and the two will live in a house Sir John will prepare for them. Willowes stays away rather longer than he had intended: this is a characteristic touch of Hardy's, for he commonly shows his characters to be blind to the obvious connection between chance and time, between delay and additional risk. At all events, a terrible thing happens: Willowes is visiting the Commedia del Arte in Venice when the theatre catches fire. Willowes is badly burnt; indeed at first the doctors despair of his life. But here, and several times during the story Hardy makes the point that Willowes's stock was altogether healthier and sounder than that of the landed gentry and nobility: Willowes has a strong constitution and he survives.

Months later, largely recovered but maimed and terribly disfigured, he arrives back in England and goes to meet his wife. To save her from worse shock, they had stopped her from going to Italy after the accident. She is apprehensive, but resolved that the loss of his good looks will make no difference to her love. Alas, the reality is too much for her. When he removes his mask, she breaks down; and he leaves her, promising to return in a year; and, if she still cannot bear the sight of him, to leave her forever. In fact, he dies after a few months, without having seen Barbara again.

Now, on the surface, the essence of the story so far is the thought that occurs to all the Grebe family when they hear the news from Venice; though only Barbara's mother, with that insensitiveness that Hardy's 'well-bred' people sometimes show, is tactless enough to voice it: what a misfortune, Lady Grebe points out,

'. . . that the one little gift he had to justify your rash choice of him—his wonderful good looks—should be taken away like this, to leave 'ee no excuse at all for your conduct in the world's eyes. . . .'

Barbara had married Willowes for his appearance, his 'wonderful good looks'. And they were gone. This is what the events mean not only to Lady Grebe but also, unfortunately, to Barbara.

But I have purposely omitted something of great importance, something which changes the whole meaning of the story, something in the light of which we are meant to read Lady Grebe's remark not only as a cruel piece of tactlessness on her part, but as bitter irony on Hardy's: the burning beams of the roof had fallen upon Willowes not because he had been slow in getting out of the theatre but because he had returned again and again to the flaming building rescuing lives. Barbara's strikingly handsome husband, with all the appearance of a glamorous and romantic stage hero, was a *real* hero. But the evidence, or at least the reminder, of this reality was his terrible disfigurement. In proving the reality, he had destroyed the appearance; and it was only the appearance that Barbara wanted.

The significance of the rest of the story will now be appreciated. Barbara reproaches herself bitterly, but eventually accepts the situation, and marries Lord Uplandtowers. The marriage is unhappy. Barbara is cold and listless; and Uplandtowers is first disappointed, then resentful that she does not bear him an heir. Then Barbara's life is transformed by the arrival of Willowes's statue: sculptured in Italy before the accident, it has long since been forgotten. But when the sculptor writes that the statue is taking up storage space, and will be sent as soon as he receives a balance of payment, Barbara sends for it. Once again she is overcome by the beauty of her first husband and with remorse for her cruelty. Barbara has a cupboard made for the statue in her boudoir; and Uplandtowers is angered by the discovery that she leaves his bed every night to worship her first husband at what is, in effect, a shrine to his memory. Uplandtowers seeks out the tutor who had accompanied Willowes on his continental tour, and with his help mutilates the statue into a likeness of Willowes after the burning. Barbara collapses in terror when she sees it: but, not content with this, Uplandtowers has a wardrobe put at the foot of their bed, and, operating the doors by means of cords, opens them to reveal the statue, its mutilated and realistically painted features lighted up by candles. This cruelty is continued until Barbara has a mental breakdown. When she recovers, she is pathetically devoted to and dependent upon her harsh husband.

Despite what critics have said, this fable is certainly not immoral; nor does it express sadism or any other uncontrolled emotion. The feeling is carefully controlled. There is no sympathy for Lord Uplandtowers, whom Hardy describes as

a subtle man when once he set himself to strategy; though in the present instance he never thought of the simple stratagem of constant tenderness.

So far as Barbara's second marriage is concerned, all the sympathy is with her. But, equally clearly, the sympathy is with her *only* here; or, if more generally, then only because it is her story: it is she who makes the choices and the mistakes, and she who suffers. To take

Willowes as a mere piece of machinery in her story is to ignore the quiet genuineness of his impact. In his brief appearances, and in the letter of farewell he leaves for Barbara, we glimpse a somewhat formal and shy man, saddened and sensitive, but of unselfish love and calm courage—a man, in short, of true gentleness and nobility, who stands out effectively from the base metal of the titled people around him. The moral sympathy, in fact, is with Willowes.

Again, the irony is double. First, Barbara and her family are blind to Willowes's real qualities; then, Barbara's remorse, obsessed with his beauty, is equally falsifying; it proves she never knew the husband she mourns for. The whole structure of the story is built on the theme of reality, of truth; truth and reality being defined by contrast to all kinds of appearances: titles, masks, pretences, romance, and sentimental remorse. But apart from the general structure, one must also point to certain details of imagery that might be obscured by the deceptive naturalism of the narrative. First, there is Willowes's *mask*, to which he is reduced by the world of appearances. Then the terrible climax of his association with this world of culture and show, is the burning of a *theatre*. Then there is the shrine-stage imagery at the end: Barbara's closet that she visits with candles is frankly a shrine, except that she not only worships but also embraces the image of her 'Phoebus-Apollo' husband (as Uplandtowers calls him). Uplandtowers ironically recalls this closet of Barbara's when he calls his own contraption a 'shrine'. But it is really a stage, with Uplandtowers himself, a diabolical showman, pulling the curtain cords, the candles having become footlights, and Barbara, the audience not 'purged', but shocked with horror. But more significant than any of these is the statue itself: the cold marble that replaces the warmth of love and living flesh and blood, the pathetic efforts of Barbara to enter the timeless [27] world of the statue, to kiss it, and protest that she was 'ever-faithful', reminds us again of Hardy's preoccupation with Time. And we realize that what happened to Willowes—the loss of his looks—was what Time would have caused eventually in any case. Hardy has contrived incidents to represent and speed up the natural process, and to bring home to us with startling clarity the weakness of Barbara's love.

Hardy's short stories merit more serious attention than they have received. Once we realize that they are fables, their apparent action

---

[27] The allusion to Keats may be unconscious, but it is significant all the same.

in the real world need not mislead us.[28] There is, indeed, nothing obscure about his symbols—which he uses again and again, showing imagination rather in their re-arrangement than in their selection. A single example will make this point clear. Superficially there appears no likeness between *Barbara of the House of Grebe* and *The Well-Beloved*; yet a little reflection shows that their themes are the same: both deny the value of appearance (beauty, the ideal, romance, the dream) and insist upon that of reality; both urge the importance of what is left in life 'when the false romance has been abstracted.' In fact, once we realize that Willowes is much more than his beauty, that his beauty is a paradox, we see that each tale might have as its epigraph 'Beauty is *not* Truth!' It is then but a step to see that, different as the stories are in their settings, plots and people, several symbols are identical: the sculpture (as an escape from time and from human reality); the world of fashionable society and show; and, finally, the mask and act of unmasking—the last with the two-fold significance of accepting reality as more valuable than beauty, and accepting time.

What Jocelyn Pierston calls 'the Well-Beloved' is an ideal, an image, a vision of beauty which he is always chasing and which he seeks to embody in his sculpture. And these two things—the vision, and the stone itself—are alike in being inhuman and fixed: fixed partly by Pierston's remorse over deserting Avice I, and his readiness to find the beauty unchanged in her daughter and granddaughter. Pierston knows that he is wrong; he tries to regain the path of reality, but he is unsuccessful. Since he seeks it through the *appearances* of Avice II and Avice III, different as he recognizes their characters to be from his original Avice, perhaps he is doomed to failure. The first real step in the right direction is taken when the rays of the early morning sun and an unfamiliar mirror suddenly reveal him to himself, no longer as 'a young man turned sixty', but as an old man. He makes sure that Avice III has no illusions about him, and, in effect, loosens the bonds of obligation she feels.

[28] An interesting example is *The Romantic Adventures of a Milkmaid*. Every 'romantic' element is ironical. Baron von Xanten is happy to gratify the harmless wishes (as he thinks) of the pretty milkmaid, Margery, whose unexpected intrusion has prevented him from committing suicide. He then realizes the truth: that for Margery he has become the centre of a romantic dream that is impairing her grasp of reality. Except for one lapse, when the Baron is tempted to take advantage of Margery's romanticism and elope with her, he conscientiously tries—again and again, and finally with success—to bring her back to her real-life commitments. The story, in fact, is a quasi-romantic fable in praise of reality, and one can well understand its unpopularity beside such romantic fables as *Axel*.

Almost to his relief, she deserts him—as he had once deserted her grandmother. . . .

Pierston recovers from a serious illness to find his values have all changed. His restless pursuit of beauty seems to him meaningless. He can now appreciate everything *except* beauty. And having grown fond of Marcia, who nurses him, he regrets that she is still beautiful: she seems hardly less beautiful, indeed, than when he had known her forty years before. Next morning, however, she comes without her make-up:

. . . The cruel morning rays—as with Jocelyn under Avice's scrutiny— showed in their full bareness, unenriched by addition, undisguised by the arts of colour and shade, the thin remains of what had once been Marcia's majestic bloom. She stood the image and superscription of Age—an old woman, pale and shrivelled, her forehead ploughed, her cheek hollow, her hair white as snow. To this the face he once kissed had been brought by the raspings, chisellings, scourgings, bakings, freezings of forty invidious years—by the thinkings of more than half a lifetime.

'I am sorry if I shock you,' she went on huskily but firmly, as he did not speak. 'But the moth eats the garment somewhat in such an interval.'

'Yes—yes! . . . Marcia, you are a brave woman. You have the courage of the great women of history. I can no longer love; but I admire you from my soul!'

The Well-Beloved is an absurd novel, perhaps, and unsuccessful; but it is difficult to share the common opinion that it is trivial. It seeks to show that the beautiful appearances which glamorize our lives are devices of cowardice; and that reality is life, and life is courage. Unlike Barbara who, having no courage herself, rejects Willowes's, the two old people at the end of *The Well-Beloved*, Pierston and Marcia, face their ugliness and their infirmities and other realities of life and time; and, for Pierston anyway, life is for the first time truly satisfying.

IX

Hardy's Poetry

DURING THE PAST few decades it has been customary to regard Hardy as a greater poet than novelist; several good essays have been written on his poetry; they are easily accessible; and less, therefore, remains to be said on this subject, particularly since it is usually agreed that the number of Hardy's poems meriting serious attention is not large in relation to the bulk of his collected verse. I am not going to quarrel with the last verdict, except to remind readers that many another great poet has left us a large mass of dreary or downright bad verse, and to suggest that the number of good poems written by Hardy may be rather larger than we think. We might agree to jettison all but a score of his poems; but there would, I suspect, be much disagreement over the twenty to be salvaged. And a sufficient reason for writing about Hardy's poetry might be the bringing of two or three neglected poems to the attention of other readers.

But my main aims are to offer a few general remarks, even if these lack originality, to help any newcomers to Hardy's poetry who may still find his rhythms difficult, and to correct errors which seem to be current about Hardy's themes. The two aims are related. I do not make the mistake of taking the themes to 'be' the poetry, but nor do I make the commoner mistake of assuming that the themes have nothing to do with the poetry at all. The themes of the poems cannot properly be separated from their rhythms, and the subtleties of the latter cannot be appreciated while the former are misunderstood.

Hardy's rhythms are not 'difficult' so much as 'unfamiliar'. Each poem, as we come to know it, will create its own rhythm with controlling certainty. The poems that seem to hesitate or stumble, do in fact hesitate or stumble; it is right to read them in this way. To find the rhythm of such poems easy and familiar would be to fail to reach the poem itself. Hardy was well aware of what he was doing:

. . . The whole secret of a living style and the difference between it and a dead style, lies in not having too much style—being in fact a little careless, or rather seeming to be, here and there. It brings wonderful life into the writing:

> "A sweet disorder in the dress . . .
> A careless shoe-string, in whose tie
> I see a wild civility,
> Do more bewitch me than when art
> Is too precise in every part.

Otherwise style is like worn half-pence—all the fresh images rounded off by rubbing, and no crispness or movement at all.

It is, of course, simply a carrying into prose the knowledge I have acquired in poetry—that inexact rhymes and rhythms now and then are far more pleasing than correct ones.[1]

There is a later reference, too, to making 'defects . . . the basis of a hitherto unperceived beauty', where he rather vaguely, perhaps, is linking both Nature's defects and 'defects' in writing.[2] And, much later, he is justly indignant when a reviewer remarks of *On Sturminster Footbridge* that one could make as good music out of a milk-cart [3]: pointing out that this was obviously the kind of effect the poem attempted.

But this sensitiveness to what the rhythm itself is doing is necessary even when we come to poems—the tragic ballads such as *The Trampwoman's Tragedy*,[4] for instance—which seem to invite a strictly metrical reading and which carry an insistent 'beat': familiarity does strange things with this regular rhythm. The regularity beats itself out, in horrified exhaustion:

> Then in a voice I had never heard,
> I had never heard,
> My only Love to me: "One word,
> My lady, if you please!
> Whose is the child you are like to bear?—
> *His*? After all my months o' care?"
> God knows 'twas not! But, O despair!
> I nodded—still to tease . . .

And so on, mechanically (in a sense, but not making the poem itself mechanical) to the end. Coming back to the poem, and rereading it,

[1] *Early Life*, p. 138; *Life*, p. 105.   [2] *Early Life*, p. 150; *Life*, p. 114.
[3] *Later Years*, p. 193; *Life*, p. 390.
[4] In addition to the usual 'Index of first lines' and table of 'Contents', recent editions of Hardy's *Collected Poems* possess an alphabetical index of titles. I shall therefore dispense with footnotes that give no more than a page reference in the *Collected Poems* volume.

we may be surprised to find that the regularity is not controlled by a formal refrain; but a refrain might in fact invite variations of tone and rhythm at an early point. It is the nervous tension beneath the clockwork which is so effective: beneath the 'inevitable' or 'mechanical' momentum of events is that one shockingly *un*inevitable nod; so wanton an act in the face of a human appeal that we cannot believe it happened; yet so completely plausible—'still to tease'—that we believe it only too well.

A Sunday Morning Tragedy exploits the same kind of insistent rhythm. Again there is no formal refrain—except for the girl's mother's (the narrator's) insistence on 'alas for me': the one formal metrical element is this 'me' rhyme that occurs in the second and fourth lines of every stanza: abab, cbcb, dbdb, and so on, right to the end, with ever accumulating horror:

> "Is there a herb . . .?" I asked. "Or none?"
> Yes, thus I asked him desperately.
> "There is," he said; " a certain one . . ."
> Would he had sworn that none knew he! . . .
>
> . . . There she lay—silent, breathless, dead,
> Stone dead she lay—wronged, sinless she!
> Ghost-white the cheeks once rosy-red:
> Death had took her. Death took not me.
>
> I kissed her colding face and hair,
> I kissed her corpse—the bride to be!—
> My punishment I cannot bear,
> But pray God *not* to pity me.

There is hardly a stumble in the rhythm (there indeed is the irony) till we come to 'Death had took her. Death took not me.' But against all the clockwork of the metre runs the equally insistent protest of the sense: that the girl's death and the desperate remedy were unnecessary. It is a *Sunday* morning tragedy not because Hardy is suggesting that a 'Christian' society should be less quick to condemn the unmarried mother (this point is made earlier), but because, as the girl lies dying, news comes that her lover has decided to marry her after all, and that the first banns have been read in the church. The assertion, only too common, that many of Hardy's poems are concerned with death and disaster, is wholly misleading: the theme of *The Trampwoman's Tragedy*, *A Sunday Morning Tragedy*, and many others lumped under this heading, is not the disaster, but the disaster's unnecessariness.

To appreciate Hardy's handling of rhythm at its simplest, we may turn to a very different poem, *The Colour*:

> 'What shall I bring you?
> Please will white do
> Best for your wearing
>   The long day through?'
> 'White is for weddings,
> Weddings, weddings,
> White is for weddings,
>   And that won't do.' . . .

The woman also rejects 'red' (since this is 'for soldiers'), 'blue' ('for sailors'), and 'green' ('for Mayings'); but the strain of reading three additional stanzas in which only these words are changed, plays havoc with the rhythm: by the fourth stanza the maid is either in exasperated impatience or in despair:

> 'What *shall* I bring you?
> Please—will *green* do?'

Surely not? Her mistress hardly ever wears green? The whole metrical structure has fallen before the attack of the sense; but a new smoothness and dignity enter with the last stanza, the rhythm reestablished:

> 'What shall I bring you
> Then? Will black do
> Best for your wearing
>   The long day through?'
> 'Black is for mourning,
> Mourning, mourning,
> Black is for mourning,
>   And black will do.'

Hardy is here only elaborating a half-remembered folk-song. Even so, what he is attempting to do with it is clear. He is setting the sense against the metre, straining the metre, giving it a burden that it cannot bear—without the most alert and subtle adjustments, without in fact the creation of a new rhythm by the reader.

The three poems I have briefly discussed are not, in my view, great poems; though Hardy himself considered *The Trampwoman's*

Tragedy to rank with his best. It has power, certainly. So has *A Sunday Morning Tragedy*. Rhythmically, all three are interesting, and in a way not so very different from the generally accepted masterpieces, *The Voice* and *After a Journey*:

> Can it be you that I hear? Let me view you, then,
> Standing as when I drew near to the town
> Where you would wait for me: yes, as I knew you then,
> Even to the original air-blue gown!

Were ever dactyls used with such sadness before? And what of

> Yes: I have re-entered your olden haunts at last;
> Through the years, through the dead scenes I have tracked you,
> What have you now found to say of our past—
> Scanned across the dark space wherein I have lacked you?
> Summer gave us sweets, but autumn wrought division?

The strange breaking rhythm (stranger still when these poems were written), changing from 'víew you, then,' to 'knew you thén' and 'I've trácked you' to 'Í have lacked yóu' has often been noticed; nor has the effect been missed—the nuances of sadness and uncertainty that seem as surely a part of the rhythm as of the sense. The redistribution of stress on a feminine rhyme is something the rudest critical yardstick can measure and, in these and a score of other poems, demonstrate. But I need not insist that the real effect depends upon the most subtle of rhythmic variations and changes which defy adequate critical analysis but which we recognize as characteristic of Hardy's tone. There is no explaining *The Voice*, beyond noting its lingering, haunting quality, its sense of loss, and the cold feeling— more subdued than in some of Hardy's poems, however—that Nature is doing nothing to comfort or redress. The poise of *After a Journey* is still more delicate; and attempts at paraphrase are unlikely to be helpful. But the poet is re-affirming what for him has been the meaning of the past, sad in the thought that the woman's spirit, seeing her life completed and in retrospect, may not agree:

> What have yóu nów found to say . . .?

He has 're-entered' the 'olden haunts' (but what of her?):

> Trust me, I mind not, though Life lours,
> The bringing me here; nay, bring me here again!
> I am just the same as when
> Our days were a joy, and our paths through flowers.

It is sad, though, that it should all need re-affirming. If the poet had always made the best of the past, would he be dwelling on it now? Is there any point, after all, in his 'journey'? The writer may truly be 'just the same as when' their 'days were a joy . . .', but he is also (the poem shows) the same man who described the uselessness of Troy's remorse and the foolishness of the lonely workman at the graveside 'in the moonlight', and the man who threw doubt on the genuineness of those black rims on the invitations to Lady Luxellian's funeral.[5]

The poems Hardy wrote in memory of his first wife vary in mood: if some, such as *The Voice*, express the greyness and coldness of his loss, others recall his unalloyed faith in

The woman whom I loved so, and who loyally loved me,[6]

And his certainty that there was never

A time of such quality, since or before . . .[7]

But in *After a Journey* we find a more complete blend of feelings than in any of the others, a finer balance, communicated through these changes in rhythm. The hesitations prepare us, show us where we must read between the lines, keep the movement in suspense until the whole poem is before us—all with beautiful control.[7a]

But, as we said, there are other poems where Hardy exercises this control, perhaps more simply, but just as surely. We need not analyse the technique in order to feel the power. The total effect, in all the better poems, is one of question rather than of statement, of opening a subject, rather than pronouncing finally; it is something in the movement, or better, the balance of the poem, which perfectly accords with Hardy's desire to let us see the possibilities, the contingencies of any situation.

There are pessimistic poems: the most optimistic of writers, spending sixty years of his life in the nineteenth century and then living on to see his books misrepresented and the people for whom he had written involved in wars and the preparation for wars, could scarcely have avoided periods of depression. But one has only to compare the most pessimistic of Hardy's poems with typical poems of Housman, to realize Hardy's resilience. Here is Housman:

. . . Take from seventy springs a score,
It only leaves me fifty more.

---

[5] See above pp. 66–7 and 105–6.   [6] *Beeny Cliff.*   [7] *At Castle Boterel.*
[7a] See the excellent analysis of this poem in 'Reality and Sincerity', F. R. Leavis, *Scrutiny* XIX.

> And since to look at things in bloom
> Fifty springs is little room,
> About the woodlands I will go
> To see the cherry hung with snow.[8]

It would be foolish to argue that this represents a totally negative
attitude. None the less it is, and it is intended to be, stoical in its
finality. And this is true, too, of

> Up, lad! When the journey's over
> There'll be time enough for sleep.[9]

And of

> [My bones] shall do my will
> Today, while I am master still;
> And flesh and soul, now both are strong,
> Shall hale the sullen slaves along. . . .[10]

The pride underlines the pessimism. The merit of the resolution is
precisely that it is an attitude adopted despite the absence of hope.
Indeed in the poem quoted last, the final emphasis is upon the
'steadfast and enduring bone'. And these, it will be agreed, are
comparatively cheerful poems. In others we are told that neither
effort nor hope avails; courage and cowardice, faith and betrayal,
come to much the same thing in the end; life itself is a mockery, and
death—though meaningless in itself—is a good release. And continually the sense is reinforced by the finality of the rhythm, and by
other qualities in Housman's language: the lapidary perfection of
phrase, the use of classical allusions and near-clichés: long-accepted
and known materials and formal techniques that would damn any
other writer, turned to Housman's own purpose, made to express an
inescapable verdict: that the only changes possible on earth are
those from night to day, day to night; that as life was, so it is, and
ever will be.

> In all the endless road you tread,
> There's nothing but the night.[11]

> . . . Then 'twas the Roman, now 'tis I.[12]

> . . . They, no help for all they try,
> Tread the mill I trod before.[13]

---

[8] *Shropshire Lad*, II.   [9] *Shropshire Lad*, IV.   [10] *Shropshire Lad*, XLIII.
[11] Ibid. LX.   [12] Ibid. XXXI.   [13] Ibid. LV.

This dry finality is quite foreign to Hardy, whose verse takes nothing for granted. It searches and doubts and questions, striving to find some other possible answer. 'This is so, perhaps. But why? Must it be always so? What margin was there, or may still exist, for free and different action?' Even when baffled himself, he sees no cause for despondency, and imagines his thrush, in 'blast-beruffled plume', as glimpsing

> Some blessed Hope, whereof he knew,
> And I was unaware.[14]

The Trampwoman's Tragedy and *A Sunday Morning Tragedy* are two of Hardy's grimmest poems. But even these, we saw, are not fatalistic: they are grimly moral. Hardy is not protesting against man's helplessness in the hands of Fate, but against his putting himself, by foolish and irresponsible actions, into such a helpless position. Mention of one or two more of these grimmer narratives may serve to make an additional point. In *A Conversation at Dawn*, the bride has despaired of marrying the man she is in love with, for he is married already; unhappily she is pregnant, and she has taken the desperate step of marrying someone else. No sooner is this done than her lover's wife dies, and he is—or would have been—free to marry her. So far the pattern is familiar: had the girl taken stock of the worst possibilities, from the very beginning, she would not have become pregnant; when circumstances changed for the better, she would then have been able to take advantage of them. Or, having got herself into a difficult position, she would still have found the happiness she sought, had she had the courage to face her troubles, and, if necessary, pay the price of her mistakes. In fact, the pattern is roughly that of *A Sunday Morning Tragedy*—but the girl is still alive, and it is she herself who faces the irony of a chance that has come too late. Encouraged by a word of sympathy from her husband, she tells him everything and asks for her release. As Hardy presents the story to us, in fact, there is a chance even at this late stage for the mesh of circumstance and convention to be cut by an act of generous humanity, an act of entire good faith. Instead, the husband turns cruelly upon his bride:

> "Even should you fly to his arms, I'll damn
> Opinion and fetch you; treat as sham
>   Your mutinous kicks,
> And whip you home. That's the sort I am."

[14] *The Darkling Thrush.*

Men indeed 'make things worse than they need be'. By contrast we may recall those moving chapters of *Jude the Obscure* in which Phillotson faces a similar problem, but rejects the promptings of convention and pride, and sets Sue free to marry Jude. And it is ironical that this civilized act is condemned by all except the hucksters and cheap-jacks, and fair-booth keepers, and other outcasts of society. They rally round the schoolmaster, and take his part, thereby of course bringing still more discredit upon him in the eyes of all the right-thinking Shaston bourgeoisie. And if nothing of this loving-kindness is found in *A Conversation at Dawn*, there are certain of Hardy's narrative poems that it irradiates. In *The Burghers*, the husband is informed that his wife is about to elope with her lover. But something in the manner of his informant, of this fellow-burgher who attempts to work upon his jealousy and indignation, grates upon the husband, and he resolves to act alone. With sword drawn, he lies in wait for his wife and her lover; but when he actually encounters them and realizes the genuineness of their love, he sees himself not as the wronged husband, but as a 'licensed tyrant'. He flings away his sword and insists upon supplying them with money for their journey. So too with the wife, in *A Wife and Another*: she too sets out in hatred and jealousy to trap her husband with the woman he loves, and she is only too successful. But their blank unhappiness is no triumph to her, and the awkwardness with which Hardy describes her feelings is not unimpressive:

> Then, as it were, within me
>   Something snapped,
> As if my soul had largened:
>   Conscience-capped,
> I saw myself the snarer—them the trapped.

Such 'largening' of the anger- or convention-constricted soul is not, perhaps, very often described in Hardy's poems; but those in which *some kind* of liberation is indicated, *some* way through the mesh, are far more numerous than the usual superficial accounts of his subject-matter indicate.

Even in 'Satires of Circumstance' (those which could be so described, as well as those so named) things can turn out fortunately. In the poem, *Outside the Window*, the man who has gone back for his walking-stick overhears his sweetheart viciously scolding her mother, and he is not too much blinded by love to take advantage of the knowledge that chance thus puts in his way. In *At the Altar Rail*, the man is saved by the woman's own honesty and good sense. And in *In the Restaurant*, although the man counsels a timid deception, the woman has a courage that would have saved the girl in *A Sunday Morning Tragedy* or the bride in *A Conversation at Dawn*:

> ". . . If you stay, and the child be born,
> It will pass as your husband's with the rest . . ."

he advises; but she replies:—

> "O you realise not what it is, my dear,
> To a woman! Daily and hourly alarms
> Lest the truth should out. How can I stay here
> And nightly take him into my arms!
> Come to the child no name or fame,
> Let us go, and face it, and bear the shame."

The 'satire' of any 'circumstance' (we infer) will fade if it is faced with courage. And in contrast to the distress of some of Hardy's trapped women, we might also set the young wife in *The Husband's View*. The 'Husband' is, indeed, somewhat coarse-grained; he has the 'animalism' perhaps, and certainly the tolerance, that Angel Clare and Henry Knight so signally lack. But he loves his wife, and his love gives him the sympathy and imagination to guess his wife's secret and to guess, too, what she may be suffering and contemplating, and he has the gumption to act in time.

Hardy has written a number of even very light-hearted poems on the subject of 'facing it, and bearing the shame': *The Dark-eyed Gentleman*, *One Ralph Blossom Soliloquizes* and *The Ruined Maid*. These are not great poems, it is true; and it might be argued that, if we are estimating the prevailing cast of Hardy's mind, they should not be allowed to weigh in the balance against those of a sadder and graver kind. There are two things to be said against this argument. One is that, for obvious reasons, sadder poems carry greater conviction, and seem more serious, *generally*; for the reader as well as for the poet, 'Our sweetest songs are those that tell of saddest thought'. The other is that Hardy has left us as many light-hearted poems as almost any other great poet; and if those we have mentioned are of no great merit, there are others that are deeply moving. There is, for instance, the tranquillity of *Regret not me*:

. . . I did not know
That heydays fade and go,
But deemed that what was would be always so.

I skipped at morn
Between the yellowing corn,
Thinking it good and glorious to be born.

I ran at eves
Among the piled-up sheaves,
Dreaming, "I grieve not, therefore nothing grieves."

Now soon will come
The apple, pear, and plum,
And hinds will sing, and autumn insects hum.

Again you will fare
To cider-makings rare,
And junketings; but I shall not be there.

Yet gaily sing
Until the pewter ring
Those songs we sang when we went gipsying.

And lightly dance
Some triple-timed romance
In coupled figures, and forget mischance;

And mourn not me
Beneath the yellowing tree;
For I shall mind not, slumbering peacefully.

And of the equally satisfying *Julie Jane*:

. . . Laugh; how 'a would laugh!
Her peony lips would part
As if none such a place for a lover to quaff
At the deeps of a heart.

Julie, O girl of joy,
Soon, soon that lover he came.
Ah, yes; and gave thee a baby boy,
But never his name. . . .

> —Tolling for her, as you guess;
>   And the baby too . . . 'Tis well.
> You knew her in maidhood likewise?—Yes,
>   That's her burial bell.
>
>   "I suppose," with a laugh, she said;
>   "I should blush that I'm not a wife;
> But how can it matter, so soon to be dead,
>   What one does in life!"
>
>   When we sat making the mourning
>   By her death-bed side, said she,
> "Dears, how can you keep from your lovers, adorning
>   In honour of me!"
>
>   Bubbling and brightsome eyed!
>   But now—O never again.
> She chose her bearers before she died
>   From her fancy men.

Only perversity could represent such poems as being 'about' a man in his grave, and a funeral. They are essentially concerned with life— lives enjoyed, and in a measure fulfilled. Their serenity lies in their freedom from any bitterness or envy (' "Dears, how can you keep from your lovers . . .?" ' and 'Yet daily dance. . . . And mourn not me. . . . I lie uncaring, slumbering peacefully'). The absence of any regrets, remorse, or hankerings after what 'might have been', is obvious enough even if the reader is unfamiliar with those other poems where Hardy deplores the way that people miss their chances of happiness, and waste the 'gleam' of the present by 'looking away'.

The man lying 'Beneath the yellowing tree . . . uncaring' had not dreamed 'that heydays fade and go'. He is thus free from the nagging time-sense that inhibits enjoyment of the present. We may remember Giles's weakness ('All night did Winterborne think over that unsatisfactory ending of a pleasant time, forgetting the pleasant time itself' . . .[15]) or Eustacia's (' "I know that I shall not love like this always . . . Love . . . will evaporate like a spirit, and so I am full of fears" ' . . .[16]) or, in still greater contrast, little Father Time's pathetic inability to enjoy life (' "I should like the flowers very much,

[15] *Woodlanders*, XXXIX.   [16] *The Return of the Native*, III. iv.

if I didn't keep on thinking they'd all be withered in a few days" '¹⁷).
But there is no need to refer back to the novels; the poems—several
of those I have already discussed as well as many others—provide
abundant evidence of Hardy's preoccupation with Time.

In the often-quoted poem *Hap*, the 'purblind Doomsters' Time
and Chance ('Crass Casualty') might as readily have 'strewn Blisses
about' the writer's 'pilgrimage as pain'. But even in this early poem,
we find something different from Schopenhauer's philosophic
resignation to the fact. The poet knows he is not doomed by a
'Powerfuller' than he; he is doomed rather by his own nature to a
perpetual investigation, often in ironical protest, of those moments
and situations when his time-sense plagues him and he misses the
'blisses' or 'gleams' of present reality. In *The Minute before Meeting*,
written a few years later, the critical detachment is clearer; the re-
iterated stress on 'expectance' foreshadowing Boldwood's pathetic
romanticism; and the anxiously awaited 'far-off heap of happiness'
that Elfride and Knight discuss [18] and agree to find unsatisfactory:

> The grey gaunt days dividing us in twain
> Seemed hopeless hills my strength must faint to climb
> But they are gone; and now I would detain
> The few clock-beats that part us; rein back Time,
> And live in long expectance never closed. . . .
>
> And knowing that what is now about to be
> Will all *have been* in O, so short a space!
> I read beyond it my despondency
> When more dividing months shall take its place,
> Thereby denying to this hour of grace
> A full-up measure of felicity.

Often the situations may seem trivial: *Faintheart in a Railway Train*
ends.

> . . . And then on the platform, she:
> A radiant stranger, who saw not me.
> I said, "Get out to her do I dare?"
> But I kept my seat in my search for a plea,
> And the wheels moved on. O could it but be
>   That I had alighted there!

And in *A Thunderstorm in Town*, the pair sit in a hansom, hidden
from the outside world by the rain on the window. The cab had

---

¹⁷ *Jude the Obscure*, V. v.   ¹⁸ *A Pair of Blue Eyes*, XVII.

already reached the woman's destination and had stopped; but time had not really been arrested:

> Then the downpour ceased, to my sharp sad pain,
> And the glass that had screened our forms before
> Flew up, and out she sprang to her door:
> I should have kissed her if the rain
>   Had lasted a minute more.

Are these poems about a mere missed kiss or missed encounter? Or about the absurdity—once the moment has passed by—of any regret? Something of the latter certainly enters into it; but it was Hardy's way, also, to consider the 'possibly great issues of little beginnings'.[19] And we cannot dissociate these particular conceptions of Time—Time as Chance—even from some of those poems, with historical references, which might be thought to stem simply from a love of the past. Such poems as *The Jubilee of a Magazine* and *Lausanne: in Gibbon's Old Garden* mention the past only to reflect upon its 'ifs' and to deplore its wasted potentialities:

> Despite your volume's gentle aim
> To straighten visions wry and wrong,
> Events jar onward just the same.

In *Lausanne*, in his former garden, Gibbon's ghost asks,

> "How fares the Truth now?-Ill?
> —Do pens but slily further her advance?
> May one not speed her but in phrase askance? . . ."

This is the point, too, of *Embarcation*: the mention of past armies—Vespasian's, Cerdic's and Henry's—comes not from an antiquarian's love of history, but from a modern's dislike of war, from Hardy's disgust that, after centuries of 'civilization',

> Vaster battalions press for further strands,
> To argue in the self-same bloody mode
> Which this late age of thought, and pact, and code,
> Still fails to mend.

These poems stress what Time has 'failed to mend'. But their protest is not defeatist. And Hardy had a positive belief in the persistence of the seed until, sometimes from a disregarded and forgotten beginning, something valuable could germinate and grow. It is thus,

---

[19] *Far from the Madding Crowd*, XVII.

in *Shelley's Skylark*, that he thinks of the 'meek life' of a creature that 'only lived like another bird', disregarded, although it 'moved a poet to prophecies'. And in the more complex 'fragment', *The Wood Fire*, the stress is upon the mean preoccupation of mean people, blind to the significance of an event that was to change the history of the West:

> —"Aye, it has been the bleakest spring I have felt for years,
> And nought compares with cloven logs to keep alight:
> I buy them bargain-cheap of the executioners,
> As I dwell near; and they wanted the crosses out of sight
> By Passover, not to affront the eyes of visitors . . ."

To those nearest the scene, the event passed off with only a minor hitch, and is now fading into the past:

> "Though only three were impaled, you may know it didn't pass off
> So quietly as was wont? That Galilee carpenter's son
> Who boasted he was king, incensed the rabble to scoff:
> I heard the noise from my garden. This piece is the one he was on. . .
> Yes, it blazes up well if lit with a few dry chips and shroff;
> And it's worthless for much else, what with cuts and stains thereon."

Despite the 'blinkered sight of souls in bond',[20] to tear Hardy's words from another context, the truth persists for others to perceive, but this does not excuse the callous indifference of those near at hand who could have done much, initially, to 'favour her advance'.

A Commonplace Day treats of the same subject; but no centuries, only twenty-four hours, have elapsed. Even this short time, Hardy feels with regret, has been quite wasted; since he himself has achieved, or projected, 'Nothing of tiniest worth'. And he speculates sadly that even if some 'impulse', some 'intent' tending towards 'the world's amendment' has been born, it has also most probably been 'benumbed at birth'. We are back to the kind of speculation we found in *A Thunderstorm in Town*: that some 'little beginning' might, with a little more effort, have had a 'great issue'.

I have argued that Hardy's sense of the 'seeds of time' and his interest in 'which grain will grow and which will not' must modify any conception we have of him as a complete determinist. But what, it might be objected, of such a poem as *The Convergence of the Twain*? Here surely is Hardy's apparently most deterministic utterance, and we cannot in all conscience, ignore it. But the

---

[20] *He resolves to say no more.*

answer, again, lies in the context: not only the context of the rest of Hardy's work, but the context of the occasion. We all know about the *Titanic* and the iceberg, or, if we do not, the poem will tell us. What we do not realize today is the amount of publicity and controversy that surrounded the event; and the final horrified realization—after all the enquiries, the whitewashing, the face-saving and recriminations—that the disaster—at all events the full extent of the disaster—had been unnecessary. Something of the complexity of contemporary feeling emerges from the reflections [21] of Conrad, for whom the event became a grotesque example of what happened when the complacency of the 'shore gang', and their love of luxury and profits, undermined the precautions and disciplines of the sea; he called the ship—

. . . a sort of marine Ritz, proclaimed unsinkable and sent adrift with its casual population upon the sea, without enough boats, without enough seamen (but with a Parisian café and four hundred of poor devils of waiters) to meet dangers which, let the engineers say what they like, lurk always amongst the waves; sent with a blind trust in mere material, lightheartedly, to a most miserable, most fatuous disaster.

There is much more, in Conrad's own tone and idiom. I have deliberately selected a passage which, although different in attitude from Hardy's poem, throws light upon it and touches upon just those points which Hardy too makes in his first fifteen lines. Even with this brief reminder of the 'historical context', we see exactly what Hardy meant, by his references in those early lines to 'human vanity', to the 'mirrors meant To glass the opulent' and to man's 'vaingloriousness'; and in the second half of the poem the Immanent Will directing the ship and the iceberg, the 'twin halves of one austere event', must seem as inappropriate—that is, as ironical—as the 'President of the Immortals' seems to the attentive reader who reaches the final page of *Tess*.

The irony is of the same kind. But the question is not whether the reader perceives it as irony so much as how he reacts to it. Does Hardy's 'determinism' make us more deterministic ourselves? or does it make us more anxious that lifeboats should be numerous enough and that they should work efficiently? May not the very animosity that has been aroused by 'Hardy's ideas' be a measure of his success with the 'phrase askance'?

[21] See 'Some Reflections on the loss of the *Titanic*' and 'Certain Aspects of the Admirable Enquiry', both reprinted in Conrad's *Notes on Life and Letters*, 1921.

Time is sometimes thought of as a line from the past, through the present, to the future. And if the will is weak (impulse, mere volition, or acquiescence), then the line serves well enough as an illustration: 'length without breadth.' But Hardy's insistence on the awareness of contingencies and chances, his sense of the 'ifs' and 'might have beens' and the 'unfulfilled intentions' of history, broadens the 'line' into a band. Within this band the human will or human choice can be exercised, not indeed between an infinite number of possibilities, but—while the various forces are in equilibrium—at least between some.

A multiplicity of causes and an ever-changing balance of possibilities: this is a world in which the 'evolutionary meliorist' can move, understood at least by the ecologist. John Crowe Ransom has said that there is no evolutionary meliorism in Hardy's poems.[22] And if he means that Hardy's poetry is not made out of these, or any other, ideas, then we must of course agree. There are many poems which are little more than versified expositions of Hardy's philosophy; and although Hardy has tried to give a few of them a kind of mythological framework, they are still not 'poetry' in a true sense. Some of them are not uninteresting, however; some have a sense of dignity; and I would regard *A Plaint to Man* and perhaps one or two others as sensible inclusions in any selection of Hardy's verse, if only because they provide interesting and useful quotations and throw light on Hardy's other writings. Other philosophical poems (*A Commonplace Day* for example) have occasions as rather flimsy excuses. But to admit that the ideas are not poetry does not mean that they are quite irrelevant. The good poetry is written not *about* the ideas, but in their context. We have seen that even the 'Veteris vestigia flammae' poems have a greater complexity and a finer poise when we recall Hardy's ideas about remorse; and that '*Regret not me*' and *Julie Jane* take on a greater or a different kind of serenity when we remember the divided aims of some of his more romantically unhappy characters. In the same way, to understand Hardy's ideas about time and chance, and his sense that some only-too-natural inertia, or some 'momentary chance or wile', may 'benumb at birth' some good intention, is to become more acutely aware also of the significance of his affirmations of hope. Certain 'intentions' persisted, even though they might be for a long time 'unfulfilled'; certain chances recurred, even in the 'flux and reflux' of change;

[22] 'Honey and Gall', *Southern Review*, Summer, 1940.

and even 'In Time of "the Breaking of Nations" ', one thing that
persisted was the human spirit:

> . . . Only thin smoke without flame
>   From the heaps of couch-grass;
> Yet this will go onward the same
>   Though Dynasties pass.
>
> Yonder a maid and her wight
>   Come whispering by:
> War's annals will cloud into night
>   Ere their story die.

X

Choice and Existence

These venerable philosophers [Hegel and his predecessors]
seem to start wrong; they cannot get away from a prepos-
session that the world must somehow have been made to be
a comfortable place for man.

Early Life, XIV. Note dated May 1886.

The spectators . . . saw only troops and battalions in the
concrete, straight lines of red, straight lines of blue, white
lines formed of innumerable knee-breeches, black lines formed of many gaiters, coming and going in kaleidoscopic change.
Who thought of every point in the line as an isolated man,
each dwelling all to himself in the hermitage of his own mind?

The Trumpet Major, XII.

. . . A little figure wending its way between the scratching
furze-bushes, and diminishing far up the valley—a pale-blue
spot in a vast field of neutral brown, solitary and undefended
except by the power of her own hope.

The Return of the Native, II. viii.

AN OCCASIONAL reference in preceding pages to Existentialist
writers must not be taken as an attempt to turn Hardy into a mere
precursor of Sartre. The differences between Hardy and the French
Existentialists are many; all the same there are similarities too, and I
believe it will be worth our while to notice these. If we do, we may
better realize Hardy's coherence and integrity, see fewer contradictions than critics sometimes ascribe to him, and notice a deeper
and more consistent interest in psychological issues. Differences
will not be obscured; and these too may prove illuminating.

Most of my references are to Sartre, for obvious reasons; a few are
to Camus or Anouilh. I do not wish to blur distinctions; Sartre himself has said that Camus was not an Existentialist but a philosopher
of the absurd, who depicted a world from which Existentialist conclusions might be drawn, but from which Camus himself drew 'only

those of classical pessimism'. Hardy's place may be rather similar: it will be remembered that Hardy once disconcerted the Rationalists by insisting that the label 'irrationalist' would suit him better. But what, despite their differences, all these writers—Hardy included—have in common is that they are concerned less with problems about the nature of the world as with subjective questions as to how the individual is to live in it. Indeed, the disorder of the world in which man must live is deliberately stressed; and the most important question is that of man's freedom. But this is hardly a single question, since so many other questions stem from it: In what sense is man free? And from what? From God, from Fate, from society, from environment, from the past? Free to choose what? Free even to change his mind, to go back? Free to impose his will upon others? What about these 'others'? Is the free subject inhibited by their opinion? By his own opinion of himself? Is the subject free to interpret the world of reality in his own way, to live perhaps in a world of his own? Has the 'real' world any 'reality' apart from the subject's interpretation of it? or apart from its appearances? How is choice 'free'? Does one choose by oneself and for oneself, unhelped by advice or by 'signs'? What have Chance and Time to do with freedom? Can one lose freedom? regain it? No matter what their particular aims are, writers so concerned will be drawn into parallel investigations and into analysing similar situations.

It is often said that Sartre's Existentialism demands to be worked out, to be demonstrated, in concrete instances, in the problems and choices of the people in Sartre's plays and novels; and that his conclusions rest as solidly upon these as upon the close reasoning of *L'Être et le Néant*. There is much truth in this; we are ultimately concerned, moreover, not with any 'philosophy' but with the personal problems, situations and choices in Hardy's books, and the conclusions—whether similar to Sartre's or not—that he suggests in these diverse impressions. None the less, this chapter will gain in coherence if I give a brief summary of Sartre's main points. These are derived in the main from his popular lecture *L'Existentialisme est un humanisme*, which, even if it does less than justice to the strength of his position, will serve our purposes and prepare the way for the Hardy references. Indeed, it may prove difficult to summarize Sartre without making brief allusions to Hardy as we go along.

Sartre's central point is best made by his own illustration of the paper-knife: a true object, conceived and made with a definite purpose in the mind of its maker, and eventually fulfilling that purpose. Indeed if the paper-knife were accused of being a failure as a screwdriver, it might with justice fall back on the excuse, " 'Tis Nater, after all, and what do please my Maker". Man, says Sartre, never has this excuse. Man finds himself in the world, and only then discovers his potentialities and works out his purposes. He comes into existence, and only afterwards makes his 'essence'. There is no 'human nature' *a priori*; man makes himself by his deeds. Sartre insists that for a believer or an atheist the problem is the same: 'nothing can save him from himself, not even the valid proof of the existence of God.' For an atheist, certainly, there is no escape: for him it is no recommendation that a 'morality' should be 'good enough for divinities': he must create a better one.

This is man's essential freedom: to choose, to act, and thus to create his own values. And he is 'doomed' to be free, in the sense that he chooses whether he wants to or not: what he does *is his choice*. Without 'human nature' or God to justify him, he must act: he *is* nothing but what he *does*. Even what he does, however, does not define him completely, because he is always free to redefine himself, to re-interpret his past. Sartre quotes Ponge with approval: 'Man is the future of man.' And he himself adds, 'Whatever man may now appear to be, there is a future to be fashioned. . . . But in the present one is forsaken.' The emphasis on forsakenness, aloneness—upon the self from which nothing can save man—does not imply any self-interest (this should be obvious), nor justify selfish or egocentric action. On the contrary it is the illusion of the self as something of importance that leads to a kind of action that is most suspect and least effective. Aims accepted in a complete sense of one's own nothingness, however, promote objective actions dedicated simply to whatever has to be done.

Every choice, including a choice not to choose, is one's own choice, made alone and therefore in anguish. One may ask for advice; but in choosing whom to ask, one has already chosen what kind of advice one wants (Tess asks her mother whether she shall confess), and one still knows oneself (as Tess does) whether one ought to take the advice or ignore it. It is still, in fact, one's own choice. As for 'signs': who is there but oneself, again, to interpret the sign? No one but Abraham himself, ordered to sacrifice his only son, can decide whether it is indeed God's voice, God's order.

That choice is 'free' does not mean it is easy. Choice is, moreover, partly conditioned. Every man is limited, sometimes burdened, by heredity and environment. All the same, the man who insists he is such-and-such by nature and can act in no other way, is deceiving himself and acting in bad faith. He must not blame nature, or the trend of events, or accident, or the 'Will', without asking whether he, as an intelligent being, cannot decide better than any such 'Vast Imbecility'.[1] Although he chooses *by* himself, moreover, he chooses as a man, and *for* all men. His choice makes human nature. Tess, 'carried on the wings of the hours', only too effectually defines human nature, denying a place, in that definition, to her 'bright intelligence' and new sensitivity.

Not that one's fetters are illusory. They are real enough: but many (one conveniently forgets) are forged from previous choices that were free at the time. A man (young Henchard, for instance) may boast of what he would have done, unburdened by an early marriage; but the marriage was his own choice. One can judge a man's intentions, Sartre says, only by his deeds. Bathsheba 'intends' to break off her affair with Troy: she goes off to Bath to see him, and tell him of her decision. But, instead, she marries him. It is not just that when she comes under his personal spell her decision is reversed, but that she has deceived herself as to the purpose of her journey. In order to break with a person, one doesn't go to him; one stays away: a point which Hardy makes very clearly.[2]

Although it is wrong to use one's limitations as an excuse, it is also wrong to ignore them completely, for this may lead to kicking against the pricks, or to separating oneself from the world of reality. Limitations are not only limitations, they are also opportunities: they are part of the substance of existence out of which life must be fashioned.[3] No man asked for life, with all its sorry conditions; but, having got it, he must make something out of it, not vainly ask for something else. And 'it is necessary', Sartre says, ' "to obey nature in order to command her"; that is to say, to insert my action in the mesh of determinism'—a statement which recalls the actions of Oak and one or two other Hardy characters, as well as the views of Mill.

[1] See Hardy's poem, *Nature's Questioning, Collected Poems*, p. 58.
[2] *Far from the Madding Crowd*, XXXII.
[3] '. . . . Every event in the world can disclose itself to me only as opportunity (opportunity taken advantage of, lost, neglected, etc.), or better still . . . everything that happens to us can be considered as a chance, that is to say can appear to us only a means of realising this being that is in question in our being . . .' *L'Être et le Néant*, quoted by Blackham in *Six Existentialist Thinkers*, VI, vii.

Moreover, despite the determining factors—even those, the most frustrating of all, imposed by oneself by past mistakes and evasions —there is a perpetual renewal, a rallying, a re-encountering of one's freedom in new contexts. Just as one does not begin life with a definition or formula, so one never attains one; every new situation demands decisions that are essentially creative. And this is true, even though there may be, indeed should be, a general commitment to a purpose: one is continually adjusting and redirecting. Man is 'a project which possesses subjective life, instead of being a kind of moss, or fungus, or cauliflower'. To define man would be to turn him into such an object in a world of other objects. But he remains a subject: free to recreate himself, until he is finally rounded off into an object in the only way possible: by death.

Hardy (it has often been noticed) has given us no childhood backgrounds, no causal explanation of character. Sartre touches on just this point:

Suppose that, like Zola, we showed that the behaviour of these characters was caused by their heredity, or by the action of their environment upon them, or by determining factors, psychic and organic. People would be reassured, they would say, "You see that is what we are like, no one can do anything about it".

The fact that Hardy's people lack causal psychological backgrounds is a measure of their freedom. And although it might be held that Hardy does in fact show the influence of heredity and environment and various determining factors upon his characters, I should like to suggest that this is not *quite* what he does. He shows the influence of environment—sometimes indeed going out of his way to show that these influences are of the most casual kind—not so much upon the characters, as upon the *actions* of his people. The influences, that is to say, are not completely, in fact only temporarily, determining. The people act in such and such a way, but they might so easily have acted differently: 'so easily' that the reader feels, often with some irritation, like the unsophisticated audience of a melodrama, urged to call out and prompt the hero or heroine so that the disaster may be averted. But the irritation is all the more intense because the person does not, or should not, need prompting: he is well aware of the course that he does not take. Thus Angel, as we saw, nearly goes back to fetch Tess, already knowing all we could tell him about

Tess's love for him; Bathsheba knows better than to send the valentine; Tess and Elfride know they should be honest with their lovers, and nearly succeed in being so; Eustacia, as Hardy tells the story, does not really wish to elope with Wildeve: she wants a sign of reconciliation from Clym, and Clym wants to give it. . . . Here then are courses of action not excluded by determining factors or by wholly determined character-traits. It was not Springrove's character to neglect his couch-grass: he was a conscientious man who had worked hard to clean the patch of ground from which the weed was taken.

In some of these situations there are unknown (and therefore, it might be argued, 'accidental') factors. Captain Vye does not know that Eustacia may be about to elope, though he does suspect that she is upset by the estrangement, and may be glad to receive the letter from Clym. He recognizes the writing and goes to give it to her; then he decides she must be asleep. Thus Eustacia does not know the letter has come. Giles does not know that Grace still loves him despite his poverty. Angel does not know that Tess will be in want, that there will be pressures from her family, and from Alec. . . . But repeatedly Hardy suggests that such unawareness of contingencies is culpable. To be unaware, is to be 'contemptibly unaware'; and his people pay heavily for it. The instance with the greatest emphasis comes in *Desperate Remedies*: Owen, Cytherea's brother, is walking home, noticing that there is some commotion in the village, and coming gradually to realize that in some way the talk relates to him. The first Mrs. Manston has been seen alive since the fire in which it was supposed she had died: so Cytherea, who has just left on her honeymoon as Manston's second wife, is probably not legally married to him after all; this fact, of urgent concern to Owen, is known to everyone else in the village; it is there, right before Owen's nose, for him to notice, and act upon. ' "If they want me, surely they will call me," he thought.' And so the precious time continued to slip by:

"How unutterably mean must my intelligence have appeared to the eye of a foreseeing God," he frequently said in after-time. "Columbus on the eve of his discovery of a world was not so contemptibly unaware" (XIII. 5).

But even when he knows the truth, Owen is fettered by conventional proprieties; it is Edward Springrove who acts, seizes the unforseen chances, and reaches Cytherea in time.

So Hardy's heroes and heroines have little excuse for not knowing, and often do actually know, what they ought to do. And the point that we have made in several contexts that Hardy's plots are woven of possibilities as well as actualities, implies a basic Existentialist concern with choice. His treatment of choosing and evading is indeed so exhaustive that to call it an exploration of the psychology of choice would be no exaggeration.

First, there are the people who pretend that the choice and the responsibility are not their own: one tosses a hymn-book ('Open, Teddy—shut, Boldwood'); another, perhaps the most agonized of all Hardy's choosers, whom we shall discuss more fully, leaves a decision to her horse; and other 'signs' are sought—but not always accepted fatalistically. Then there are those who, having chosen a course of action and having at last, perhaps, chosen wisely and constructively, allow some slight but unnecessary element of chance to come between the decision and the deed: Tess is not the only one who entrusts a package or a letter to the possible caprice or delay of chance, when a personal delivery into the very hands of the other person would have obviated all misunderstanding. And we cannot doubt that Hardy is indicating the difference between such trusting casualness and the fully-committed, resolute action that is possible to an Egbert Mayne. Napoleon's indignant complaint will be remembered too: a message of any importance should have been entrusted to at least six messengers.[4] If six are sent, and all are intercepted, one might justifiably perhaps, speak of 'bad luck'; but for only one messenger to be sent is carelessness. Hardy clearly contrived certain incidents to suggest this too common human weakness of allowing chance to creep in; but there are also many situations of a more general kind where chance enters decisively simply because action is postponed. It is not even that, like Eustacia, people let 'events fall out as they may, rather than wrestle hard to direct them'; it is simply that they delay, and the time itself, by mathematical necessity, increases the odds of something going wrong.

Anyone who has thought about the subject knows well that the chooser always values what he has rejected: to choose A instead of B is almost inevitably to discover, afterwards, that A was 'wrong,' and that B would have been 'right'. This is true of some of Hardy's characters,[5] but it is only one symptom of the general weakness of

---

[4] See p. 85 above.
[5] See quotation from *A Pair of Blue Eyes*, pp. 146–7 below.

preferring the remote or the inaccessible, and despising reality. Hardy never tired of deploring the romanticist's habit of 'looking away' from the small but satisfying glow of real life to some perhaps illusory 'anticipated heap [of happiness] far away'.[6] Hardy criticizes not only Eustacia for lacking the 'homely zest for doing what she can' with real life, but Wildeve too—that 'Rousseau of Egdon':

To be yearning for the difficult; to be weary of that offered; to care for the remote, to dislike the near; it was Wildeve's nature always. (III. vi)

These romantic natures in *The Return of the Native* are almost incapable of choice, because they can choose resolutely and whole-heartedly only what they think they have lost. Eustacia's love for Wildeve varies inversely with his accessibility, and the degree of her commitment to him. When she thinks she has won him, her affections at once cool:

She was, then, secure of him at last. Thomasin no longer desired him. What a humiliating victory! . . . (I. xi)

Once, though, feeling Thomasin was a real rival for Wildeve's love, Eustacia had offered herself to him. And this of course, had the effect of cooling *his* feelings:

'. . . The scales are balanced so nicely that a feather would turn them.'
    'But don't you really care whether I meet you or whether I don't?' she said slowly.
    'I care a little, but not enough to break my rest. . . .' (I. ix)

Later, however, we are told:

The old longing for Eustacia had reappeared in his soul: and it was mainly because he had discovered that it was another man's intention to possess her.[7]

And so through nearly every one of Hardy's books. Fancy, the reader feels, never takes Dick seriously till he leaves her and goes off nutting alone, and she thinks she has lost him [8]; Bathsheba marries Troy in haste, in the agony of hearing he has seen a woman more beautiful than she.[9] Grace, when she gives up the thought of marrying Giles at once discovers that

---

[6] '. . . A thin widespread happiness, commencing now, and of a piece with the days of your life, is preferable to an anticipated heap far away in the future'—Elfride to Knight: *A Pair of Blue Eyes*, XV.
    [7] *The Return of the Native*, III. vi.   [8] *Under the Greenwood Tree*, IV. i.
    [9] *Far from the Madding Crowd*, end of XXXVII.

'When a man has been refused you feel pity for him, and like him more than you did before.'[10]

And when Fitzpiers hears this, and realizes that Grace's affections are not quite disengaged, his own indecision vanishes, and he at once proposes to her. In *The Trumpet Major*, Festus Derriman's interest in Matilda Johnson revives only when he thinks John Loveday is winning her; and Margery, the 'romantic milkmaid', abandons her romance and is reconciled to Jim only when the latter acquires some of the glamour of the unattainable by pretending to fall in love with the widow Peach. A factitious choice, based entirely on such jealous feelings, tragically twists the natural course of events in the story *To Please his Wife* [11]; and the absurdity of such choices is treated humorously in *Tony Kytes, the Arch Deceiver*.[12] I need hardly remind the reader of examples in *Jude*, since so much of the plot hinges on them: Sue consummates her love for Jude only after meeting Arabella and obscurely feeling that Arabella wants him back; Arabella behaves in much the same way; and neither woman is very happy about her choice during her periods of possession. Indeed the one thing that keeps alive Sue's love for Jude is the fact that she never commits herself to him legally and irrevocably. In the serial version there is even another example: when Jude's affections begin to cool, Arabella, instead of seducing Jude and telling him she is pregnant, pretends to have another lover.

It is difficult to recall one of Hardy's novels or stories which does not at some point or other focus our attention upon the meaning of choice; but in four or five, what we may call the 'agony of choice' is a major theme, worked out in an intricate pattern of choices and re-choices, whilst some degree of freedom is lost or attained. As we might expect, it is in the earliest of such stories that Hardy analyses a simple choice most elaborately and explicitly. Elfride, in *A Pair of Blue Eyes*, is on her way from Endelstow vicarage to St. Launce's where she is to marry Stephen:

She turned in the saddle and looked back. They were now on an open tableland, whose altitude still gave her a view of the sea by Endelstow. She looked longingly at that spot.

During this little revulsion of feeling, Pansy had been still advancing, and Elfride felt it would be absurd to turn her little mare's head the other way. 'Still,' she thought, 'if I had a mamma at home I *would* go back!'

---

[10] *The Woodlanders*, XIX.   [11] *Life's Little Ironies*.
[12] One of 'A few crusted Characters' in the same volume.

And making one of those stealthy movements by which women let their hearts juggle with their brains, she did put the horse's head about, *as if unconsciously,* and went at a hand-gallop towards home for more than a mile. By this time, from the *inveterate habit of valuing what we have renounced directly the alternative is chosen,* the thought of her forsaken Stephen recalled her, and she turned about and cantered on to St. Launce's again.

This miserable strife of thought now began to rage in all its wildness. Overwrought and trembling, she dropped the rein upon Pansy's shoulders. . . .[13]

There follows the 'choice' to which we have referred: to be 'led whither the horse would take her'. But this does not prevent her from again rechoosing, as the reader will remember, and again regretting her rechoice!

But this is only the beginning: a few chapters later, Henry Knight decides to buy Elfride some ear-rings. As he knows nothing about jewellery, it is not surprising that he has difficulty; but Hardy takes Knight's 'agony of choice' into the realm of farce, making him thoroughly unhappy about the expensive pair he has bought, unable to go back to the shop to change them, and finally buying others and disposing of the first pair by selling them for a fraction of their value (XX). But even before this, the ear-rings have become a symbol of a dubious choice for both Knight and Elfride: Knight has put before her a hypothetical choice between a pair of ear-rings and a 'well-chosen little library of the best music', and Elfride, although she prides herself on being musical, has finally been forced into admitting that she would prefer the ear-rings. Knight is beginning to be fascinated by Elfride; but there is no doubt of his disapproval. So even his buying the ear-rings represents a choice for Knight: a concession to the female vanity and weakness of someone to whom he is, none the less, going to make a proposal of marriage. Then, when they are offered to Elfride, they become the centre of a quite new situation of choice: they are virtually a declaration of Knight's love; so Elfride has to choose between Stephen, about to arrive back from India, and Knight. Painfully—her previous choices are nothing to this one—Elfride chooses to stand by Stephen. The choice is reversed very simply: the nearness of death, on Beeny Cliff, sends her into Knight's arms. The nearness of death is now a distinct

[13] *A Pair of Blue Eyes*, XI. Hardy italicized Elfride's '*would*'; the other italics are mine.

factor in the story (the Luxellian tomb; the sudden death of Mrs. Jethway . . .): it could conceivably have made Knight value the living reality of Elfride rather more highly; but it doesn't. And at the end of the story we again have the farce of a choice—on Knight's side at least—determined only by the presence of a rival, merging into the grimmer farce of choices, both Stephen's and Knight's, which death has made too late anyway.

'The nearness of death' (we said) clarifies the choice for Elfride. For Knight too, of course, the trilobite's hint of extinction produces a desperate surge of the will to live. And the same is true of many images of death in Hardy: they lead people to more modestly objective action, and perfectly illustrate Sartre's remark about life being found 'on the far side of despair'. Henchard's return from Ten Hatches, his impulse to suicide overcome, is not unlike Matthieu's return from the river in *Les Chemins de la Liberté*. Apart from the images of this kind that I have mentioned before, we may recall the man-trap in *The Woodlanders* which affects Grace and Fitzpiers precisely as the horror of the cliff incident affects Knight and Elfride, sending them into each other's arms (XLVII). Then there is the grim situation Baptista Heddegan finds herself in on her wedding night—the corpse of her first husband laid out in the adjoining room.

Such grim reminders do not invite fatalistic acquiescence. They provoke fight. And so, in Hardy's stronger characters, do other disconcerting 'signs'. What could have been more discouraging than the 'sign' that met Reynard in *The First Countess of Wessex* when, after many delays, he comes to claim his wife? Betty, the victim of her mother's ambition, had been only a child when she had gone through the ceremony of marriage with him, and she has been at home since. She has, moreover, fallen in love with someone else; and, as the time of her husband's arrival draws near, she is desperate and rebellious. She tries to infect herself with small-pox; and then, on the very evening of Reynard's arrival, she elopes with her lover. When they stop at an inn, the first signs of small-pox are seen on Betty's face; and, appalled, her lover takes her back home. She is still little more than a child; he is not much older; and as he helps her back up the ladder, he shrinks from her embrace.

In the dining parlour, as it was called, the now sick and sorry Betty was startled to see at that late hour not her mother, but a man sitting, calmly finishing his supper. There was no servant in the room. He turned, and she recognised her husband.

'Where's my mamma?' she demanded without preface.

'Gone to your father's. Is that—' He stopped, aghast.

'Yes, sir. This spotted object is your wife! I've done it because I don't want you to come near me!'

He was sixteen years her senior; old enough to be compassionate. 'My poor child, you must get to bed directly! Dont be afraid of me—I'll carry you upstairs, and send for a doctor instantly.'

'Ah, you don't know what I am,' she cried. 'I had a lover once; but now he's gone! *'Twasn't I who deserted him. He has deserted me*; because I am ill he wouldn't kiss me, though I wanted him to!'

'Wouldn't he? Then he was a very poor slack-twisted sort of fellow. Betty, *I've* never kissed you since you stood beside me as my little wife, twelve years and a half old! May I kiss you now?'

Though Betty by no means desired his kisses, she had enough of the spirit of Cunigonde in Schiller's ballad to test his daring. 'If you have the courage to venture, yes Sir!' said she. 'But you may die for it, mind!'

He came up to her and imprinted a deliberate kiss full upon her mouth, saying 'May many others follow!'

She shook her head, and hastily withdrew, though secretly pleased at his hardihood. . . .[14]

Out of the very desperateness of the situation, a man like Reynard can create life: the worst chances and appearances become the very means he needs to win his wife's love. Unlike Hardy's weaker characters, too, he is quite unmoved by Betty's unwantedness, though she flings it in his face: he remains free. But even much weaker characters, looking for signs and promptings and advice, may react against them, and establish their independence. Though Tess acquiesces more than once in what 'was to be', and gives way sometimes to superstitious misgivings, she does not always do so: she refuses to be depressed by the red-painted texts ('I don't believe God said such things'), and arrives home after that encounter rather strengthened than otherwise; and if she asks for her mother's advice about confessing to Angel, she no sooner receives it than she realizes its worthlessness. And Bob Loveday, chasing after Matilda, but with his brother's sensible warnings in his head, sits down to think. First in a 'strife of thought' as agonized as Elfride's, he at last grows calmer:

---

[14] *The First Countess of Wessex* (*A Group of Noble Dames*). The two sentences are italicized by me.

This strife of thought was so well maintained that, sitting and standing, he remained on the borders of the spring till the shadows had stretched out eastwards, and the chance of overtaking Matilda had grown considerably less. Still he did not positively go towards home. At last he took a guinea from his pocket, and resolved to put the question to the hazard. 'Heads I go; tails I don't.' The piece of gold spun in the air and came down heads.

'No, I won't go, after all,' he said. 'I won't be steered by accidents any more.'[15]

Is there so much difference between these examples and the way Sartre shows Orestes asking Zeus for a sign?

ELECTRA: . . . See what comes of being a pious young man and asking counsel of the gods [*She is convulsed with laughter and can hardly get the words out.*] Oh noble youth, Philebus,[16] darling of the gods! "Show me a sign," you asked. "Show me a sign." Well, now you've had your sign — a blaze of light round that precious sacred stone of theirs. So off you go to Corinth! Off you go!

ORESTES [*staring at the stone*]: So that is the Right Thing. To live at peace . . . always at perfect peace. I see. Always to say "Excuse me," and "Thank you." That's what's wanted eh? [*He stares at the stone in silence for some moments*] The Right Thing. *Their* Right Thing. . . .[17]

Needless to say, Orestes does not slip off to Corinth; he stays in Argos, and acts.

Sartre's idiom, it might be argued, is very different from Hardy's. But is it? Is it not relevant to recall Hardy's disgust with a morality 'good enough for divinities' but 'scorned by average human nature'?[18] or the suggestion in his 'Aeschylean phrase' that man should not condone a scheme of things that is so obviously a travesty of 'justice' and that 'sports' with human lives?

Even in love, one can be free: Owen Graye remembers his father saying, 'Blindly you will love if you love at all, but a little care is still possible to a well-disciplined heart'.[19] It is possible at least for a time, according to Ethelberta:

'At the beginning of caring for a man—just when you are suspended between thinking and feeling—there's a hair's-breadth of time at which the question of getting into love or not getting in, is a matter of will—quite a

15 *The Trumpet Major*, XX.
16 Electra has so far refused to call Orestes by his real name.
17 *Les Mouches*, II. i.
18 *Tess*, XI.
19 *Desperate Remedies*, I. 4.

thing of choice. At the same time, drawing back is a tame dance, and the best of all is to stay balanced awhile.'[20]

Hardy's more passionate heroines do not find it so easy to 'stay balanced awhile', it is true. Perhaps they deceive themselves into thinking they are still 'balanced' when in fact they have overstepped the brink.

There is an interesting parallel from one of Miss Iris Murdoch's books, relevant here because she is consciously developing a Sartrian theme. In her monograph on Sartre,[21] she notes that Sartre illustrates 'bad faith' by the state of mind of the woman who leaves her hand limply in the grasp of her lover; and her own Michael, in *The Bell* behaves in much the same way:

... A mist of emotion, which he did not attempt to dispel, hid from him the decision which he was taking: which indeed it seemed to him he had taken by letting Nick, without comment or withdrawal, lay his hand upon him. He knew that he was lost, and in making the discovery knew that he had in fact been lost for a long time. By a dialectic well-known to those who habitually succumb to temptation he passed in a second from the time it was too early so struggle to the time when it was too late to struggle.

There is no need to refer back to the close parallel of Cytherea and Manston[22] since Hardy's women have a general tendency to act thus: like Elfride, letting 'their hearts juggle with their brains' and making some stealthy movement 'as if unconsciously', or like Bathsheba going to renounce Troy 'blind to the obvious fact that the support of a lover's arms is not of a kind best calculated to assist a resolve to renounce him'. But the heroine most pathetically skilful at 'choosing not to choose' in this way is Tess. We have already seen, and Hardy describes in detail, the way she slides into acquiescences to Angel's importunities. There is, of course, no reason why she should not marry Angel—choosing this course openly, being honest with herself over her feelings and honest with Angel over her past. But she does not do this. She knows in her heart that unless she is frank with Angel, she must not marry him: and yet this is just what she finds herself drifting into doing. And there are other similar acquiescences on Tess's part: for example, those she makes to Alec, the precise nature of which Hardy leaves us to infer.

[20] *The Hand of Ethelberta*, VI. In *The Return of the Native* (II. iii) Eustacia's early 'fancy' for Clym prompts a similar reflection that even 'in the most gigantic passions there is a time when they are in the hands of the weakest will.'
[21] *Sartre : Romantic Rationalist*, Iris Murdoch, 1953.   [22] Quoted on p. 102 above.

It is significant that Hardy several times alludes to Tess's ability to dissociate her mind from her body. It is from a reverie of this sort that she slides insensibly into actual sleeping and dreaming before the first of her disasters (IV); later she vividly describes the separation of her mind and her body to the astonished dairyman Crick (XVIII); and finally, when Angel finds her living with Alec at Sandbourne, he realizes 'that his original Tess had spiritually ceased to recognise the body before him as hers—allowing it to drift, like a corpse upon the current, in a direction dissociated from its living will' (LV).

The sensations experienced by a woman who, in bad faith, leaves her hand in that of her admirer, are described by Sartre thus:

> The aim is to postpone the moment of decision as long as possible. We know what happens next; the young woman leaves her hand there, but she *does not notice* that she is leaving it . . . the hand rests inert between the warm hands of her companion—neither consenting nor resisting—a thing.
> . . . Finally while sensing profoundly the presence of her own body . . . she realises herself as *not being* her own body, and she contemplates it as though from above as a passive object.[23]

That Hardy should have described Tess's sensations as being very much the same is not particularly remarkable: the remarkable thing is that Hardy, like Sartre, describes these sensations as typical of those which accompany actions made in bad faith. Hardy's analysis of Tess's 'bad faith' is extraordinarily tolerant and sympathetic; none the less, it is consistent and it goes deep: few modern authors—even amongst those whom we habitually consider far more psychologically sophisticated than Hardy—could have achieved it.

Being tossed in raging 'strife of thought', 'staying balanced awhile', or deceiving oneself when one is already 'lost' in acquiescence, these are not the only possibilities. There are times when Hardy's people act in all good faith, and choose firmly. They may have misgivings, but they choose all the same. Then some accident happens to annul their decision, and they have the same choice to make all over again. But clearly no situation is quite the same the second time it is encountered; the mere fact of having made his choice before has changed the chooser. Besides, time, knowledge and reflection have changed the perspectives, even if the context has not

[23] *L'Être et le Néant*, I. II. II.

changed. A second choice, therefore, is always a significant psychological event. Of the many critics who have remarked upon Hardy's
use of accident and coincidence, I know of none who has pointed out
that his ingenuity in this matter is used less often, perhaps, to make
some startling change in the situation, than to *un*make some change,
to bring events full circle, so that almost the same choice is encountered a second time. Wildeve's mistake over the marriage licence is
not exactly an accident: it is seen by Mrs. Yeobright, Eustacia,
Wildeve himself and perhaps even by Tamsin as a reflection of his
half-heartedness. Wildeve, in fact, has not really chosen. But for
Tamsin, the matter is quite different: she has chosen. For her, therefore, the hitch is a reprieve. Her feelings for Wildeve have not,
apparently, been very strong; and now she suffers a considerable
setback and disillusionment. 'I put it to you,' says her Aunt, 'would
you at this moment agree to be his wife if that [24] had not happened
to entangle you with him?' Knowing she no longer loves him enough
to justify marrying him, Tamsin refuses to answer; but she persists
in her choice. *The Mayor of Casterbridge* is full of second chances
and rechoices: a few are genuine re-interpretations of the situation,
but most are pathetic re-iterations of Henchard's obstinacy and
pride against his better sense, as when he quarrels repeatedly with
Farfrae, or persists in deceiving Elizabeth-Jane headlong to his own
undoing. Indeed, as so often in Hardy's novels, we have at the very
beginning a glimpse of a typical behaviour-pattern in little. Henchard
is getting drunk in the furmity tent, and attempts to sell his wife
(chapter I). Twice he tries; and the second time an accident reprieves him: a swallow enters the tent, and everyone's attention is
distracted and the whole affair is forgotten—except by Henchard,
who begins all over again. Actually he has two more chances of re-
versing his choice, for both Susan and Newson are reluctant at first
to take him at his word: far from being dogged by a malicious fate,
it is far more as if he were determined to wear out the patience of a
favourable one. In *Jude the Obscure*, Sue marries Phillotson knowing
she cannot love him; she gets a divorce; then remarries him. Jude
foolishly marries Arabella, not wishing to do so, but feeling that he
must; the recovery of his freedom is an even more gratuitous piece
of luck than Sue's: but he remarries Arabella later. And the most
extraordinary rechoice is that offered to Viviette and Swithin in *Two
on a Tower*. Sir Blount Constantine, Viviette's husband, is reported

[24] I.e. the engagement, followed by the hitch over the marriage licence.

to be dead. The marriage has not been a happy one; and for years Sir Blount has been exploring in Africa. His death does not greatly change Viviette's situation, but it frees her to marry Swithin. They marry secretly: the very secrecy is in part a récognition on Viviette's side that there are arguments against the alliance. News then comes that Sir Blount is indeed dead, but that he was still alive at the time of Viviette's and Swithin's 'marriage'—which was not, therefore, legal. No matter: they are in love; a second ceremony is all that is necessary to put things right. But then Viviette finds the letter written by Swithin's uncle—discovers, in fact, that he has inherited a fortune to carry on his research, provided that he is unencumbered with a wife (as technically he still is—since the marriage was not legal) and remains so until a certain age. Swithin's uncle has, indeed, tried to protect him against her. But, except for the legacy, the letter tells her nothing she does not know already—unless one counts the realization that others are ready to pass upon her the judgement she has already secretly passed on herself: she has befriended Swithin and bought him a telescope only because she is in love with him; she is no longer rich enough to provide him with the additional equipment and opportunities he needs; she is considerably older than he is; she has 'caught' him, and does not much care about anything else. The situation is unchanged by the letter—except that she knows, instead of merely suspecting, that she is blighting Swithin's potentialities and his hopes. She loves him passionately; but now, for the first time, unselfishly. Despite his protests, she refuses to marry him till the stipulated time is up; and packs him off to South Africa to work in a southern hemisphere observatory. Viviette is one of Hardy's real heroines. She pays heavily for her decision because, although she does not know it, she is pregnant. But she makes something quite new of her choice, and of Swithin's life, even though she ruins her own.

Pierston's marriage to Marcia at the end of *The Well Beloved* is another rechoice in complete freedom. It is not a turning back to the past; it re-interprets Pierston's future, what is left of it, and the whole meaning, for him, of love and marriage.

There are many other examples, some which I have mentioned in earlier sections of this chapter. A list of those who make, unmake, then remake the original choice would include not only Fitzpiers, Grace, Angel, Eustacia, Wildeve, Pierston, Marcia, Sue, Jude, Farfrae, Bob Loveday and so on, from the novels, but also many

figures from the short stories such as Millborne (in *For Conscience'
Sake* [25]), Jolliffe and Joanna (in *To Please his Wife* [26]), Barnet (in
Fellow Townsmen [27]), Christine (in *The Waiting Supper* [28]), and
others. And the fact that I have lumped together many dissimilar
examples does not weaken my argument, but rather strengthens it:
Hardy is tireless in his exploration of choice and freedom in different
contexts.

But another point can be made too: from this exhaustive exploration we are led to see the conditions under which a choice is free and
good: not when it is made in jealousy, or remorse, or 'for conscience'
sake'; but only when it accepts the past and the present creatively,
to make something new of them in the future.

Hardy had indeed a typically existentialist way of regarding Time:
seeing it tragically, perhaps, but still essentially as a 'becoming', as
meaningless except in terms of an implied future. Consider:

The moment upon the face of it was critical; and yet it was one of those
which have to wait for a future before they acquire a definite character as
good or bad.[29]

Or this:

The very next morning brought round a circumstance which, slight in
itself, took up an important position between the past and the future of the
persons herein concerned.[30]

Or any of the references to the 'contemptibly little suggesting
possibilities of the infinitely great'.[31]

In terms of human pretensions, too, 'being' is essentially meaningless. What counts is the way a man is oriented to the future, to
what can be done. To become 'somebody'—'Sir John' Durbeyfield,
for instance, or our brave Sergeant Troy in spurs and uniform in
All Saints' Church—is to risk becoming ineffectual. And to touch

[25] *Life's Little Ironies.*   [26] Ibid.   [27] *Wessex Tales.*
[28] In the volume, *A Changed Man.*
[29] *The Hand of Ethelberta*, I.   [30] *Desperate Remedies*, III. i.
[31] *Far from the Madding Crowd*, XIV. Hardy's readiness to believe in the 'possibly
great issues of little beginnings' which we noticed in the Poems, has been an odd ground
of contention. Thus Alfred Noyes's protest (quoted in *Later Years*, XVII) 'that he
[Noyes] had "never been able to conceive a Cause of Things that could be less in any
respect than the things caused" ' is apparently regarded by Miss Evelyn Hardy as completely demolishing Hardy's position. But a 'Cause of Things . . . less . . . than the
things caused' is of course no *reductio ad absurdum*, but something that the existentialist
and evolutionist find it easy to conceive. *L.Y.*, p. 218; *Life*, p. 410.

rock bottom (we have made the point before) and become nothing, as Oak does in *Far from the Madding Crowd*, and Angel and many another hero much later in their respective stories, is to discover that although there is no ready-made meaning in life, a meaning can be created.

We have already noticed that the 'psychology of the object'—the loss of freedom when one finds oneself an object in the eyes of others —is a favourite theme of Hardy's; here is Thomasin:

'I am a warning to others, just as thieves and drunkards and gamblers are,' she said in a low voice. 'What a class to belong to! Do I really belong to them? 'Tis absurd! Yet why, Aunt, does everybody keep on making me think that I do, by the way they behave towards me? Why don't people judge me by my acts? Now, look at me as I kneel down here, picking up those apples—do I look like a lost woman?'[32]

And in two of the more 'philosophical' chapters of *Tess of the d'Urbervilles*, Hardy discusses Tess's 'thought of the world's concern at her situation' just before and just after the birth of her baby, and tries to distinguish between what her predicament is in fact, and what the 'world's concern' makes it appear. In *The Waiting Supper*, again, Christine allows incipient gossip about herself and Nicholas to discourage her from marrying him—a change of mind which brings her much unhappiness. I mention these additional instances to show that Hardy returns to the theme consistently; but the incidents I mentioned earlier [33] when a person is *suddenly* deflated by the discovery that he or she is an object in another person's universe (like Sartre's instance of someone looking through a keyhole who suddenly realizes he is being observed) may well seem more striking: Tess turning back because she hears herself being criticized by Angel's brothers, Elfride dismayed at references to herself in Knight's diary, Sue's distress over the gossip and so on.

In Sartre's work, this concern is clearly crucial. Treated briefly in *L'Existentialisme est un humanisme* and exhaustively in *L'Être et le Néant*, there are many instances in the novels and plays: the people in *Huis Clos* frozen into a vicious circle of behaviour, forced to justify themselves in each other's eyes and in the eyes of the world they have left; Hugo in *Les Mains Sales*, with the photographs of himself, and his image of himself as the revolutionary hero; Goetz,

---

[32] *The Return of the Native*, II. ii.   [33] See pages 71 and 78–80 above.

in *Le Diable and le bon Dieu*, ineffectual for all his violence, till he
abandons the image of himself as anti-Christ or Saint and concentrates simply upon aims and deeds outside his own ego; Daniel,
in *Les Chemins* who insists on being seen and accepted as
himself, a coward, a paederast, a sinner—if by no one else, then by
God. 'I am *seen*, therefore I am', he writes to Matthieu. Sartre deals
also with those who seek to define themselves in extreme isolation:
an expedient far more desperate than the 'crusoeism' which tempts,
rather than completely takes possession of Hardy's characters:
Franz, in *Les Sequestrés d'Altona*, is the extreme pathological
example.

But there is also the isolation that is man's normal heritage. Like
Hardy, Sartre sees man as fulfilling himself by rejecting the beaten
paths. In *Les Mouches*, Orestes discovers that man is outside Nature;
and he braves Zeus's taunts, and rejects his invitation:

ZEUS: Your vaunted freedom isolates you from the fold; it means exile,
 . . . Come back to the fold. Think of your loneliness; even your sister
 is forsaking you. Your eyes are big with anguish, your face is pale and
 drawn. The disease you are suffering from is inhuman, foreign to my
 nature, foreign to yourself. Come back. I am forgetfulness, I am peace.
ORESTES: Foreign to myself—I know it. I know it. Outside nature, against
 nature, without excuse, beyond remedy, except what remedy I find
 within myself. But I shall not return under your law; I am doomed to
 have no other law but mine. Nor shall I come back to Nature, the Nature
 you found good; in it are a thousand beaten paths all leading up to you
 —but I must blaze my own trail. For I, Zeus, am a man, and every man
 must find his own way. Nature abhors man, and you too, god of gods,
 abhor mankind.[34]

There is no need to return to man's isolation from Nature: we have
stressed this point sufficiently in earlier pages, and the little description of Tamsin alone on the Heath, used as the third epigraph to
this chapter, is a vivid reminder. But there is also a striking similarity
between Sartre and Hardy in the way they describe the price paid
for this isolation. Compare Zeus's taunts, 'Your eyes are big with
anguish, your face is pale and drawn . . .' with the descriptions of
some of Hardy's heroes. There is Knight, whose mouth and eyes
were 'younger and fresher than the brow and face they belonged to,
which were getting sicklied o'er with the unmistakable pale cast',[35]
and Somerset, too, his face

[34] *Act III.*   [35] *A Pair of Blue Eyes*, XIII.

showing dominant speculative activity . . . which . . . had played upon his forehead and temples till, at weary moments, they exhibited traces of being over-exercised. . . . Briefly, he had more of the beauty—if beauty it ought to be called—of the future human type than of the past.[36]

We may recall, too, that when Angel returned from Brazil, 'mentally aged a dozen years', he was morally improved out of all recognition. Even Oak does not go through life with his round 'rising-sun' face and almost ear-to-ear smile: at the hiring fair, he is described as 'paler', his eyes are 'more meditative' and 'an ordeal of wretchedness' had left other marks.[37] He too is morally improved. Hardy's description of Clym [38] is almost too well-known to mention, but a phrase that follows the more hackneyed sentences, remarks upon the 'isolation' of his look.

Clym is perhaps the most 'isolated' of Hardy's heroes; for despite Hardy's insistence upon man's isolation from nature and God, we have seen that he notices, only to deplore, man's isolation from his fellow-men. His sense of the need of human beings for one another, 'in brotherhood bonded close', is a point of difference from Sartre. It is a difference which might not seem fundamental in the final analysis; but Sartre is more uncompromising, a fact that is reflected in the more dramatic and political quality of his characters, and of their choices and decisions. The cost of a mistake or an omission is not just the loss of individual happiness, but something which reaches much further. Hardy admires courage (Oak, Willowes, Reynard) but has none of Sartre's hatred of cowardice. Nor does Sartre share Hardy's tolerance of failure and of 'intentions'. But on this last point, too, it would be easy to misrepresent the difference as more fundamental than it is. Hardy, it is true, stresses the importance of 'intentions'. The only difference in a failure, Knight tells Elfride, is 'that the last chapter is wanting to the story'.[39] And Angel re-adjusting his ideas about Tess, asked himself,

Who was the moral man? Still more pertinently, who was the moral woman? The beauty or ugliness of a character lay not only in its achievements, but in its aims and impulses; its true history lay, not among things done, but among things willed.[40]

On the surface, that is certainly unlike Sartre; but the importance of the 'things willed' in Angel's argument is that he wishes, at long

---

[36] *A Laodicean*, I.   [37] *Far from the Madding Crowd*, VI.
[38] *The Return of the Native*, II. vi.
[39] *A Pair of Blue Eyes*, XIX.   [40] *Tess*, XLIX.

last, to help Tess to bring some of these 'things' to fulfilment. If they remain in the realm of 'unfulfilled intentions' they may *excuse* Tess, but they are certainly not going to do her any good or bring her any happiness. On this matter—the futility of good intentions, of 'being' without 'doing'—Hardy is as uncompromising as Sartre. He would, clearly, have denied that only the deed defines a person; all the same, only the deed counts in terms of happiness.

When Sartre attacks those who excuse themselves by saying,

'I admit I have never had a great love or a great friendship; but that is because I have never met a man or a woman who was worthy of it; if I have not written any very good books, it is because I have not had the leisure to do so . . .'

his point is not merely that there is no reality apart from the deed, that 'there is no love apart from the deeds of love', and so on, but that in default of a perfect action, there is always a direction to take, a provisional if imperfect action out of which something may be made later. And just this point is discussed repeatedly in Hardy's novels—in criticism of Eustacia (especially), Angel, and others who reject reality; and it is—though ambivalently—the theme of the poem which stands first in every collected edition of Hardy's verse: *The Temporary the All.*

In an earlier chapter [41] we noticed Hardy's interest in the relationship between reality and appearance—or, better, between reality and the interpretation of appearance. This phenomenological interest has a wide range of application, from Jude's attempt to put up with Arabella ('His idea of her was the thing of most consequence, not Arabella herself'), and the insignificance of the label on Tess's marmalade jar,[42] to the tragic change that took place, not in Tess but in Angel's view of her ('Nothing had changed since the moments when he had been kissing her; or rather nothing in the substance of things. But the essence of things had changed'[43]). It is not the thing that matters, but the way we take it. When Christopher Julian expresses horror at the notion of Ethelberta's marriage to Montclere, imagining it will 'tear her heart out like a claw', his sister pulls him up:

'You are too warm about it, Kit—it cannot be as bad as that. It is not the thing, but the sensitiveness to the thing which is a true measure of the pain.'[44]

[41] Chapter VIII, pp. 105 ff. above.   [42] *Tess*, XIV.   [43] Ibid. XXXV.
[44] *The Hand of Ethelberta*, XL.

Faith is right: Kit had overestimated Ethelberta's vulnerability. Ethelberta is not depicted with the love and pity that went into the creation of Tess and Sue; but there are things about her that Hardy admired. Not her insensitiveness, but her refusal to be hurt. It is this refusal—not any blunting of their sensitiveness—which might have saved Sue and Tess, Knight and Angel.

In this phenomenological approach—I mean in this desire of Hardy's to make us, or his characters, see the same thing in two or more different ways, a desire upon which his ironical contrasts often hinge—there is more than a little that adumbrates the French Existentialists. I am thinking now not so much of Sartre as of those plays of Anouilh where the pure love of the young and innocent is framed within the lusts and intrigues and cynical realism of their elders. The effect is not simple disillusionment: the cynicism also has the effect of defining, framing, the innocence and purity. The time sense is heightened nervily and tragically; and the purity of youth, lovely, fragile, and intensely real, and yet already somehow absurd, is threatened by the world's stain. 'Threatened'—but is it destroyed, or does it survive under a different guise? There is a seeming contradiction at the heart of some of Anouilh's most dramatic effects: that both his young lovers and his disillusioned sceptics are most convincing when they are most theatrical. But neither Sartre nor Anouilh would see this as a contradiction: whether a man 'is' a hero or merely 'acts' heroically, is the same thing. Who is the real lover in *Ring round the Moon*—the innocent, romantic and ineffectual Frederic, or his cynical twin, Hugo? And who is the real Colombe, in the play of that name? the one for whom Paul brings the bouquet, or Julien's faithful wife? Pathetically Colombe denies her love for Julien; but is this only because he insists that she shall avow it? Is it only the demand that kills the love?

We turn in dismay from Julien, shocked by his rejection of Colombe, much as we turn from Angel Clare.[45] Hardy repeatedly deals with the theme of purity, repeatedly gives it some flaw (Tess's past, Elfride's prevarication . . .) which looms large but should be

---

[45] Another tragically absurd scene occurs in *The Return of the Native*, when Clym tries to bully Eustacia into avowals of love and explanations of her behaviour (Book V, Chapter iii). Critics have been severe upon the staginess of Clym's speeches, and the awkwardness of the whole scene; but this, of course, is the whole point. Clym is making a 'scene', escaping from reality and from his real love for Eustacia into a piece of atrocious acting.

discounted,[46] and repeatedly defines the purity by setting it within a frame of the worn, the tawdry, the old and disillusioned, or (sometimes) the only seemingly worthless. There is no missing the theme of 'purity' in *Tess*: Hardy calls our attention to it in the subtitle. Tess's purity is framed first by the sordidness of her family (her mother busily exploits the commercial possibilities of her daughter's beauty like the parents of a typical Anouilh innocent), then by the Trantridge folk, with their sweaty dancing and drinking and loose morals ('a whorage' Tess calls them in her innocence—and partly her ignorance); and Tess remains innocent to the end (Hardy insists), although it is round a 'fallen woman', a whore, that Angel and Alec try to erect their frame. But how often Hardy does this kind of thing may not be realized. For instance, in *Two on a Tower*, Viviette's romantic love for Swithin is framed first by the misalliance of her first marriage, and then, after the arrival of her brother Louis, by all the conventional parties and social climbing that prepare the way for the degradation of her marriage with the bishop. But there are several carefully contrived small touches too. There is the scene, for instance, where Viviette, surprised by Louis's arrival, bundles Swithin off in a hurry; he dons an old overcoat of Sir Blount's and is mistaken by the countrymen for Sir Blount's ghost. By such means (for there is no getting round the literal fact that Swithin has been turned out of the house by his 'wife') Hardy nurses the reader's misgivings as to whether Viviette's pure and romantic affair with Swithin is perhaps as great a misalliance as her first marriage. A similar 'framing' is given to Elfride's and Stephen's romance in *A Pair of Blue Eyes*. The purity of their boy-and-girl love is grotesquely parodied by the romantic machinery that masks the marriage-of-convenience between Elfride's father and the rich widow Troyton: each couple is deceiving the other, both meet secretly by moonlight, and both elope (and on the very same day) for marriage at a discreet distance from home. Again, Betty's romantic love affair in *The First Countess of Wessex* is contrasted with the seemingly loveless marriage forced on her by her ambitious mother, and with the real misalliance of Betty's mother and father. The curious structure of *The Well Beloved* leads to similar *montage* contrasting youth and age; and *Jude*, also by its very structure, presents us with similar effects:

[46] For a different existentialist treatment of a somewhat similar situation, see Henri's marriage with Nadine in *Les Mandarins*. Henri is quite aware of Nadine's deceit, but he is prepared to interpret it in a constructive way. He behaves, in fact, as Angel should have behaved, and later tried to behave.

the 'pure' and 'ideal' nature of Sue's and Jude's union being framed first by the aridity of Phillotson's home and school, and then by the fleshy coarseness of Arabella and Cartlett. The scene at the Wessex Agricultural show, where Hardy vividly presents the second contrast, will be recalled: the Cartletts—'this pot-bellied man and florid woman'—meet at what is for them the normal centre of interest, the bar; but Arabella has been watching Sue and Jude: and that

more exceptional couple and the boy still lingered in the pavilion of flowers—an enchanted palace to their appreciative taste—Sue's usually pale cheeks reflecting the pink of the tinted roses at which she gazed. . . .[47]

It is, indeed, one of the serenest times of happiness and fulfilment that Hardy gives them. Other effects of 'framing' may be remembered: in *The Woodlanders*, for instance, at a time when we are seeing events largely through Melbury's eyes, it seems that Grace's youth and sensitivity may be crushed through the rough-and-ready life offered by Giles: the party he gives for the Melburys (when the reader is as relieved as Giles and Creedle to know that the slug on Grace's plate was at least 'well boiled') is a hilarious piece of framing for Grace's rather fragile beauty.[48] And in *Under The Greenwood Tree*, Fancy is presented in much the same way: an image of youth and refinement framed by a rustic and insensitive way of life.

But these effects, though not so paradoxical as Anouilh's, have their measure of ambiguity, and some of them are highly complex. Fancy is not only the most 'innocent' thing in Mellstock; she is also the most capricious and sophisticated. Sue at her 'purest' has provoked bitter reactions from readers—just as she did from Jude himself. Viviette, despite appearances, proves that she loves Swithin purely and selflessly. The kiss that Reynard gives Betty may be calculated, and is certainly a dramatically heroic and theatrical gesture; but it has the instant effect of making her 'real' love and romantic elopement seem utterly *un*real and of banishing her lover for ever.[49] In fact, Hardy often shows the contamination of innocence to be only an illusion. Grace, threatened by the contamination of Society (by the genteel education that makes her talk nonsense to Giles, and that nearly throws her into Mrs. Charmond's toils) and by the rudeness of rustic life (not so rude, as she comes to realize), is actually contaminated by other things—by a loveless marriage and a

[47] *Jude the Obscure*, V. v.   [48] *The Woodlanders*, X.
[49] See above, pp. 148–9.

worthless husband; and yet, out of this experience and from only this raw material, she is able to make something well worth while in the end.

It is strange that, despite his own explicitness, Hardy's preoccupations with choice and rechoice, and the re-interpretation of life's raw material should have been ignored. But this is partly because the implications of his attitude are unpopular. Indeed it is relevant to notice that critical reaction to Sartre and Camus is much the same as it is to Hardy. When Camus visited England in 1953, a dramatized version of *The Outsider* (*L'Étranger*) was broadcast, and a talk by Camus himself. For these an official B.B.C. commentator sought to prepare us with the words:

Whether Camus is truly an Existentialist is perhaps a matter for a family quarrel between himself and Sartre, but his work (especially here) is laden with a pessimistic sense of human loneliness and futility that are among the artistic fruits of the creed. . . . Camus may well strike many of us as the exemplar of a stultifying view of life.

This commentator saw no absurdity in mentioning later in his article that the two men he was stigmatizing for their 'futility' and 'stultifying view of life' had been active in the French Resistance during the German occupation; just as those who denounce Hardy's pessimism in similar language see no absurdity in recounting also the persistent efforts of his long and active life, his liveliness into old age, and his consciousness of misunderstanding but refusal to be discouraged; they even see no contradiction in telling us that he left a will, made not long before his eightieth birthday making provision for children that might still be born to him. In *Existentialism and Humanism* Sartre says of his critics:

Their excessive protests make me suspect that what is annoying them is not so much our pessimism but more likely our optimism. For, at bottom, what is alarming in the doctrine . . . is . . . that it confronts man with the possibility of choice.

This may well be true; and what appals critics of Hardy too may be the courage of his attitude, his sense of man's responsibility, and his insistence that man can achieve something, as Oak and one or two others do, alone. And when Sartre says, 'The business of any morality is to consider human life as a match that can be won or lost and to teach man how to win', we are inevitably reminded of Hardy's 'Pessimist's Apology', and other practical notes of his about 'playing the sure game'. It is the fact that one is called upon to *do something*, not merely withdraw, that makes Hardy so much less acceptable than Schopenhauer.

I referred to Camus near the beginning of this chapter, and should like to end it with some brief notes based on his play, *Cross Purpose* (*Le Malentendu*). The plot is closely similar to that of Lillo's *Fatal Curiosity*: a man returns to his family after many years of absence abroad; he is now rich, and he dreams of relieving their poverty and bringing them happiness. Finding they are now keeping an inn, he lodges with them for the night without revealing his identity: this they discover only after they have murdered him for his money. Admittedly he is foolish to delay his revelation until he has worked on their feelings, drawn them out on the subject of the son who went away and never returned, talked of their poverty, and otherwise dramatized his return. But his motives are understandable. He naturally trusts his own family; he is the last person to see the risks of 'reversals and recognitions'. The irony of the situation might well have appealed to Hardy, and it requires no effort to imagine the complications, the missed hints, the opportunities, the delays, the hesitations ('he thought he would tell them that very evening; then he thought he would not') which Hardy might have introduced. Camus handles them well; but it is mainly upon the despair of Jan's relations that he concentrates: that of the mother and sister who have killed him, and of the wife who has lost him. At the final curtain, Maria, the wife, calls to God to have pity on her; and upon the threshold there suddenly appears the Old Manservant, a bearded patriarchal figure, who says in 'a clear firm tone':

What's all this noise? Did you call me?
MARIA [*Gazing at him*]: Oh! . . . I don't know. But help me, help me, for I need help. Be kind and say that you will help me.
OLD MANSERVANT [*In the same tone*]: No.

The monosyllable harshly summarizes the scene that has just been enacted between Martha (Jan's sister) and Maria, and underlines the motif that Camus harps on throughout Martha's cruel despair: the evil mistakes are not just untoward accidents; they—and not recognition, love, understanding—are the natural order of things, the raw material of life. Man, if he wants something different, must make it himself. God will perform no miracle to bring Jan back to life.[50]

Hardy has several exactly parallel effects—more convincing than the statements of some of the 'philosophical' poems—when he uses a vain appeal to God, just as Camus uses Maria's, to underline man's isolation and his own inescapable responsibility. At Elfride's tomb, Knight prays, 'May God *not* have mercy on me'; the mother in *A Sunday Morning Tragedy* prays God *not* to pity her; Clym, realizing that he had caused the death of two women, says, 'If it had pleased God to put an end to me, it would have been a good thing for all. . . . My great regret is that for what I have done no man or law can punish me.' Angel, less quick to blame himself, is at least quick to see that 'God's *not* in his heaven; all's *wrong* with the world'; and his final refusal to comfort Tess by talking of a reunion in heaven is not far, in its effect, from Camus's curtain line. And so we could refer to Henchard's will ('. . . that I be not buried in consecrated ground . . .') and Troy's assumption (derided by Hardy) that Providence would pity and forgive him, as additional recognitions in different character contexts, that there is no excuse and no forgiveness for mistakes. Of the early nineteenth-century translators and adaptors of Lillo's *Fatal Curiosity*, it has been said: 'These irresponsible romanticists . . . were anxious to blame their own evil doings on some supernatural power.'[51] To both Camus and Hardy the supernatural power is beyond such an appeal, and for any 'ill-judged execution' of the originally perhaps 'well-judged plan of things' man is partly to blame, and must alone find the remedy.

Maria (the observer might say) was comparatively innocent. The point is, though, that she has everything to lose, and she allows events to take their course. This is where she is like one of Hardy's characters, and where Hardy would appreciate Camus's treatment. On the other hand the degradation of character that led up to this foulest kind of murder, and the murder itself, would have interested Hardy little. He condemns few as sinners and criminals; there are many misled people in his books, and a few who are selfish and cruel; there are a few, too, who trifle with others' feelings: but it is the very innocence (in the Trampwoman's teasing or Bathsheba's) that Hardy focuses upon, rather than sin or crime. What he most deplores

[50] The allusion to Lazarus (Martha and Mary) is clear; but there is no room, even without these allusions, for misunderstanding.
[51] Werner P. Friedrich, *Outline of Comparative Literature*, Chapel Hill, 1954.

is blindness to possibilities, carelessness, casualness, 'human action in spite of human knowledge': not evil.

Edwin Muir once accused Hardy of being 'partial to man', of 'taking the evil from man's shoulders' and putting the responsibility instead upon the Universe.[52] This neatly summarizes the popular idea of Hardy; but tolerant, or even 'partial' as Hardy may be, I believe he seems more tolerant than he is. He exaggerates his own tolerance as a way of underlining his plea: human nature is good enough in intention, and in potentials; then why not the extra care, the intelligence, the effort of will, that would make it good enough in fact? Human nature is good; but goodness is not enough. By emphasizing man's essential goodness, Hardy concentrates more effectively upon the one area of blame: man's lack of will, his taking life too easily, his imagining that it is the kind of trivial game where the players can afford to 'act like puppets',[53] to be 'so contemptibly unaware'.

This, after all, is the crux of the matter. Different as Hardy and the French Existentialists may be, they have this in common: they refuse to regard life as a trivial game, and insist that it is a serious contest in which a man may, only too easily, lose. It is a commonplace of criticism that Sartre's existentialism was a philosophy of wartime, one geared to the difficulties and demands of the Occupation, useless in time of peace. It is by such criticism that optimists try to justify a return to a normal state of blissful unawareness, to a world that 'must somehow have been made to be a comfortable place for man'. It is by such means (it is not too much to say) that we are lulled to a sense of security despite 'peacetime' developments that might conceivably destroy a hemisphere. The *Late Lyrics and Earlier* preface makes it clear that Hardy foresaw such a possibility. In so far as Hardy's 'Immanent Will' is not a mere negation of Providence, but something positive—a myth of an anti-Providence—we can make sense of it, and of all Hardy's writings, only if we see it, not as depriving man of responsibility, but as intended to tone up his efforts and his opposition, to create in him precisely this wartime alertness.

[52] *Essays on Literature and Society.*   [53] See above, p. 75.

XI

Conclusion

... The new fragment of truth is more wanted, more adapted to the needs of the time, than that which it displaces. ... No sober judge of human affairs will feel bound to be indignant because those who force on our notice truths which we should otherwise have overlooked, overlook some of those which we see.

J. S. Mill

IN HIS OWN copy of the essay *On Liberty*, Hardy marked for double emphasis the sentence I have italicized above; and it is a sobering reminder of how much—in my efforts to redress the balance—I may have omitted from my account of Hardy. There are several omissions I should have liked to make good; but I must limit myself, at this stage, to a few points not too far removed from those discussed in earlier chapters.

First, about Hardy's tragic sense: it is sometimes felt that Hardy's tragedy differs in some essential respect from other, or from 'real' tragedy. One critic dubs it 'naturalistic', and many, as we have seen, put the blame on Hardy's fatalism. To the last subject I need not return, except to remark that even were Hardy as fatalistic as he is popularly supposed to be, this would indicate nothing unusual or unorthodox about the tragedy: Greek tragedy is often fatalistic, and so is Elizabethan. If Hardy's tragedies differ in this respect, they may indeed be *less* fatalistic. But the essential difference lies elsewhere. Arthur Miller's lawyer-commentator in *A View from the Bridge* helps us over the stile when he says of his hero, Eddie, that 'he allowed himself to be wholly known'. This is what the typical tragic hero does. His weakness lies in going too far, not in holding back: *hubris* and *hamartia* are inseparably connected. The hero pits his whole self, or characteristic self, against circumstance, against Fate; and it is in the very completeness with which he does this, allowing himself 'to be wholly known', that he invites disaster.

Hardy's typical heroes are different. They don't go too far; they hold back. They fail, often, precisely because they do not let themselves be 'wholly known'. The novels are seldom concerned with very high aims; or, if they are, these aims shift. Fitzpiers, Pierston, Clym, Jude, Angel—all have ambitions and worthy aims; but what the plot is mainly concerned with is a more modest effort, aside from these ambitions, to attain love and happiness. Some (Fitzpiers and Pierston, for instance) finally succeed; but most fail when the goal is almost reached, when all that is necessary, perhaps, is to stretch out the hand for whatever has been waited and worked for. Again we may quote: 'What is Wisdom really? *A steady handling* of any means to bring about any end necessary to happiness.'[1] Too often the effort is not 'steady', but intermittent, or abandoned just too soon. Giles might have married Grace; Tess might have won the affection and support of Angel's parents; even more easily might Elfride and Knight have found the happiness they longed for; Sue and Jude actually attained happiness and then wantonly cast it away. . . . The weakness of misgiving, of turning back, is not the typical Aristotelian 'tragic weakness', it will be agreed. An exception appears to be Henchard, who seems driven to disaster by his energy and pride. But it is not to disaster, only to near-disaster, that he drives himself. Repeatedly he regrets some rash act, seeing clearly his own folly (as when he bitterly regrets his lie to Newson). He hides his need to love and be loved; refuses to 'be wholly known'; allows himself to be misunderstood: and it is from this that the final disaster comes. The same is true of Eustacia. She had something of the mind òf the tragic heroine, 'forswearing compromise'[2]; but she also had more than a little affection for Clym, and it was by compromising with such realities, by 'allowing herself to be wholly known', that she might have escaped the final disaster.

But Eustacia is a typical heroine neither of tragedy nor of the Wessex novels. We are clearly not meant to feel a great deal of sympathy with her, and some readers feel none at all. When, for instance, Eustacia withdraws into herself, and makes no effort to effect a reconciliation with Clym, we feel none of the admiration that we feel for Tess when, under somewhat similar circumstances, Tess refuses to influence Angel's decision after the confession.

Tess's respect for Angel's freedom, her withdrawal from a situation from which a more selfish woman would have salvaged much, must

[1] *Desperate Remedies*, I. 5. The italics are mine.   [2] *The Return of the Native*, I. vii.

not be taken as evidence that Hardy was acclaiming the virtues of renunciation, of withdrawal from a struggle in which, as Schopenhauer maintained, only the insensitive and unscrupulous could win. The event is one of a series, and the reader receives a totally different final impression: that as long as something can be done, the real virtue lies in remaining alert and prepared for such opportunities to do it as may arise; that the real virtue, in fact, is in re-engagement. It is indeed in *Tess* that Hardy disclaims any sympathy with Schopenhauer's doctrine of renunciation: he describes Angel's father's 'creed of determinism' as—

. . . such that it almost amounted to a vice, and quite amounted, on its negative side, to a renunciative philosophy which had cousinship with that of Schopenhauer and Leopardi.[3]

In only one of the novels does Hardy seem to put the final emphasis upon withdrawal. In *The Trumpet Major*, the nobler, more unselfish, more intelligent of the Loveday brothers, gives up his claim to the heroine (whom he has a very real chance of winning) to his amiable but comparatively worthless brother. He devotes himself to bringing about a re-union between the two, and then says goodbye to the girl he loves, and to his family:

The candle held by his father shed its waving light upon John's face and uniform as with a farewell smile he turned on the doorstone, backed by the black night; and in another moment he had plunged into darkness, the ring of his smart step dying away upon the bridge as he joined his companions in arms, and went off to blow his trumpet till silenced for ever upon one of the bloody battlefields of Spain.

That is the last paragraph of the book. The patriotic cues evoke a comfortable response, perhaps, and obscure for a moment some of the implications. In any case to call the train of events a Schopenhauerian withdrawal is perhaps to oversimplify, to set aside the possibility of irony. None the less, it still seems odd that this book, in which there is a stress, unusual in Hardy, upon the *acceptance* of a fatalistic pattern, should be almost universally regarded as his most lighthearted novel.

Hardy's attitude is distinctive, and his position assured. He avoided the ready-made stoicism of Housman as certainly as he rejected the anodynes of Romanticism and the optimism of the Victorians. More

[3] *Tess*, XXV. And see footnote to p. x above.

tolerant than George Eliot, and less uncompromising in his moral judgements, he is in some ways more logical in his agnosticism. For, while she saw an order which mysteriously and arbitrarily survived the divine order in which she no longer believed, Hardy saw none. He held fast to the one fact of human kinship, and the human kind's chances of creating something out of life's difficulties.

But his historical importance matters less than the interest he holds for the modern reader. This has been shown sufficiently, I think, in my last chapter. But instead of concentrating there on the turn of Hardy's thought in the direction we think of as liberal and continental (or, whatever we think of it, at least not Puddletown-Malthouse-rustical), I might as logically have pointed to parallels in some of the younger English writers of today. I am not attempting any judgements about comparative merit, nor am I suggesting that writers such as Braine, Amis or Miss Murdoch have taken anything consciously or unconsciously from Hardy or from one another. It is rather that they have certain preoccupations in common: that they are all concerned exhaustively with love and sex, with human will and freedom, with choices and rechoices, and with happiness; and that similar aims and preoccupations beget similar methods.

At all events, all these writers use a type of narration in which every event is provisional, taking its values from other events before and after; and they adopt a narrative attitude of what one might call ironical behaviourism. I mean that a fictional character's deeds are less clear than what is done *to* him, less clear than what 'happens'. The person's actions fall far short of what he might do or even of what he intended to do. His course is uncommitted, not really chosen. We noticed that Hardy looked forward to one day writing 'an account of human action in spite of human knowledge, showing how very far conduct lags behind the knowledge that should really guide it'. But if this is what Hardy wanted to do in *The Dynasts*, it is also what he had been doing in his novels from the start: when he shows Cytherea failing to withdraw her hand from Manston's, or Fancy Day flirting with the idea of deserting Dick for Parson Maybold, or Elfride turning her horse's head by 'one of those stealthy movements by which women let their hearts juggle with their brains', or Bathsheba resolving to renounce Troy and at the same time hurrying to Bath to see him (to go no further than his first four books), he is doing just that; but one could as well say he was pre-figuring the sort of self-deception that so fascinates Mr. Amis in his heroes ('by an internal holding of telescope to blind eye, he had been keeping off what he had been up to'[4]).

Miss Murdoch is even more interested in such evasions and the private worlds to which they lead, but does she tell us more of the psychology of such indulgences or of the difficulty of shaking ourselves free of them, of re-engaging in the world of others, than we learn from Henchard, Eustacia, Boldwood, Timothy Petrick, Pierston, and Margery, the romantic milkmaid? Whether she does or not, she puts the same emphasis on re-engagement: the truth lies, as one of Miss Murdoch's characters puts it, in 'blundering on', in renewing contacts with reality and with other human beings, and in resisting the temptations of isolation, of 'crusoeism'. Tess, with her baby, withdraws from the community when most are ready to accept her; Eustacia and Mrs. Yeobright arm themselves against the encounter which might have cleared up the misunderstandings and saved them both; Henchard, misjudging public opinion in Casterbridge, fancies himself shunned, and finally is shunned indeed. He brings upon himself the most terrible of punishments: distrust and disbelief when he at last tries to save from disaster those he has loved.

Lascelles Abercrombie makes the wise remark that Eustacia, by 'mistaking the indifference of [the Heath's] motion for malignity, does actually turn it into malignity on herself and on the others'. And this is true of many of Hardy's other persons: by shrinking from circumstances, they do in fact become powerless against those circumstances. Clearly Hardy and Miss Murdoch share an interest in this problem: the choice between re-engaging in the world of reality or drifting into a world of one's own. Different as their attitudes may be, they meet often on common ground: we have already noticed that Michael in *The Bell* and Cytherea in *Desperate Remedies* find that with the hands of their lovers upon them it is already 'too late to struggle'; there is a kinship between the gipsy in *The Sandcastle* and Hardy's 'Mephistophelian visitants'; there is the scene in the same book of Miss Murdoch's when Felicity tries to impose her will upon the external world by black magic just as Susan Nunsuch

---

[4] Admittedly this is self-critical: Bowen (in *I Like It Here*) is seeing through himself. But Hardy's characters often do this too. Apart from the moods of self-reproach (in Henchard, for example), there are some remarkable self-discoveries: for instance Melbury's realization that even when he doesn't intend to boast about Grace's accomplishments his tongue takes on an 'independent personality' (*The Woodlanders*, chapter VII).

does in *The Return of the Native*—and both authors are to some degree ironical about the success of their respective witches; there is Rosa's discovery that she is an object fixed in the world of others by the tell-tale photograph, and her retreat from Mischa—a loss of courage much like Tess's at Emminster; there are the occasional virtuosities of ingenious contrivance (Oak's victory over the storm, the rescue on the Cliff Without a Name, Manston's duping of the postman and his substitution of the photographs . . . and, in Miss Murdoch, the salvaging of the bell, the rescuing of Mor's son . . .) as if to show how effectively a man may pit himself against circumstance if he acts with complete determination; and there are in both writers, unless I am much mistaken, similar obsessions with the truth, with communication, with chance and with time.

Whether Miss Murdoch has been directly influenced by Hardy I should very much doubt. But the point I wish to make is that the modern reader—familiar with Miss Murdoch's narrative method, or with that of any of these ironically behaviouristic writers—should have no difficulty in understanding Hardy. With Mr. Braine's 'Vodi' or Mr. Amis's 'Bastards' Headquarters' (*Take a Girl Like You*) or Mr. Nabokov's 'Aubrey MacFate' (*Lolita*) in mind, the reader does not have to make heavy going of the 'President of the Immortals' or Eustacia's 'colossal Prince of the World'. The tone is not identical, admittedly, but it is comparable. In Mr. Amis, indeed, Hardy's pessimism is replaced by a far more unnerving optimism; I mean that whereas in Hardy events turn out absurdly wrong when they might, with good sense and good faith, have been guided aright, in Mr. Amis's world things go absurdly right with his heroes even when Fate has been outrageously baited and things should logically and with 'justice' have gone wrong. Such loading of the dice in favour of the hero would have been accepted by our Victorian forefathers without question; that to us it seems absurd, improperly and shockingly funny, would have seemed to Hardy a healthy sign; but cannot we go further and say that our incredulity (that Jim Dixon proves so 'lucky' or that Patrick Standish retrieves the affections of Jenny Bunn) derives very largely from what we have got from Hardy? Hardy himself has shocked certain critics by offering an alternative happy ending to *The Return of the Native*, bringing Venn back to marry Thomasin; of another happy re-union he himself is said to have offered a cynical explanation: these 'contradictions' do not represent a lack of seriousness or integrity, but a confidence in having made his point: in having destroyed the Victorian fictional world; of having established his own, and of being able to convey it to many readers (despite the obtuseness of others) without fear of lost tones and overtones.

Hardy was not always so confident. And it is here perhaps, in his occasional lack of confidence in his power to communicate through a range of tones, that we may explain the comparative weakness of the 'bad' novels. 'Comparative' weakness, because it is a popular fallacy that a great gulf separates two groups of Wessex novels: inspired masterpieces and dismal failures.[5] Even if it is conceded that two or three are not very good, they are still essential parts of Hardy's work. Whether they can be recommended to the general reader or not, they are of absorbing interest to the critic.

Where, apart from this lack of confidence, does their weakness lie? *The Well Beloved*, *A Laodicean* and *The Hand of Ethelberta* have tiresome 'society' episodes; but these are hardly more tiresome and intrusive than two or three of the rustic scenes in some of the others. A worse flaw, apparent also in *Desperate Remedies*, lies in the irritating naivety of the young hero of each novel. Pierston to some extent, and Somerset, Chris and Edward to a much greater, are awkward and incompetent as soon as they fall in love. We can see that Hardy intended this: by the touches of comedy, by the fact that the same sort of awkwardness is shown by inexperienced lovers in some of the other books (by Angel, by Stephen Smith and Henry Knight, by Boldwood, by Dick . . .), and finally by the fact that much of the awkwardness later disappears, and we can hardly miss the point of the change. All the same, these young lovers are a shade *too* awkward; they seem to embody an awkwardness in Hardy himself. On the other hand there are good things even in *The Hand of Ethelberta*, which I regard as the worst of Hardy's stories. But I shall try to make my points *a fortiori*, by briefly discussing not that book but the one which is, I think, popularly supposed to be the worst, namely *A Laodicean*.[6]

It is a contrived book; and the contrivance which has attracted most ridicule is Dare's attempt by means of a faked photograph to blacken Paula's image of Somerset. But to make another comparison

[5] George Wing divides them into 'Bulls', 'Inners' and 'Outers', implying (rightly, I believe) that not one misses the target.
[6] Hardy himself does not seem to have thought of the book as a failure; he presented copies of it to several people he admired, including Mrs. Henniker.

of the kind suggested a few pages back, can the modern reader, with Iris Murdoch's Calvin Blick in mind, fail to see what Hardy was suggesting? He brushed aside photographic technicalities [7] in his impatience to show the effect of the photograph upon Paula and to explore an area of the psychology of loving which this grotesque incident seemed to open up. Once again Miss Murdoch comes to my help: in her discussion of Sartre, she refers to Proust's analogy that 'what I receive in the presence of the beloved object is a negative that I develop later'. [8]

This romantic image, 'developed' and cherished in the absence of the beloved object, is threatened (as surely we all know) even by a somewhat candid but unflattering photograph. Dare's trick did more than threaten; it destroyed Paula's cherished image—not merely by presenting a distorted likeness, but by the sudden manner of presentation, as if by accident, and so that Paula and all her friends saw it and discussed it. The essence of Paula's and Somerset's love affair had lain in its private, romantic and uncommitted nature; but suddenly Paula sees herself as in danger of being committed to a very different George Somerset, who had been passed from hand to hand, a shameful object, a piece of public property. The production of the photograph is the climax of Dare's campaign to misrepresent Somerset—it crystallizes that whole campaign for the reader—and, until much later, when the deception is discovered, it determines Paula's course of action.

Like Calvin Blick, Dare is partly a symbolical figure. He is gambler, and 'a student of probabilities'. We meet him at the gaming tables, and elsewhere, thumbing through his one book, De Moivre's *Doctrine of Chances*. And when he constructs a spy-hole through the wall of Paula's gymnasium, we are told that 'Dare, even without a settled plan in his head, could arrange for probabilities'. Dare, in fact, is the personification of Chance, just as his father, William De Stancy, putting all his trust in patience and waiting, personifies Time: 'Time and I against any two', he quotes; and at the end of the book he upbraids Dare and claims that he would have won Paula but for Dare's trickery: 'Time was all I required.' De Stancy and Dare are indeed the 'Doomsters', Time and Chance, that so nearly wrest Paula from Somerset's hands.

[7] Had it not been for his illness, Hardy might have taken more care with the details. His phrase about a 'device known in photography' is certainly incautious (*A Laodicean*, V. iv.).

[8] *Sartre : Romantic Rationalist*, IX.

There is another sense in which De Stancy is 'Time': he is history and the past. Except for the past (a doubtful asset, as we learn in an early chapter from Charlotte) the De Stancys have nothing. The father, Sir William, has long since sold De Stancy Castle, and squandered the money. Before the story opens the Castle has been bought by Paula's father and inherited by Paula herself. Paula Power is, of course, the 'Laodicean' of the title. Her inclinations are fairly clear from the start, yet she is almost as expert in evading a final choice, in 'staying balanced awhile', in letting events choose for her, as Elfride; and the choice she finds most difficult of all is precisely this one between the old and the new, between William De Stancy with his family's historical past, and Somerset, the young architect of the future. Even when she has broken off her arrangement to marry De Stancy and become reconciled finally with Somerset, the same choice between the old and the new has to be made all over again over the question of the castle. For Paula's castle is burnt, and she and Somerset are at first uncertain whether to restore it. Not, however, for long:

'We will build a new house from the ground, eclectic in style. We will remove the ashes, charred wood, and so on from the ruin, and plant more ivy. The winter rains will soon wash the unsightly smoke from the walls, and De Stancy Castle will be beautiful in its decay. You, Paula, will be yourself again, and recover, if you have not already, from the warp given to your mind . . . by the mediaevalism of the place.'

'And be a perfect representative of "the modern spirit"?' she inquired; 'representing neither the senses and understanding, nor the heart and imagination; but what a finished writer calls the "imaginative reason"?'

'Yes; for since it is rather in your line you may as well keep straight on.'

'Very well, I'll keep straight on; and we'll build a new house beside the ruin, and show the modern spirit for evermore. . . . But, George, I wish—' And Paula repressed a sigh.

'Well?'

'I wish my castle wasn't burnt; and I wish you were a De Stancy!'

That is the end of the book. But to say that Paula is 'a Laodicean to the end' is to miss the point. Whatever her regrets, she has made her choice and endorsed it. Though the past itself—a bastard past, warped and evil, in the person of Dare—has tried to destroy the castle, it is not burnt to the ground, and Paula and Somerset can rebuild it. They choose not to turn back, but to 'keep straight on'.

Guerard calls her 'the charmingly modern' Paula, but complains that she degenerates early into a 'paragon of Victorian smugness and evasion'. But surely Hardy's point (there are parallels elsewhere [9]) is that Paula was responsive and natural until Somerset tried to be possessive. She had begun to cool a little before the arrival of the disillusioning photograph. But although one might accuse her of warming to her lover again only when she thought she had lost him (a thought that does indeed add excitement to the final pages) Paula had made her choice and made it firmly, as soon as she knew the truth about De Stancy and Dare, and realized that Somerset had been wronged. Against the advice of her aunt and the dictates of propriety, she went in pursuit:

> . . . They left the maids and baggage at the station; and, hiring a carriage, Paula told the coachman to drive them to such likely places as she could think of.
> 'He'll never forgive you,' said her aunt, as they rumbled into the town.
> 'Won't he?' said Paula, with soft faith. 'I'll see about that.'[10]

Clearly she is a 'Laodicean' no longer!

In a note prefixed to the book for the 'Wessex Edition', Hardy speaks of the 'changing of the old order in country manors and mansions', but for his own part, he declines to romanticize the old, saying that the 'romantic issues' are 'not necessarily restricted to a change back to the original order'. He knows well the romantic attraction which the past holds for Paula, but he is concerned to show its fraudulence and inadequacy. At the end, she too distrusts it and will take no more chances with its evil influence: she insists on marrying Somerset before returning home:

> 'I will never return to that castle as Miss Power. A nameless dread comes over me when I think of it—a fear that some uncanny influence of the dead De Stancys would drive me again from him. . . .'[11]

Earlier she feels the 'strange spell', the 'weird romanticism . . . as if the historic past had touched her with a yet living hand . . .'[12], needing, but not entirely wishing for, the strength to shake herself free. At all events, the need for the new, the honest and the frank—whatever the seductions of the past: this is the book's theme. And the subtitle, 'a story of today', gives a hint of the way Paula should resolve, and finally does resolve, her Laodicean hesitations.

Paula decides; and sets off on Somerset's trail through Normandy.

[9] Vide supra, pp. 145 ff.
[10] Op. cit. VI. I.   [11] VI. III.   [12] III. IV.

But Hardy still keeps the theme before us in the texture of the narrative, in the scenes through which Paula passes, and in her reluctance to abandon the 'romantic' completely:

It had been her sudden dream, before starting, to light accidentally upon him in some romantic old town of this romantic old province. . . .[13]

Later, as Paula was walking down a street—

She was transported to the Middle Ages. It contained the shops of tinkers, braziers, bellows-menders, hollow-turners, and other quaintest trades, their fronts open to the street beneath stories of timber overhanging so far on each side that a slit of sky was left at the top for the light to descend, and no more. A blue misty obscurity pervaded the atmosphere. . . .[14]

But when she at last caught a glimpse of him, it was in a wide street 'with customary modern life flowing through it'.[15] And—still more disillusioning—she found he was hurrying 'to the railway', which of all things, as the reader will recall, held for Paula the most modern and unromantic associations. Later still, in Caen:

She still persisted in her wish to casually encounter Somerset in some aisle, lady-chapel, or crypt. . . .[16]

She misses him again, however; and when she finally catches up with him, the encounter is in Étretât, a modern resort with beach and Casino, where there are 'no old churches' to provide a romantic setting for their reunion.

In their chase, Paula and her aunt encounter someone else trailing Somerset: his father. And conversation between the three has the effect of sifting over the same values. The old and conventional are not always rejected; but there is a careful selection from both the new and the old.[17] So the whole finale of the book is not just the successful ending of a chase; it is rather the choice of a future, and the steady realization of its meaning.

But it is not merely at the end of the book that the theme, given in the subtitle and preface, is worked into the narrative. It is in the plot itself from the start, in the mesh of Paula's dilemma, or series of dilemmas. It is in our first impression of that 'mixed young lady', as

[13] Op. cit. VI. I.   [14] Ibid.   [15] Ibid.   [16] VI. II.
[17] The note quoted at the foot of p. 25 above, about the 'true political principle' that is neither 'Conservation' nor 'Radicalism', was written while Hardy was at work on *A Laodicean.*

Somerset calls her; in the embarrassment of Somerset's twofold function, first as Paula's lover, longing for favours and liberties, and second as her architect, bound by social and professional conventions. It is in the anomalous position of Charlotte: a De Stancy, but not a typical one. . . . There is a relevance to the theme even in the way Paula's telegraph cuts through the delays which Dare and De Stancy need for the maturing of their plots. To turn back to a major point: the main theme—Paula's hesitation between making a new life for herself and being engulfed in the 'weird romanticism' of the 'historic past' and the intrigues of the De Stancys—gives a new and special point to the tension between Hardy's twin strands of narration, the tension between what actually happens and what ought to be happening. And it is especially appropriate perhaps that the two strands are finally brought together (though there are some earlier ironically close shaves) by the intervention of Charlotte, the only De Stancy who is modern, and who has the honesty, good-sense and warmth of a real human being.

Not that her brother William is without interest: he is a pessimist, but of the wrong kind; one 'seasoned in ill-luck', who sees *only* the worst, and lacks the resilience and courage that might enable him to see and take advantage of a tide in his favour.

There are other points of interest too; but I do not wish to persuade my readers that the book is better than it is, only that it may be better or more interesting than it is reputed to be. The 'tedious illness' that 'laid hold of the author soon after the story was begun in a well-known magazine', so that it had to be 'strenuously continued by dictation' doubtless explains—partly at least—why Hardy did not do justice to his material, and why he failed, especially, to exercise that greater and more subtle control demanded by a narrative of this sort—a narrative, I mean, that is not entirely realistic. Even so, *A Laodicean* is well worth reading; it presents, as we have noticed, a slightly different treatment of several familiar themes; and for the Hardy student it can hardly fail to throw light upon his other books.

Short Bibliography of Hardy's Main Works[1]

Except where otherwise indicated, the first date is that of publication in book form.

The Poor Man and the Lady.
  [Never published in original form. Written 1867–8. Some passages and scenes were used in later books, e.g. *Under the Greenwood Tree*. The central plot, very little altered, formed the basis of *An Indiscretion in the Life of an Heiress*. The MS. is known to have been destroyed.]

Desperate Remedies. 1871.
  Written 1869–70.

Under the Greenwood Tree. 1872.
  Written 1871; but some passages written earlier were incorporated (see above).

A Pair of Blue Eyes. 1873.
  Written between 1871 and the spring of 1873. Serial in *Tinsley's Magazine*, 1872–3.

Far from the Madding Crowd. 1874.
  Written between the spring of 1873 and July 1874. Serial in the *Cornhill*, January to December 1874.

The Hand of Ethelberta. 1876.
  Finished in January of that year; by then the serial had been running in the *Cornhill* for six months.

The Return of the Native. 1878.
  Written 1877–8. Serial in *Belgravia* during 1878.

Fellow Townsmen. 1880.
  New Quarterly Magazine; as paper-bound book in U.S.A. same year. Revised for inclusion in *Wessex Tales*.

The Trumpet Major. 1880.
  Written 1879–80. Serial in *Good Words* 1880.

A Laodicean. 1881.
  Written 1880–1. Serial in *Harper's*, December 1880 to December 1881.

Two on a Tower. 1882.
  Written 1881–2. Serial in the *Atlantic Monthly* May–December 1882.

---

[1] For all details the reader is referred to Professor R. L. Purdy's excellent bibliography, to which I am, of course, greatly indebted.

The Romantic Adventures of a Milkmaid. 1883.

    Written 1882–3. Printed in the *Graphic*, Summer Number 1883, and as paper-bound book in U.S.A. same month (June).

The Mayor of Casterbridge. 1886.

    Written 1884–5. Serial in the *Graphic* (weekly instalments) January to May 1886.

The Woodlanders. 1887.

    Written 1885–7. Monthly instalments in *Macmillan's Magazine*, May 1886–April 1887.

Wessex Tales. 1888.

    All the stories had been published previously in magazines, and one ('Fellow Townsmen' *q.v.*) as a paper-back book. Dates as follows: 'The Distracted Preacher' 1879; 'Fellow Townsmen' 1880; 'The Three Strangers' 1883; 'Interlopers at the Knap' 1884; and 'The Withered Arm' 1888.

A Group of Noble Dames. 1891.

    The stories had all been published before, sometimes in more than one version: 'The Duchess of Hamptonshire' 1878; 'The Honourable Laura' 1881; 'The First Countess of Wessex' 1889; 'The Lady Penelope' 1890; and the remaining six stories—'Barbara of the House of Grebe', 'The Marchioness of Stonehenge', 'Lady Mottisfont', 'The Lady Icenway', 'Squire Petrick's Lady' and 'Anna, Lady Baxby' —also in 1890.

Tess of the d'Urbervilles. 1891.

    Written 1888–90. Bowdlerized serial version in the *Graphic*, July–December 1891. Details of the novel's dismemberment and restoration and of incidents published separately are provided by Professor Purdy in his bibliography.

Life's Little Ironies. 1894.

    All the stories (including the 'Few Crusted Characters') had appeared in magazines: 'A Tradition of 1804' 1882; 'A Tragedy of Two Ambitions' 1888; 'The Melancholy Hussar' 1890; 'A Few Crusted Characters' and four stories—'The Son's Veto', 'For Conscience' Sake', 'On the Western Circuit' and 'To Please his Wife' in 1891; and 'The Fiddler of the Reels' 1893.

Jude the Obscure. 1895.

    Written 1890–5. Serial in *Harper's* December 1894 to November 1895. Again, the text was drastically 'revised' for serial publication and restored for publication in book form.

['The Spectre of the Real' was written in collaboration with Mrs. Henniker in 1893 and first published in the Winter Number of *Today* in November 1894. It was revised and included in her volume of stories *In Scarlet and Grey*, 1896. The reader's impression that the story was planned and written mainly by Hardy and that Mrs.

Henniker's contribution was limited to a few descriptive passages is borne out by the correspondence quoted by Purdy. Hardy took the initiative too over the title which reflects his obsession with the 'dream and reality' theme: 'I have provisionally substituted "The Spectre of the Real", he writes. '—"The Looming of the Real" is perhaps almost better. I have also thought of . . . "A Shattering of Ideals".'

At the climax of the story a husband, like Angel, is disillusioned over his bride's past and, unlike Angel, shoots himself. There is, however, a good deal more to the story than this.]

The Well Beloved. 1897.

This novel was written, however, in 1891–2, and published as a serial in the *Illustrated London News*, October to December 1892. It was revised for publication in book form.

Wessex Poems. 1898.

Note: Hardy's poetry is now so well known that it is hardly necessary to say that he had been writing poetry for many years. Some of the poems are dated as early as 1865 and 1866 (when Hardy was about twenty-five). Many, in this and later volumes, are not given a date, but some of these can be dated from the time of their separate publication or on other evidence. Despite a group of early poems printed near the beginning of *Wessex Poems*, the general arrangement is not chronological. The first *Collected Poems* appeared in 1919. In this and later editions the same arrangement has been kept, and the divisions (*Wessex Poems, Poems of the Past and the Present*, etc.) preserved, and the prefaces printed in their places. In *Wessex Poems* and in most subsequent printings of this volume, appear some drawings by Hardy, but these do not appear in the 1912 Wessex Edition of Hardy's Works, nor (so far as I know) in any edition of the *Collected Poems*.

A few poems were published as separate books or pamphlets, e.g. 'The Convergence of the Twain' (1912) and 'Yuletide in a Younger World' (the latter as No. 1 of the *Ariel Poems*). I know of only one poem, published thus, which has not been 'collected': 'Domicilium'. But this, Hardy's earliest known poem, is printed in *Early Years*. The poem contains a near-apology for using a pathetic fallacy; and it is interesting that a country boy of about eighteen should be so self-conscious in his use of language; it suggests that the same man at fifty did know what he was doing, using a 'well-known trope' on the last page of *Tess*.

Poems of the Past and the Present. 1901.

The Dynasts. Part I: 1904; Part II: 1906; and Part III: 1908.

Begun 1897 (but projected earlier), finished 1907.

Time's Laughingstocks. 1909.

(Poems.)

A Changed Man. 1913.

All the stories had been published before, mostly in magazines. 'What the Shepherd Saw' 1881; 'The Romantic Adventures of a Milkmaid' (see above) 1883; 'A Tryst at an Ancient Earthwork' and 'A Mere Interlude' 1885; 'Alicia's Diary' 1887; 'The Waiting Supper' 1888; 'Master John Horseleigh, Knight' 1893; 'The Duke's Reappearance' and 'A Committee Man of the Terror' 1896; 'The Grave by the Handpost' 1897; 'A Changed Man' and 'Enter a Dragoon' 1897.

Satires of Circumstance. 1914.

(Poems.)

Moments of Vision. 1917.

(Poems.)

Late Lyrics and Earlier. 1922.

(With the 'Apology' explaining his 'evolutionary meliorism'.)

The Famous Tragedy of the Queen of Cornwall. 1923.

Apparently begun in 1916 (projected earlier still) and laid aside. Finished 1923. Text revised for second edition, 1924.

Human Shows, Far Fantasies. 1925.

(Poems.)

Life and Art. 1925.

'Essays, Notes and Letters collected for the first time with Introduction by Ernest Brennecke Jr.'

This collection was not sponsored by Hardy, but it is a useful republication of otherwise almost inaccessible material. It contains the early 'How I built myself a house' (1865), 'The Dorsetshire Labourer' (1883), 'The profitable Reading of Fiction' (1883), 'Candour in English Fiction' (1890), and some other articles and letters of interest.

Winter Words. 1928.

(Poems.) Prepared for publication, and prefaced with an 'Introductory Note' but printed posthumously.

The Early Life of Thomas Hardy. 1928.

'By Florence Emily Hardy'—but really an autobiography on which Hardy had been working for several years before his death. Hardy's intention in this and the following volume was to forestall misrepresentation: he had been greatly angered by Hedgcock's book, and by Brennecke's *Life of Thomas Hardy*.

The Later Years of Thomas Hardy. 1930.

The second volume of the 'autobiography', but the final chapters, written by Mrs. Hardy herself, complete the book.

Note: Substantially the same two volumes (with the same pagination, etc.) were re-issued in 1933, but re-titled *The Life of Thomas Hardy*. This is also the title of the completely new edition, in one volume, published in 1962.

An Indiscretion in the Life of an Heiress. 1934.

First published in the *New Quarterly Magazine*, 1878. Reprinted by Mrs. Hardy because of the special interest the story holds as an adaptation of the main plot of *The Poor Man and the Lady*. (See chapter IV above.)

Our Exploits at West Poley. 1952.

Written 1883. Published originally as a serial between November 1892 and April 1893 in *The Household* (U.S.A.). The story was lost, and was traced finally by Dr. R. L. Purdy, who wrote an introduction to the book for the Oxford University Press.

Note

A list of Hardy criticism with pretensions to completeness would fill many pages. A twenty-page-long 'Selected Checklist' was published in *Modern Fiction Studies* (Purdue University) in 1960, having been compiled by Dr. Maurice Beebe, Mrs. Bonnie Culotta and Mrs. Erin Marcus. I am indebted to this valuable list, and I recommend it to others.

OTHER BOOKS AND ESSAYS CONSULTED INCLUDE THE FOLLOWING:

Abercrombie, L. *Thomas Hardy : a critical study*, London, 1912.

Archer, W. *Real Conversations*, London, 1904.

Bailey, J. O. *Thomas Hardy and the Cosmic Mind*, Chapel Hill, N.C., 1956.

Baker, E. A. *History of the English Novel*, Vol. IX, London, 1938.

Barzun, J. 'Truth and Poetry in Thomas Hardy', *Southern Review*, VI (Summer 1940—Hardy Centenary Number).

Blunden, Edmund. *Thomas Hardy*, London, 1941.

Brennecke, E. *Thomas Hardy's Universe*, Boston, 1924.

Brown, D. *Thomas Hardy*, London, 1954.

Cecil, Lord David. *Hardy the Novelist*, London, 1943.

Chew, S. C. *Thomas Hardy*, *Poet and Novelist*, New York, 1928.

Child, Harold. *Thomas Hardy*, London, 1916.

d'Exideuil, P. *The Human Pair in the Work of Thomas Hardy*, trans. by F. W. Crosse, London, 1930.

Dobrée, B. 'Thomas Hardy' in *The Lamp and the Lute*, London, 1929

Goldberg, M. A. 'Hardy's Double-visioned Universe', *Essays in Criticism*, VII, 1957.

Guerard, A. J. *Thomas Hardy*, *the Novels and Stories*, Cambridge (Harvard University Press), 1949.

Hardy, E. *Thomas Hardy : a critical biography*, London, 1954.
    'Thomas Hardy: Plots for five unpublished short stories', *London Magazine*, V (November, 1958).

Hardy, Florence Emily. (See bibliography of Hardy's own books, pp. 179 ff. above, with which Mrs. Hardy's biography is listed.)

Hawkins, D. *Thomas Hardy*, London, 1950.

Holloway, J. *The Victorian Sage*, London, 1953.
    The Charted Mirror, London, 1960.

Kettle, A. *Introduction to the English Novel*, vol. II, London, 1953.

Laird, J. *Philosophical Incursions into English Literature*, London, 1946.

Leavis, F. R. 'Reality and Sincerity', *Scrutiny*, XIX (1952).

Leavis, Q .D. 'Thomas Hardy and Criticism', *Scrutiny*, XI (1943).

Lucas, F. L. *Ten Victorian Poets*, London, 1940.

Muir, E. *Essays on Literature and Society*, London, 1949.

Osawa, M. *Studies of Thomas Hardy's Literature*, Tokyo, 1949.

Porter, Katharine A. 'Notes on a Criticism of Thomas Hardy', *Southern Review*, VI, Autumn 1940.

Purdy, R. L. *Thomas Hardy, a Bibliographical Study*, New York, London, Toronto, 1954.

Richards, I. A. *Science and Poetry*, London, 1926.

Rutland, W. R. *Thomas Hardy, A Study of his Writings and their Background*, Oxford, 1938.

Stewart, J. I. M. 'The Integrity of Hardy', *Essays and Studies* (English Association), 1948.

Weber, Carl J. *Hardy of Wessex*, New York, 1940.

Introduction to *Tess of the d'Urbervilles*, Modern Library, 1951.

Webster, H. C. *On a Darkling Plain*, Chicago, 1947.

Wing, G. *Thomas Hardy* (Writers and Critics Series), London, 1962.

Index

Index 187